# BANGOR 1883-1983
# A STUDY IN
# MUNICIPAL GOVERNMENT

# BANGOR 1883-1983

## A STUDY IN
## MUNICIPAL GOVERNMENT

Peter Ellis Jones

CARDIFF
UNIVERSITY OF WALES PRESS
1986

© University of Wales, 1986

British Library Cataloguing in Publication Data

Jones, P. Ellis
  Bangor 1883—1983: a study in municipal government.
  1. Bangor (Gwynedd) — Politics and government
  I. Title
  352.0429'25     JS4030

ISBN 0-7083-0909-7

Printed in Wales by CSP Printing of Cardiff

To
ANNE, ANGELA AND JENNIFER
WHO SHARE MY LOVE
FOR BANGOR

# PREFACE

IN 1883 Bangor received its Charter of Incorporation, became a municipal borough and elected a council to manage its civic affairs. After the radical restructuring of local government in 1974, Bangor was redesignated a community and a community council replaced the borough council. Although the two councils have had markedly different functions there are many strands which have united them other than the fact that both have been called the Bangor City Council. This council has made a vital contribution to the life and development of the city and the occasion of its centenary is an appropriate time to record at length that contribution.

Two broad themes are highlighted in this centenary history of the City Council. The chronology of the growth of the wide range of welfare and protective services which the council provided and administered for the well being of the citizens of Bangor is an obvious focus of attention. Equally important is the examination of the membership of the council, of those who were involved in the decision making process, their place in the local status and class hierarchy and their political, denominational and linguistic affiliations. This is done in the context of the political, economic, social and cultural milieu of both the local and wider setting. Short biographical sketches of the mayors and chief officers, the leading actors in the drama of events, are given as a tribute to those who probably made the greatest contribution to the council's progress over the years. Administrative structures which preceded the granting of the charter are reviewed in Chapter 2 and the events which led up to the city's petitioning for a charter in 1883 are recorded. As a backdrop to the study a short history of the development of Bangor from earliest times to the present is outlined (Chapter 1). The book is written primarily for the citizens of Bangor in the hope that it may nourish in them a greater awareness of and deeper insight into their rich inheritance.

A chronological approach has been adopted in presenting the material. Consequently, the period is divided into four sub-periods, each of which marks a significant stage in the evolution of the council.

The two world wars, which had such dramatic consequences for the life of the nation as a whole, are obvious demarcation points and a third is provided by the reorganization of local government in 1974. Two chapters are devoted to each of the three periods covering the history of the borough council; the leading chapter records the evolution of services provided and the following one deals with aspects of the human drama. Although the separation of events from those who were involved in them may be justly criticized, the decision was made on the grounds that the treatment of each aspect is thereby simplified.

Local government has not been a particularly fruitful field for historians. This is especially noticeable at the borough and urban district level, certainly as far as Wales is concerned. A recent classic history of Wales, covering much the same period as this study, scarcely mentions it. Where a study of a local council does exist it is often confined to a chapter or two in a volume dealing with a town's history. There is no substantial work focusing specifically on town government in Wales over the past hundred years or so and in the absence of comparative studies this work describes events as they are unfolded in one community and no particular conceptual framework is constructed. Only after a number of comparative studies of small towns has been undertaken can general principles be established.

Since the book is aimed at the general reader, footnotes have been confined in the main to the identification of actual quotations and the acknowledgment of sources not given in the bibliography. The 1982 value of certain sums of money is frequently presented in brackets according to a conversion scale prepared by E. Barry Bower, and printed in the *Sunday Telegraph*, 5 September 1982.

The study has arisen out of my own interest in the evolution of the urban morphology and social geography of Bangor rather than from any active involvement in the process of local government. Lack of personal experience of the system has placed me at a disadvantage and I must take responsibility for omitting items that might have been important or interpreting matters with a lack of perception. However, despite the fact that people in local government have rarely kept diaries, letters or papers, there is no dearth of readily available documents to aid the researcher. Remarkably full records of the borough council were deposited in the Gwynedd Archives at the re-organization of local government in 1974 and there are reports of council affairs and meetings in the local press. Council and committee minutes record in clinical terms the decisions taken but they do not present the arguments used in the debates. Up to the Second World War meetings of the council were reported in full in the press, often taking several columns of the fine print; speeches were sometimes reported verbatim, local opinion was expressed in leader columns and details of new projects and biographies of council members were given. Since the 1950s, however, coverage of council affairs has been sparse and fragmented into 'newsy' items with little discussion of issues. To overcome this deficiency partly I have been privileged to discuss aspects of the council's work with some of its past and present members and officers and I would like to record my thanks to the following in particular: Iris Parry and Vivian Lewis, former mayors, and W. Elwyn Jones and George Gibbs, former and present town clerks respectively. Vivian Lewis, Frank Woodcock, Haydn Jones and George Gibbs have read a draft of some chapters and I am glad of the suggestions they have made. I have been given every assistance too by the staff of the Gwynedd Archives, the National Library of Wales and the University College Libraries at Aberystwyth and Bangor.

I am particularly indebted to Professor J. Gwynn Williams for persuading both the Bangor City Council and the University of Wales Press Board to take joint responsibility for financing and publishing the book and to the members of the Council and Board for their ready willingness to co-operate in the venture. George Gibbs, Town Clerk, and John Rhys, Director of the Press Board, have shown infinite patience and understanding during the preparation of the book. I am grateful to the Press Board's Reader for the valuable suggestions he made and to Mr Iwan Llwyd Williams, Assistant Editor at the Press Board, for the efficiency with which he has seen the work through the press. It is to my wife Anne, however, that I owe the greatest debt of gratitude; besides typing most of the manuscript she has given me unfailing support and generous encouragement at all times.

PETER ELLIS JONES

*Aberystwyth*
June 1985

# FOREWORD

WHEN Bangor City Council attained its centenary the Council felt that it would be appropriate to record its history in a book which would appeal to the general public. We were fortunate in having Peter Ellis Jones to complete this task because he has always shown real interest in the history and development of Bangor.

We feel privileged that this book (at least in Wales) is the only major work on a borough council and few towns have had their histories recorded in such a manner. This book will provide a most useful contribution to the rich inheritance of Bangor.

CHRISTINE NORRIS
MAYOR, CITY OF BANGOR

# CONTENTS

# LIST OF ILLUSTRATIONS

---

# LIST OF TABLES

# ACKNOWLEDGEMENTS

———

*Map* 2. Base map reproduced from the 1963 Ordnance Survey 1:10,560 map with the permission of the Controller of Her Majesty's Stationery Office. Crown copyright reserved.

*Plates* 1 & 4(ii).  U.C.N.W. Archives.

*Plates* 2, 4(i) & 10.  Douglas Gowan from City Council Collection.

*Plates* 3, 4(iii), 4(iv), 5, 6(i), 6(ii) & 6(iii).  Gwynedd Archives.

*Plates* 6(iv) & 7.  Sir W. Elwyn Jones.

# CHAPTER 1

## THE HISTORICAL BACKGROUND

A CORRUGATED ridge and furrow phenomenon, whose orientation lies from north-east to south-west, affords the topographic base upon which Bangor is built. The northern ridge, that on which Upper Bangor is built, is slightly lower in elevation, less steep sided and more flat topped than the parallel ridge to the south, Bangor Mountain. In the valley between the two ridges flows a small stream, the Adda, on whose southern bank the original settlement was founded. The Upper Bangor ridge is bounded by the depression occupied by the Menai Strait to the north and from the summit of Bangor Mountain the land slopes in a southerly direction to the valley of the River Cegin. The sea to the north and east and the River Cegin to the south form natural boundaries but in the absence of a natural feature to the west the boundary of the city has moved successively in that direction in response to urban growth. From this varied and attractive site impressive views may be obtained across the sea of south-east Anglesey and the Great Orme's Head and, towards the south, of practically the whole sweep of the Snowdonia range of mountains.

FROM THE SIXTH TO THE MID-EIGHTEENTH CENTURY
The well-watered and sheltered Adda Valley, having access to the coast and the Strait passage, was a propitious site for the founding of an early Celtic cell and for the development of the settlement which later gathered around it. The genesis of the settlement must be viewed against the background of the missionary activity during the sixth century A.D. which propagated the Christian faith in the lands bordering the Irish Sea. The source of its inspiration was the surviving Christian-Roman tradition of south-west Gaul and its lines of movement lay along the western seaways of the continent and these islands. Where their mission among the indigenous population showed some promise of fulfilment the missionaries established permanent 'cells' from which they would minister to the converted and thereby extend the network of pastoral care.

Among the Celtic missionaries was a certain Deiniol who was a member of a tribe which had been transferred by the Romans from south-east Scotland to north-west Wales in the fourth century to defend that portion of the western seaboard against the incursions of the Irish. Inspired by the evangelical movement, Deiniol became a missionary and established a cell in the Adda Valley in 525 A.D. There is reason to believe that his cell became a monastery where men were trained for the ministry of the Celtic Church. In time, the monastery probably consisted of a number of beehive-shaped cells made of stone, timber and turf and a small stone built church. This cluster was gathered within a boundary fence constructed of wattle. Bangor in fact 'as a common noun . . . denotes the upper or boundary part of a wattle fence'.[1] The monastery assumed the role of a mother church having responsibility for the guidance and support of a number of daughter churches situated within its sphere of influence. Tradition has it that Deiniol was consecrated bishop in 546 and that the territory over which he held spiritual authority probably coincided with the Principality of Maelgwyn Gwynedd who favoured him with his patronage. Later bishops exercised their episcopal rights by succession from St Deiniol.

The early ascendency of Bangor may be attributed to the leadership of Deiniol and to the patronage he received from the Princes of Gwynedd who endowed the church with land and the bishop with privileges. Important factors contributing to the maintenance of that predominance, however, were the central position of Bangor within the territory of the Princes of Gwynedd and its accessibility by land and sea. Significantly, when the church was reorganized on the Catholic model following the Norman penetration of North Wales in the eleventh century, Bangor was chosen as the centre of a new diocese. Despite the turmoil of succeeding centuries Bangor persisted as the seat of a diocesan bishop and wielded exclusive spiritual authority throughout north-west Wales. About the middle of the thirteenth century, members of the Black Friars of the Order of St Dominic founded a friary in Bangor. The presence of the friary emphasizes the dual role of Bangor in the medieval period as an ecclesiastical and an educational centre, functions which persist to the present day.

The bishop also exercised secular authority over large areas of north-west Wales. Lands vested in him by the Princes of Wales were confirmed and supplemented by the Crown after the death of Llywelyn ap Gruffudd, the last Prince of Wales, in 1282. Among his landed estates was the Manor of Bangor, *Maenol Bangor*, whose boundaries roughly coincided with the present parishes of Bangor and Pentir. He was authorized to hold annual fairs and a weekly market at Bangor and to operate ferries over prescribed stretches of the Menai Strait.

The parlous condition of the church and the disintegration of the manorial system in the fifteenth and early sixteenth centuries resulted in the alienation of land within the bishop's manors and the emergence of a new landowning class. By the mid-sixteenth century only small scattered portions of the manor remained in the bishop's possession. Coincident with the decline in the influence of the bishop as a secular lord went a decline in his spiritual influence; the bishops of Bangor were all Englishmen who rarely visited their diocese. However between 1494 and 1533 the cathedral underwent major reconstruction and a residence was erected for the bishops who increasingly spent more time in Bangor. These developments were symptomatic of the spiritual awakening of the time which culminated in the Protestant Reformation. One consequence of the Reformation was the dissolution of the monasteries and the friary at Bangor was among those dissolved in 1538. The friary and its possessions eventually fell into the hands of Dr Geoffrey Glynne who, in his will dated 1557, bequeathed his property to trustees who were charged with the founding of a free grammar school in Bangor 'for the better education and bringing up of poor men's children'. The school came to be known as Friars School.

Bangor therefore entered the modern period as a diocesan, educational and market centre, yet one should not be deluded about the scale of these functions. John Leland wrote during his itinerary through Wales, 1536-9, that Bangor 'hath ii fayres a yere, but skant a market every week'[2] and almost two centuries later Brown Willis recorded that only 'a small market was kept in Bangor every week'.[3] Friars School had very few pupils and the small staff at the cathedral administered to a sparse, widely scattered rural community. Nothing much changed until almost the end of the eighteenth century. Engravings by Lewis (1740) and Sandby (1776) portray Bangor as a small cluster of houses lining the two roads which met at the market cross adjacent to the dominant building, the cathedral. Maps[4] of the same period indicate that the number of houses did not exceed one hundred which suggests a population of some five hundred souls.

MID-EIGHTEENTH CENTURY TO 1883

Two factors were to radically change this almost medieval image of the city in the last quarter of the eighteenth century: improvements and developments in the road network led to a big increase in the number of people passing through and staying in Bangor and the exploitation on a commercial basis of the slate rock in the nearby hills provided employment for hundreds of workmen in quarrying, transporting and manufacturing slate. Suddenly, the small, isolated, self-sufficient rural backwater was tossed onto the rising tide of industrial and economic expansion which accompanied the Industrial Revolution in Britain and in a brief span of time the character of the city changed out of all recognition.

Chronologically it was improvements in the road system and a shift in the relative importance of the Strait ferry crossings which activated change locally. Before 1718 the royal mails between London and Dublin were conveyed along the North Wales coast and crossed the Menai Strait by the ferry which operated between Aber and Beaumaris. In that year the post office began to use the shorter and less hazardous Porthaethwy ferry situated some 715 metres east of the present suspension bridge. Bangor immediately found itself on the main route between the two capital cities; it succeeded Beaumaris as the principal post town in the area and clearly responded positively to its new position for Browne Willis, writing in 1721, observed that 'the town of Bangor, as it is on the great road from London to Holyhead, is well accommodated with inns'.[5]

Since the Porthaethwy ferry had become the principal crossing of the Strait before the laying down of the turnpike road system later in the century it is natural that the system should focus on the Porthaethwy crossing. The Anglesey Turnpike Act, 1765, authorized the improvement of the road from Holyhead to the Porthaethwy ferry and in 1772 the difficult and dangerous stretch of road around the Penmaenmawr headland was rendered suitable for wheeled vehicles by the Caernarvonshire Turnpike Trust. As a result the first regular daily (except Sunday) coach service between Chester and Holyhead was inaugurated in 1776. By 1777 the whole stretch of road between Shrewsbury and Conwy, via Llanrwst was turnpiked and in 1780 a Shrewsbury innkeeper, in collaboration with London innkeepers, commenced a stage coach service between Shrewsbury and Holyhead using this route. Road improvements encouraged the Post Office after 1785 to convey the mail in post-chaises rather than on horseback and in 1780 carriers began operating a regular schedule of waggons between Caernarfon and Chester via Bangor. Lord Penrhyn had a road for carriages constructed from Llandegai to the head of the Nant

Ffrancon valley in 1794 and extended it to Capel Curig in 1800. This road was superseded in 1802 by one constructed by the Capel Curig Trust which ran from Llandegai to Betws-y-Coed and the Post Office selected this route for the carriage of mails in 1808. Such was the increase in traffic converging on the Porthaethwy crossing that due to the shortcomings of the ferry itself, agitation arose for a permanent crossing of the Strait. A bill for building a timber bridge was presented in Parliament in 1786 but it was dismissed on second reading.

Improvements in and extensions to the road system, the inauguration of regular coach and waggon services and the provision of accommodation for those who used the roads greatly stimulated travel and trade. Bangor, standing at the focal point of the new road system, greatly benefited from these improvements. W. Hutton, who visited Bangor in 1797, noted that 'what great matters are done for the improvement of Bangor are . . . done by the clergy, the Irish mails and the stages'. Referring to Snowdonia, Hutton remarked 'the improvement of the roads and particularly the daily communication between England and Ireland brought (the mountains) into notice. The English traveller ventured to climb her precipices, descend her glens . . . and now the vast influx of annual visitors enrich her with their wealth'.[6] Scores of travellers who came to explore the newly found countryside stayed in Bangor and some of them committed to print their impressions of the city. The Rev. J. Evans who toured North Wales in 1798 considered Bangor to be 'particularly eligible as a place of residence . . . being whitewashed and covered with slates (the houses) have a neat and comfortable appearance. The variety of views and pleasant walks, sea, . . . and great Irish and London road passing through the place, are inducements not usually met with together'.[7] Yet even before the end of the century this idyllic view of the city was being tarnished by the quickening pace of economic activity.

The catalyst for change was the development on capitalist lines of slate quarrying on the Penrhyn estate in the vicinity of what was later to become the town of Bethesda, some five miles south of Bangor. When Richard Pennant, the son of a wealthy West Indian sugar planter became the outright owner of the estate in 1781 he found it in a parlous condition due to years of neglect. However, applying his considerable wealth and entrepreneurial flair he initiated improvements in agriculture, he pioneered new slate quarrying and manufacturing techniques and he recruited a wage earning labour force on a scale hitherto unprecedented for this area. To facilitate the conveyance of heavy slate products to markets in Britain, Ireland and even the U.S.A., Pennant constructed a quay at the mouth of the River Cegin in 1786,[8] soon to be known as Port Penrhyn, and a novel iron tramway to link the quarry to the port in 1801. These improvements gave the Penrhyn enterprise a headstart over all the other slate quarrying districts in Caernarvonshire and provided a model for their future development. So successful was the undertaking that A. H. Dodd in his review of the economic history of Caernarvonshire stated unequivocally that 'the crucial turning point in the economic development of Caernarvonshire came when . . . Richard (Pennant) secured . . . control over the Penrhyn inheritance'.[9]

Although the wars with France between 1793 and 1815 had an adverse effect on the slate trade, the sixty or so years which followed the ending of hostilities were years of progressive and substantial growth. Shipment of slate from Port Penrhyn climbed from 25,000 tons in 1815 to over 80,000 tons in 1840 and reached a peak of 135,000 tons in 1862. Between 1852 and 1876 over 100,000 tons were shipped each year.[10] In 1852 a standard gauge railway line was laid down to link the port with the mainline railway between Chester and Holyhead, and in 1855 a second quay was constructed at the port, both improvements being undertaken to increase its export capability. Demand for roofing slate was buoyant throughout this period as the rate of residential and industrial construction steadily increased both at home and abroad in response to the rapid growth in population and the migration of people to the growing industrial towns. Traffic at the port was not of course all in one direction. Coal from Liverpool, Preston and Chester was the most important cargo but timber, lime, malt, porter, flooring and ridge tiles and bricks also figured prominently among the list of imports. Cargoes of sundry items, principally from Liverpool, included a wide range of articles produced in the metal, engineering and textile factories of the new industrial towns and these were distributed not only in Bangor itself but throughout its tributary area.

Industries processing slate blocks brought down from the quarry were established at Port Penrhyn and adjacent sites. These were of two kinds. Firstly there was the manufacture of wood framed writing slates at the port itself. Hyde Hall observed in 1810 that 'there was an establishment for polishing and framing school slates (at Port Penrhyn) of which a number unaccountably great are constantly exported'.[11] Bingley visited the same works in 1814 and described it as 'one of the most extensive manufacturies of writing slates in Great Britain' and stated that between 300 and 400 dozen were on average manufactured every week.[12] In 1828 the number manufactured amounted to over 300,000 units a year.[13] Writing slates continued to be manufactured at Port Penrhyn into the present century.

The other type of slate manufacturing involved the production of sills, lintels, door steps, paving and flooring squares, kerbstones, gullies, mantlepieces, ridges, billiard tables, cisterns and dairy and pantry slabs. These works, using steam driven machinery, were located in Hirael (two) Garth (three) Upper Bangor and Glanadda and in 1854 works were built adjacent to the railway station.

Traffic at the port gave rise to a shipbuilding industry at Hirael and Garth. One of the first ships to be launched at Hirael was the *Bangor and Liverpool Packet* in 1808, which was built to convey passengers and goods to and from Liverpool, thus establishing an early connection between the two ports which has been maintained to the present day. The *North Wales Gazette* reported that 'the great concourse of spectators, the fineness of the day, a high tide and guns firing rendered (the launch) a pleasing sight'.[14] The launching of a ship in Bangor was an occasion for celebration; the log book of Cae Top School records the fact that the children were taken down to the shipyard at Garth to witness a launching in 1872. Between 1834 and 1851 twenty-one ships were launched from the two yards aggregating 1,345 tons and manning the boats gave employment to hundreds of young men from Bangor.

Returning to the other generator of economic activity which was discussed earlier, the importance of the road link between London and Holyhead was greatly enhanced following the passing of the Act of Union between Britain and Ireland in 1801. The Act made it necessary for Irish peers, Members of Parliament, civil servants and judges to make several journeys each year to and from London. Much needed to be done, however, to improve the road connection and in particular the crossing of the Menai Strait. Pressure from Irish Members of Parliament led to the passing of an Act in 1815 establishing the Holyhead Road Commissioners who were authorized to spend a large sum of money on improving the road and constructing a bridge across the Strait. Thomas Telford was appointed surveyor and engineer to the commissioners and the suspension bridge over the Strait which he designed was opened in 1826. One result of these improvements was the reduction in the time of the journey from

London to Holyhead from forty-one hours and twelve minutes to twenty-eight hours and six minutes.

Pigot's Directory, 1828-29, records that Bangor 'derives considerable benefit from its being on the great thoroughfare between Holyhead and London and Chester' for scores of travellers stayed at its hotels and inns every week. Many of these were enlarged and several new ones were built. Among the most elegant hotels along the London to Holyhead road were the Penrhyn Arms and the Bangor Ferry or George Hotel. Titled persons from dukes to baronets, often accompanied by their wives, families and servants patronized them, as did Members of Parliament, government ministers and officials, high ranking army officers and members of the legal profession.

It was not only by road that travellers came to Bangor, however. A regular steam packet service between Liverpool and the Menai Strait was inaugurated in 1822 and the arrival of the first packet, the *Albion*, was hailed as 'a new era in the commerce and intercourse of the Principality with the great western metropolis (Liverpool) and the manufacturing town of Manchester'.[15] A correspondent writing in the *North Wales Gazette* in 1824 reported that 'the influx of company into this town (Bangor) and the adjacent towns of Beaumaris and Caernarvon during this last fortnight . . . is unprecedented – every vehicle and horse for hire is in constant requisition . . . To the steam packets with their splendid accommodation is this country mainly indebted for the vast increase in wealth that is now circulating'.[16] Two hundred and thirty passengers landed off the steamer *Prince Llywelyn* on 23 August 1824 'rendering incalculable advantages to this neighbourhood'.[17] The prospect of increased trade from this source also induced inn and hotel keepers to improve their properties and to erect signs such as the 'Liverpool Arms', the 'Liverpool Packet' and the 'Albion'.

Bangor in the first quarter of the century, therefore, was developing as a tourist centre and local entrepreneurs quickly exploited the sea coast to provide facilities for bathing, an activity which became popular at this time. Bathing huts were placed on the beach at Hirael and sea water baths were constructed along the coast at Garth. In its issue of 2 June 1808 the *North Wales Gazette* carried an article on 'Bangor as a sea bathing place', in which the hope was expressed that Bangor would become one of the finest sea bathing places in North Wales.[18]

Less spectacular perhaps than its function as a port, with its ancillary trades and occupations and as a centre for travellers and tourists, was the service function of the city. Its weekly market, held on Fridays, and its three fair days had their origin in the middle ages, as we have already seen. Indicative of its growing status as a market centre was the building of a market house with a granary for grain and covered stalls for meat at Glanrafon in 1804. Hyde Hall was of the opinion that marketing in Bangor greatly improved after that time. This must have been so since a much larger market hall was built at Waterloo Place in the High (or Market) Street in 1817. About this time, however, properties along the High Street had either been converted into shops or had been built for that purpose. Trading, therefore, became a more permanent daily feature and the range of goods and services provided broadened in scope. By mid century, in the section of High Street between Lon-y-Popty and the present day Glynne Road, 84 per cent of premises functioned as retail or service outlets. A branch of the North and South Wales Bank had been established at the Old Bank (now Lloyds Bank) and there was a post office at 240 High Street. In addition, there were three hotels and twenty-seven public houses.[19]

Further evidence for the increasing importance of Bangor as a regional centre is afforded by the founding in the city of two institutions which were to play an important part in its future development. Firstly, the Caernarvon and Anglesey Loyal Dispensary was built in 1810 on a site near the Penrhyn Arms Hotel and visible from Beaumaris 'so that the loyal and charitable inhabitants of Anglesey could always see it'.[20] The initiative for founding a dispensary which would provide for the medical needs of people in the two counties came from Dean Warren and members of the local clergy and gentry. At a public meeting in 1842 it was resolved to attach an infirmary to the dispensary but the site was not appropriate for this. Consequently a site alongside the Holyhead Road in Upper Bangor was selected and the Caernarvonshire and Anglesey Infirmary was opened there in 1845. In the same year another institution, the workhouse of the Bangor and Beaumaris Poor Law Union was built about a mile from the centre of the city on the road to Caernarfon. The Poor Law Amendment Act, 1834, created unions of parishes to administer the Poor Law and stipulated that a workhouse should be erected in the town which acted as the market town for a group of parishes. Sixteen parishes in south east Anglesey and five in Caernarvonshire were grouped to form the Union, confirming the fact that Bangor was the market and service centre for much of south-east Anglesey as well as for its hinterland south of the Strait.

An important landmark in the development of the city was the coming of the railway in 1848. Once on the mainline between London and Holyhead, Bangor became accessible to travellers and tourists from all over the country who used it as a base to view the two bridges which now spanned the Menai Strait and visit the mountains of Snowdonia. Hopes were expressed in the *North Wales Chronicle* in March 1851[21] that Bangor would become the 'Brighton of Wales'. Hotels such as the Penrhyn Arms and the George were greatly enlarged and some new ones were built especially near the station, for instance, the Railway Hotel (1850), British Hotel (1851), Belle View Hotel, Upper Bangor (1851); a number of temperance hotels also opened along the High Street, mainly by the conversion of existing buildings. However, during this period it was the private lodging house rather than the large hotel which was the popular holiday accommodation for middle class families. Even if not built specifically for that purpose, the terraces of three and four storey houses built in Upper Bangor in the 1850s and 1860s made ideal lodging houses. There were fifty such houses in Upper Bangor in 1874 mainly in Menai View Terrace, College Road and Snowdon View Terrace and nineteen in Garth.[22]

Largely for the convenience of tourists Richard Harrison in 1851 erected 'a very commodious and convenient bath establishment at the bottom of Dean Street', containing tub and shower baths supplied with fresh and salt water at warm, tepid and cold temperatures.[23] Two years later another entrepreneur sited a number of bathing machines on the beach at Gored y Gut and in 1859 six local gentlemen entered into partnership to build a bathing facility at Siliwen on the shores of the Strait. This comprised a section of the foreshore for women bathers and another for men, each with its battery of changing huts; between the two sections they erected a building which housed two cisterns, one of which was filled with fresh water the other with sea water, the water being heated for bathing purposes. Adjoining the bath house they erected a cottage, which is still standing, to house the superintendent of the facility.[24]

The extension of the railway in 1852 to Caernarfon, in 1867 to Amlwch and in 1884 to Bethesda also increased the accessibility of Bangor to its market area, thereby enhancing its role as a service centre. Between 1851 and 1883 the number of shops on High Street increased by 50 per cent and their variety was extended. The railway also greatly altered the retail and wholesale distribution of goods; in essence it exposed the city to the competition of the expanding trading and manufacturing towns of England. Tradesmen were able to visit wholesale houses in the large cities with greater ease and to select items from their large ranges of goods. An advertisement in the *North Wales Chronicle* in May 1851 illustrates this point: it informs readers that John Parry of New London House 'had just returned from London with all novelties of the season in silk, mercery, linen and woollen drapery'[25] and soon shops were being stocked with an ever expanding range of manufactured articles. Goods from large wholesale houses could be delivered with greater speed and regularity thus saving traders a part of their normal warehousing costs. English firms established agencies and warehouse facilities in Bangor to increase their sales and services e.g. brewery companies, cleaners and dyers, sewing machine manufacturers, shipping lines and fire and life insurance companies. Furthermore the strategic position of Bangor in the rail network encouraged representatives of large wholesale firms to reside in Bangor and to use it as a base for their operations; eleven commercial travellers lived in Bangor in 1883 and each had an extensive ground covering much of North and Central Wales. Faced with competition from manufactured products, on the other hand, there was less scope for local craftsmen and between 1851 and 1871 the number of braziers decreased by 40 per cent, boot and shoe makers by 25 per cent and carpenters, joiners and cabinet makers by 24 per cent.[26]

Several government departments located their regional offices in Bangor after 1850 for the same strategic reason, for example, the District Registry of the High Court of Justice for Caernarvonshire and Anglesey (1858), the Admiralty Court, with jurisdiction over the coast of North Wales between Chester and Aberystwyth, a Bankruptcy Court, an office of the County Court, the District Registry for births, marriages and deaths and the offices of the Inland Revenue and Surveyor of Taxes for the counties of North Wales. These gave employment to a number of professional men and civil servants.

Bangor's nodal position in the rail network was a factor in its being chosen in 1858 as the site of the Normal College for the training of teachers in schools established by the British and Foreign Schools Society. The college buildings were opened in 1862 but it was 1870 before its full complement of fifty students was attained.

The University College of North Wales came into existence as a direct result of the findings of a departmental committee appointed by the government in 1880 to enquire into the state of intermediate and higher education in Wales. In its report, published in 1882, the committee recommended the establishment of a University College in North Wales and another in South Wales. Bangor was among the thirteen towns in North Wales which competed for the honour of providing a site for the northern college. Each town was asked to submit a statement of claim to three arbitrators who were to consider each statement and make a recommendation as to the most favourable location. Its focal position in the rail network of North Wales was one of the principal advantages claimed for Bangor by the local committee which was set up to prepare and submit the claims of Bangor. The statement claimed that there were 200,000 people residing within a twenty-five mile radius of Bangor and that the whole of North Wales could be reached within two and half hours' travelling time by rail from Bangor.[27] Bangor's claims found favour with the arbitrators who announced their decision on 24 August 1883.

The establishment of the Normal College and the University College strengthened Bangor's traditional role as a centre of learning which it had inherited from medieval times, even though the fortunes of its Tudor Grammar School sank to a very low level under the headship of the Rev. W. C. Totton (1838-67). At his death in 1867 the school, which had very few pupils, closed its doors and did not reopen until 1873.

It would be appropriate at this juncture to summarize the urban functions of Bangor at the time of its incorporation in 1883. Data from the 1881 Census reveal that it was the servicing function of the city which dominated the employment structure i.e. business, professional and personal services, various branches of the distributive trades and communications.[28] Local needs for clothing, furniture, leather goods, footwear and coaches were still being met in part by artisans, albeit a declining number of them. The only manufacturing industry which supplied a market wider than the local one was the slate industry.

Bangor had emerged as a regional centre of some importance in North Wales by the 1880s. Its population had increased from about 1,350 in 1801 to 9,000 in 1881, while the population of the tributary area for which it acted as the principal servicing centre had increased from about 10,000 to 27,000 in the same period. (Appendix, Table 11). After Wrexham it was the largest town in North Wales and some of its institutions, such as the cathedral, hospital, grammar school, teachers' training college and newspaper and government offices cast their influence far beyond the city's immediate market area.

Growth of this magnitude in the population was inevitably

accompanied by the physical growth of the city.[29] The original settlement focused on the cross roads adjacent to the cathedral where the road from Conwy to Caernarfon met the road from the Porthaethwy ferry to Glasinfryn. During the early decades of the century settlement spread along each of these roads; the main thrust was in an easterly direction down the High Street and substantial three and four storey houses and shops lined both sides of this street. Smaller properties flanked the road to Caernarfon towards Pendref and small two storey cottages in the main were built along Lon-y-Popty on the road across Bangor Mountain and at Glanrafon on the road to the ferry. Behind the buildings which dressed the main east to west road and out of sight from that road there developed small clusters of meanly built, tightly packed two storey terraces which housed members of the poorer classes e.g. Kyffin Square, Berllan Bach and Mountain Street.

Adjacent to the coast and close to the port there developed, principally in the 1820s, the working class district of Hirael. Here on land leased from the Dean of Bangor, the Rev. John Warren, and laid out in a grid iron pattern, were built about 300 houses. Practically all were small in size, in terrace formation and at high densities; they completely lacked basic amenities and Hirael soon became a classic slum area with a high incidence of illness and high mortality rates. Juxtaposed with these dwellings were slate and shipbuilding yards, an iron foundry and craft workshops.

Lying midway between the port district of Hirael and the commercial core around the cathedral there developed a similar settlement of about 370 mainly working class houses in grid iron pattern on a field which belonged to the Dean of Bangor; its major axis, Dean Street, ran at right angles to High Street.

The most active period of house building occurred in the twenty-five years following the end of the Napoleonic Wars. Approximately 1,100 houses were built, trebling the number of houses which existed in 1815. Just as an acute shortage of land for building on the narrow floor of the Adda valley became apparent the Penrallt Estate came onto the property market in 1833. Extending in an arc from Garth to the vicinity of the present day railway station it occupied the whole of the northern ridge that lay within the borough. Two separate centres of settlement developed on it. The first was at Garth, where houses were built to accommodate those who were primarily employed in activities connected with the sea – sailors, boatmen and shipwrights. A little later, and soon after the arrival of the railway, on the summit of the ridge and on either side of the Holyhead road the suburb of Upper Bangor began to take shape. Initially the area developed as a working class district with two storey terraced houses for artisans and railway workers, e.g. Hill Street, Albert Street and Victoria Street. Shortly afterwards, however, more substantial three and four storey terraced houses were built as private residences and lodging houses, e.g. Menai View Terrace and Summer Hill Terrace (now College Road). Large detached and semi-detached villas, each individually designed and decorated and standing in spacious grounds were built on the periphery of the settlement. Prosperous shopkeepers and traders, the professional classes and retired rentiers moved to live in the more salubrious and healthy elevated site of Upper Bangor.

These five discrete settlement nuclei are clearly visible on the map of Bangor in 1851. (Map 1). Another nucleus developed after 1850, with the coming of the railway, in the Glanadda area. Outside the borough until 1883, it was another essentially working class district with a high percentage of railwaymen among its inhabitants. The reason for the rather unusual development of the city in this manner rather than by expansion from a central core is entirely due to the disposition of land which was available for building upon. Neither the Bishop's park nor the land belonging to Friars School, occupying much of the valley floor between the cathedral and the coast, was available. Several strategically placed fields near the city centre, much of the former Penrallt Estate (after 1842) and the whole of Bangor Mountain were part of the Penrhyn Estate. After the death of Lord Penrhyn in 1808 the estate had passed into the hands of trustees who were not permitted to sell any of the land; when they infrequently leased land for building it was for the erection of superior residences.

Each one of the clearly differentiated settlements became a distinct community with its own places of worship, school, post office and local shopping centre and with strong community affiliations. The city grew after 1850 by outward expansion from each of these cores, a process of gradual coalescence which was almost complete by the outbreak of the First World War. Even so, a strong community spirit and local pride still persist in Hirael, Garth, Upper Bangor and Glanadda.

THE PERIOD 1883-1914

At the time of incorporation Bangor was nearing the zenith of its rapid nineteenth century growth. Even though its population increased by 23 per cent between 1881 and 1911 this was the smallest increase recorded in a thirty year time span since the census was first taken in 1801; it should also be pointed out that figures for 1891 and afterwards include Glanadda which was not incorporated into the borough until 1883. This modest increase in the population of Bangor was accompanied by a small decrease in the population of its tributary area over the same period. (Appendix Table 11).

The reasons for this pattern are not far to seek. Fundamental weaknesses appeared in the economic supports of the city and of the region for which it functioned as the principal service centre. The demographic haemorrhage which had afflicted the rural portion of the hinterland since the 1850s accelerated as a flood of cheap grain and foodstuffs entered the country and mechanization on the farms reduced the need for labour. It spread also to the slate quarrying district around Bethesda. From its peak in 1881 the population of this district fell by 8 per cent over the next thirty years, following a trend which was experienced by all the slate quarrying districts in Caernarvonshire. Demand for slate in both home and foreign markets slumped after about 1878 and although there was a revival in the 1890s it was short lived. Damaging strikes in the Penrhyn Quarry in 1896-7 and 1901-4 compounded the problems the industry was facing in trying to maintain its share of the market into which roofing tiles had intruded; in fourteen of the years between 1883 and 1914 production at the quarry dropped below 75,000 tons per annum, a little more than half its peak in the 1860s. In 1880 the tonnage of slate transported by rail from Port Penrhyn exceeded for the first time that shipped by water and this trend continued throughout the period. In consequence the number of mariners recorded in Bangor fell from 270 in 1871 to 81 in 1911. Shipbuilding ceased after 1878 and the number of works processing slate fell from nine in 1883 to four in 1910. Redundancies in the slate and allied industries led to unemployment and the migration of young men from the city.

As old traditional crafts and industries stagnated and declined, however, so new employment opportunities arose to help sustain the local economy. Among the activities which showed evidence of progressive growth were those connected with the railway. A branch line to Bethesda was opened in 1884 and one to Pentraeth and Red Wharf Bay from Holland Arms in 1907; these lines strengthened the ties of these districts with Bangor. Traffic on the railway system more than doubled in the period; between 1880 and 1900 the number of passenger services leaving Bangor increased from thirty-three to eighty-three. The station was extended in 1880 and a locomotive shed,

engineering workshops and carriage repair workshops were constructed. In consequence, employment was created and in 1898 the
railway company built an estate of seventy-five houses adjacent to the
station to accommodate its employees. By 1911 nearly 400 persons
were employed by the company which became the largest single
employer in the city.

The second area of growth was in the field of education. At the
beginning of the Michaelmas Term 1884 the University College,
occupying temporary premises in the former Penrhyn Arms Hotel,
opened its doors to fifty-eight students. Within fifteen years student
enrolment had risen to 300 and the need for purpose built buildings on
a permanent site became apparent. Eventually the city council
presented the college authorities with a site and in 1911 the new
buildings situated in Upper Bangor were opened.

In response to a demand for training facilities for teachers, the
governing body of the Normal College decided in 1907 to increase the
number of students in training to 200, eighty of whom were to be
women. In 1911 a new complex of buildings, including four halls of
residence and a residence for the Principal, was built on a site
adjoining that of the existing college. When in 1891 fire gutted the
college established in Caernarfon to train men students to teach in
schools belonging to the National Society, the governors decided to
build a new college in Bangor for 160 women students. St Mary's
College was built in 1893 on a site on Bangor Mountain. Two colleges
which had been established to train ministers for the Independent
religious denomination, one at Bala and the other at Bangor were
united in 1886 at Bangor. Six years later a college for the training of
ministers for the Baptist denomination moved to Bangor from
Llangollen. It is clear that by the early years of the century Bangor had
emerged as the centre *par excellence* for higher education in North
Wales. An estimated 750 students enrolled in the city's colleges in
1913. The colleges provided employment for about fifty academics
and many ancillary staff, and landladies and traders derived a
considerable income from the student population.

Another significant development in this sphere was the evolution of
Bangor as a centre for Grammar School education. In consequence of
an act passed in 1889, the administration of the endowments of Friars
School passed to a governing body appointed by the County Council.
This body decided to sell the old school building and its lands and to
build a new school on the Upper Bangor ridge; the new Friars School

opened in 1900. About the same time a County Grammar School for Girls was established in Upper Bangor.

The third area of growth was in a traditional activity, the tourist industry. Although Bangor had declined in importance as a tourist centre when more popular seaside resorts sprang up along the North Wales coast, it received a much needed fillip when the pier opened in 1896. Thereafter, thousands of day trippers and longer stay visitors disembarked from the pleasure steamers which ran a regular schedule of services from Liverpool to the North Wales resorts during the summer months. Lodging house keepers, shopkeepers and others derived benefit from this influx which integrated ideally with the occupation of the city by students during the winter months.

On balance then, the economy of Bangor continued to expand during this period and its service centre activities were consolidated. The number of retail and service trade establishments along the High Street increased by 20 per cent.[30] Significant increases were also recorded in shops dealing in various branches of the clothing and footwear trades and in institutional and professional establishments, e.g. banks, insurance offices, accounting firms and agencies. The period also witnessed the colonizing of the High Street by multiple shops; in 1883 there was only one, Dicks Shoes, but in 1914 there were fourteen. Among the pioneers were Liptons, Maypole, Star and E. B. Jones (groceries), Waterworths (fruits and vegetables), British Argentine (meat), W. H. Smith (stationery), Briggs and Dicks (shoes) and Boots Chemists.

Bangor also developed during this period as the entertainment centre for the surrounding district. Seaside vaudeville on the pier, popular in the Edwardian period, gave way firstly to the live theatre and then to the cinema; matinée performances were held and late trains arranged for the convenience of patrons who came into town from the villages nearby. Football and cricket too attracted considerable support; in 1896 Bangor footballers were top of the Welsh League and won the North Wales F.A. Cup and the Welsh Senior Cup.

Physical growth in the town during this period expressed itself in the form of accretions to the existing settlement nuclei and the following main developments may be noted. In Upper Bangor high class detached and semi-detached villas and terraced houses were built between College Road and the Strait, along the road to Garth and in the Victoria Park area. Houses for the artisan class were built on the old Friars School estate between the Dean Street and Hirael settlements, in the Sackville Road area, where the council built its first municipal houses and near the railway station at West End, Glanadda and the entrance to the Belmont tunnel. Among the public buildings erected in the period were the town clock (1886), post office (1909), library (1907) and museum (1909). The most impressive building was that of the University College (1911) which, perched on the Upper Bangor ridge and overlooking the city, gave to it an entirely new townscape feature [Plate 9(i)].

THE PERIOD 1914-1945

The main effect of the First World War on Bangor was to intensify its economic problems. Production of slate at the quarry dropped to about 26,000 tons and there was little activity at either Port Penrhyn or the slate works. Bangor was too remote to attract industries related to the needs of war and its only contribution to the war effort was to supply men for active service and to provide military training facilities, homes for refugees and hospitals for wounded servicemen.

The history of Bangor between the two World Wars must be viewed against a background of the economic depression which plagued the nation for much of the period. Throughout the country it was in those areas which depended upon primary industry for their economic support that the effects of the depression were most acutely felt. Recessional trends in agriculture and in the slate quarrying industry, apparent in the years preceding the war, intensified in the post-war period.

Wartime prosperity enjoyed by the farming community came to an abrupt end with the general fall in prices in 1921 and 1922. The industry failed to recover before the economic storm of 1929 broke and throughout the 1930s agriculture remained in a depressed state. Production of slate at the Penrhyn quarry rose sharply after the war as the government gave generous subsidies to builders of both private and local authority houses to meet the great demand. Production climbed to 50,000 tons in 1920 but a sharp fall in prices in 1921 led to stagnation in the building industry and it was not until 1933 that output again reached that level; it was then maintained until the outbreak of the Second World War.

Arising from a progressive contraction in these industries and in the ancillary trades which supported them there was unemployment and a migration of people out of the area on a hitherto unprecedented scale. At the height of the depression in 1930-31 over 35 per cent of the work force at Bethesda was out of work and over 16 per cent at Bangor.

Large numbers of employees at the city's slate works became redundant as substitutes were found for their products. Lack of work forced large numbers of people to seek work outside the area. An overall decrease of 6.5 per cent was recorded between 1911 and 1931 in the population of Bangor and its tributary area, the largest fall occurring in the rural districts where there was both outmigration and natural decrease, i.e. deaths exceeded births. Bangor itself recorded a decrease of 276 people between 1911 and 1931, the first significant fall in numbers since census data were collected in 1801. This is a deceptively low figure, however, since the University College was in session in 1931 but not at the time of the 1911 census. If the 600 or so students at the University were excluded from the 1931 total, the population of Bangor would have shown an 8 per cent fall between 1911 and 1931. This trend undoubtedly continued throughout the 1930s in both the city and its hinterland.

Not until the clouds of war were gathering in 1938 did the government take the first positive initiatives to provide alternative employment. Funds were then made available to build a factory at Glanadda which was leased to Messrs. Daimler for the production of components for their Pegasus aircraft engines. During the war several hundred people gained employment there.

Despite the effects of the depression and of outmigration there is evidence to suggest that Bangor strengthened its position as a regional centre. In the first place the inter-war period was one in which substantial progress was made in raising living standards generally, and secondly, the expansion in the number of rail and road services from Bangor and in the number of privately owned motor vehicles made it possible for people to visit the city more frequently and to spend more money there. These factors combined to create a greater demand for goods, services and entertainments which helped in part to counteract the effects of unemployment and outmigration. The balance was probably delicately poised. The number of commercial outlets along the High Street increased by less than 3 per cent between 1910 and 1938 though this does not of course take into consideration the fact the the retail sales area of a number of shops was extended by the redevelopment of ground floors and by the conversion of first floors into retail sales and office accommodation. In fact, the number of offices along High Street doubled during the period, mainly in first floor premises. Several national multiple stores such as Bradleys, Burtons and Hepworths (clothing), Freeman Hardy and Willis and Olivers (shoes), George Masons and Irwins (groceries), Astons (furnishings) and Woolworths established branches.

Evidence of growth is also apparent in two groups of regional institutions which were located in Bangor, namely educational establishments and hospitals. The termination of the hostilities of war saw the return of men to the University College and the Normal College to resume their studies and a post-war peak of 672 students was attained at the University College in the 1920-21 session. Numbers fell later yet the average number of students enrolled in the five years preceding the Second World War was 571 compared with 332 for a similar period before the First World War. A large building programme to house the science departments on a site along Deiniol Road was activated in 1924 and when completed the transfer of the college from its original Penrhyn Hotel site was accomplished. Increased numbers of students at the Normal College after the war induced the authority to purchase the George Hotel, near the suspension bridge, to accommodate its men students. During the 1930s two new schools were built: a girls' Grammar School at Ffriddoedd (1939) to replace the one in Upper Bangor and a Higher Grade School on Deiniol Road (1936).

Hospital services continued to expand. New wings were added to the Caernarvonshire and Anglesey Infirmary in 1923 and 1932 and in 1936 the infirmary was recognized by the General Nursing Council as a training school for nurses. In 1911, 221 persons were treated as in-patients; the corresponding figures for 1921, 1931 and 1945 were 474, 1,149 and 3,542 respectively. The hospital built for the Guardians of the Poor Law Union in 1916 was converted into a children's and maternity hospital in 1938. New wards were also added to the Isolation Hospital (1937) which now took in patients from adjoining local authority districts.

Bangor succeeded in attracting yet another important regional institution during this period. The British Broadcasting Corporation began transmitting programmes in both English and Welsh from studios in Cardiff in 1923 and Swansea in 1924. Pressure mounted in the late 1920s and early 1930s for the establishment of a studio and improved transmission facilities in north Wales. Bryn Meirion, a large house in Upper Bangor, became vacant in 1934 and by the end of 1935 the B.B.C. had converted it into a studio in which a wide variety of programmes in English and Welsh were produced. It also erected a transmitter across the Strait at Penmon in 1937.

Bangor was able to improve its position as a regional service centre largely because of its strategic location with respect to the rail and road network of the area. Traffic on both networks increased, particularly on the roads, due to a big expansion in the number of motor vehicles in use. The first application by a bus company for a licence to operate passenger services from Bangor was made by a Llandudno company in 1912; in 1913 companies in Bangor, Bethesda and Caernarfon were granted similar licences. The Bangor Blue Bus Company was formed in 1921 and by 1928 it was operating along ten routes, employing over a hundred men and running a fleet of thirty-five buses. Many of the bus operators, however, used inferior vehicles, had no proper timetables and competition between them made the task of co-ordinating services very difficult. This state of affairs was remedied by the Road Traffic Act of 1930 which established a more rigid licensing system. The Act benefited the larger enterprises at the expense of the smaller and helped to enable the Crosville Motor Company, whose original provenance was the Chester and Wirral area, to acquire an almost complete monopoly of public passenger bus services in the area by 1935. The company built a major depot in Bangor in 1931 from which it directed a greatly expanded, efficient and co-ordinated bus service. By the late 1930s nearly 300 buses were leaving Bangor daily for the surrounding districts and express coaches maintained a regular connection with Birkenhead and Liverpool. One of the effects of the development of bus services was to complete the process begun by the railway after 1859 of extending the influence of Bangor into south-west Anglesey, an area which had traditionally looked towards Caernarfon as its market centre, using the ferry as a transport link.

Undeterred by the growing volume of road traffic the railway company carried out a major reconstruction scheme at the station in 1924. Throughout the period the number of scheduled train departures steadily increased to reach a peak of ninety-eight in 1939. In the years immediately before the Second World War about 250,000 passengers arrived at Bangor station each year.[31]

Even though the inter-war years were years of modest development, the physical appearance of the city changed considerably. Inducements by the government to local authorities to build houses to help mitigate the chronic housing shortages of the post-war period and, in the 1930s, to replace slum dwellings, resulted in the building by the council of nearly 900 houses. Some of these were built as infilling in vacant plots in the built up area or as a part of a redevelopment project, but the greatest number was built on large estates on the periphery of the city at Penchwintan, Maes Tryfan, Brynllwyd and Maesgeirchen. Another 500 private houses were built on estates at Meirion Lane and Belmont and as ribbon developments along Ffriddoedd Road and Penrhos Road. Many more houses were built during this twenty year period than at any similar period in the city's history. Built at much lower densities they occupied more land and the effect was to greatly extend the built up area; to keep pace with the westward march of the city, its boundaries in that direction were extended in 1934. On the other hand, 580 houses were declared unfit for human habitation and were demolished, thereby erasing some of the oldest districts, notably the Dean Street area.

The Second World War witnessed an infusion of new life into the veins of the city. At the outbreak of war hundreds of government sponsored evacuees from Liverpool were assigned to Bangor and many more people came of their own accord. Boys from the Liverpool Collegiate School shared lessons with Friars boys and students from the University of London attended lectures at the University College. Perhaps the most notable evacuees from 1940 to 1942 were members of the Variety Department of the B.B.C., including artistes of nationwide renown such as Tommy Handley and Sandy MacPherson. Also for the first time in Bangor's history, opportunities of employment for both men and women were provided in light manufacturing industries orientated towards the war effort, e.g. aircraft components at Brynllwyd, naval ships at Dickie's yard in Garth and at Saunders Roe's works outside Beaumaris.

THE PERIOD 1945-1974

The Second World War marks a significant turning point in the economic life of Bangor and its hinterland, as it did in the life of the nation as a whole. For the purpose of analysis the period between 1945 and 1974 may be divided into two roughly equal parts. From 1945 to the late 1950s employment opportunities in the region's primary industries continued to decline and the failure to attract new forms of manufacturing employment on a significant scale led to the intensification of the inter-war economic syndrome of low rates of economic activity, high levels of unemployment, low wages and outmigration of the more active and better qualified persons of working age. Between the late 1950s and the early 1970s the situation changed dramatically: government policy encouraged the siting of light industry in peripheral areas of the country and there was a big expansion in tertiary and quaternary employment. Living standards rose appreciably and business and service activities benefited.

Immediately after the war demand for slate to repair war damage and roof new houses sent production levels up to 20,000 tons in 1946 (about half the level of output in the 1930s). The industry was not able to compete however with mass produced tiles and production was down to 7,000 tons in 1964 when a construction company, McAlpines, secured a 51 per cent interest in the quarry and spent about half a million pounds on a modernization scheme. Production climbed back to 10,000 tons in the early 1970s but rationalization and mechanization reduced the workforce to under 300. No slate was shipped by sea from Port Penrhyn after the war and in 1952 the narrow gauge railway line connecting the quarry and port was dismantled. Lack of demand for slate products led to the closure of the three remaining slate manufacturing works by 1952. Slate handling and manufacturing, which had been a cornerstone of the city's economy for decades was no longer carried on. Wartime factories at Brynllwyd and Beaumaris however continued in production, albeit orientated to peace time needs.

The weakness of the economic base is revealed in the census data for 1951 and 1961. Apart from Bangor and Menai Bridge all the rural and urban districts within Bangor's sphere of influence declined in population. Although Bangor recorded an increase of nearly 1,200 people, it must be emphasized that whereas over 1,000 students were enumerated in 1961, the colleges were on vacation at the time of the 1951 census. There was therefore a net loss of population from the area as a whole in the 1950s.

A dramatic change occurred in the demographic situation during the 1960s. For the first time since 1891 every local government district in the area recorded an increase and the overall increase of nearly 10 per cent was nearly twice the national average; Aethwy Rural District registered an increase of 17 per cent which is remarkable bearing in mind the fact that this area had been losing population consistently for over a century.

What factors were responsible for this change in fortunes? Prominent among them are the inducements given by the government in legislation passed in 1958 and 1960 to manufacturers to locate their plants in the peripheral areas of the country. Further, under the Industrial Development Act of 1966 the whole of North Wales was designated a Development Area and an array of incentives, grants and tax advantages was offered to manufacturers who located their factories in this area. In response to the legislation, industrial estates were opened in Llangefni (1958) and Llandegai (1965). The largest single industrial investment in the region was a factory built by

Messrs. Ferodo near Caernarfon in 1961-62 providing employment for nearly 1,000 people. By the early 1970s nearly 3,000 jobs had been created in light manufacturing, requiring a wide range of skills and giving employment to a significant number of women.

The second factor in the regeneration of the economy of the area was the expansion in the monies the government allocated to further and higher education and in the encouragement it gave to young people to study at these levels. In an expanding national economy there were urgent demands from industry and commerce for qualified scientists, technologists and managers and in response to these demands the government approved in 1958 a large expansion programme at existing universities and the founding of seven new ones. A comprehensive development plan was commissioned at the University College and a number of new buildings, each reflecting in their brick, concrete and glass structures the architectural tastes of the decade, were erected. Between 1960 and 1970 the number of students almost doubled and there was a corresponding increase in the number of academic and ancillary staff.

Expansion in the 1960s was not confined to the University College: in 1960 the duration of the training course for teachers at Colleges of Education was extended from two to three years and throughout the 1960s and early 1970s the two colleges took in more students in order to satisfy the demands of schools for teachers. Both the Normal and St Mary's College doubled in size and large extensions were added to them. Further and technical education was not neglected in this affluent decade. Bangor was chosen in 1957 as the site for Caernarvonshire's new Technical College which was planned to provide National Certificate courses in engineering, building construction and science among an array of vocational and general studies courses at lower levels. About 100 full time teaching and ancillary staff were employed there at the end of the decade. Furthermore the city's schools grew in response to a rising birth rate up to the mid-1960s, the extension in the period of full time schooling and the greater participation in education beyond the statutory period.

Another reason for buoyancy in the local economy was the rising demand for retail, financial, commercial and personal services which was brought about not only by higher population numbers but by greater affluence in particular. During the summer months this demand was augmented by the needs of tourists. Although Bangor was no longer a centre for long stay visitors, thousands of tourists passing through the cathedral city or staying in holiday accommodation of various sorts within reach of the Anglesey beaches and Snowdonia mountains would visit it and make use of its service facilities. One manifestation of affluence was the steady growth in the number of privately owned motor cars and this trend inevitably led to more frequent visits being made by people living within the city's hinterland. In time it had the effect of concentrating urban services in Bangor at the expense of smaller centres. The demand for services was met by the employment of more personnel and by the extension and redevelopment of a high percentage of premises along the High Street, by the building of a sixty unit shop and office complex at Wellfield in the heart of the commercial core and by the siting of supermarket stores nearer the periphery.

Growth in the field of health and hospital services was particularly apparent. Between 1937 and 1968 the number of admissions to the C. and A. Hospital increased from 1,908 to 6,768 and the number of operations from 1,361 to 4,817. The number of outpatients increased from 3,108 to 29,044 in the same period. A large extension was added to the C. and A. Hospital (1963) and to the St David's maternity, children's and geriatric hospital (1966). New group headquarters were built on the St David's site in 1968. Nearly 800 people were employed in the city's hospitals and health establishments in 1970, making the service the second largest single employer after the education service.

Finally, Bangor's role as a regional centre was consolidated during the period. A new government office block was built in 1957 to house the offices of the Inland Revenue, Employment Exchange and National Assistance Board (Glynne House) and a new telephone exchange, incorporating office accommodation for various government departments, was built on Deiniol Road in 1953. With the rationalization of postal services in 1970, Bangor became the postal centre for an area which included the whole of Anglesey and the greater part of Caernarvonshire. Cultural activities at the University College attracted allied institutions such as the north Wales offices of the Arts Council, British Council and Workers Educational Association, an Open University centre and the headquarters of the Welsh Theatre Company. The presence of renowned departments of agriculture and the environmental sciences, with the research facilities and skilled personnel attached to them, was a factor in the choice of Bangor for the regional offices of the National Agricultural Advisory Service and the headquarters and research station for Wales of the Nature Conservancy. To the B.B.C.'s radio studio was added a television studio and the I.B.A. also established a television studio.

Further consideration might be given to the impact of an increase in motor car ownership on the economic and social life of Bangor and its region. Its effect on the public transport system, a major employer of labour, was dramatic. Rail services were the first to be pruned; one by one all the branch lines radiating from Bangor were closed and by 1969 only the main line between London and Holyhead remained. Contraction and rationalization led to the closure of the locomotive maintenance and cleaning sheds (1965) and the engineering head-quarters and various workshops (1966). Railway staff dwindled from 550 persons in 1954 to 135 in 1970 and in the following year the station could not even support a full time station manager. Bus services also felt the impact of the motor car and as services contracted, staff at the Crosville Depot shrank from 208 in 1952 to 105 in 1970. The rail service and many of the bus services were kept going primarily as a social service and were supported by money funded by local and central government.

Increased volume of road traffic gave rise to congestion in the city itself and, at peak travelling times, along the main roads into the city. The problem was particularly acute at the suspension bridge and was exacerbated during summer months by the flow of tourist traffic. In an attempt to maintain the city centre as a viable commercial area, land in the twilight zone bordering the business core was scheduled for car parking and the High Street itself was pedestrianized.

Perhaps the most significant effect of greater mobility was the opportunity it afforded people who worked in town to satisfy their preference for living in the country. The Report of the Royal Commission on Local Government in England highlighted this trend and claimed that 'decentralization of population from towns into surrounding areas, and often deep into rural districts, has become a main feature of present day life'.[32] Decentralization in the Bangor area has resulted in substantial growth in a number of small towns and villages around the city, particularly along a stretch of the north shore of the Strait between Llanfairpwll and Beaumaris. There was a 26 per cent increase in the population of this strip between 1961 and 1971, contrasted with a small decrease in the population of Bangor itself, if persons in private households only are considered. Llanfairpwll, Menai Bridge, Llandegfan, Tregarth, Bethesda and Llanfairfechan became as much suburbs of Bangor in the early 1970s as were Penrhos and Maesgeirchen in the 1930s. On the other hand, greater mobility made it possible for people living in the districts around Bangor to commute to work rather than to have to move there to live. Growing employment opportunities in Bangor during the 1960s and 1970s therefore were a factor in halting migration from the traditional agricultural and slate quarrying areas of its hinterland. In term time the daily flow to work was augmented by students studying at the city's colleges; in 1971, for example, 587 students or 23 per cent of students at the University College lived in lodgings, flats, cottages and caravans outside the borough boundary.

Separation of residence from workplace has resulted in the growing interdependence of urban and rural areas. Whilst Bangor provides a range of employment opportunities for people living in the surrounding countryside, scores of Bangor residents too, leave each day to work in factories and industrial estates which have been built out in the country on green field sites. The growing economic and social interdependence of urban and rural areas was stressed in the Report of the Royal Commission on Local Government in England and concluded that 'it seems inevitable that all these forms of interdependence . . . will intensify'.[33] The principle that the division between town and country for local government purposes is no longer relevant was accepted in the Consultative Document on the Reform of Local Government in Wales whose proposals were embodied in the Local Government Act, 1972. Under this Act, which came into force on 1 April 1974, Bangor's status as a municipal borough was swept away and with it its mayor and council as constituted in 1883. New administrative arrangements reduced the status of the city to that of a community but at the same time preserved the title of mayor for the chairman.

Physical growth of the city during the period 1945 to 1974 was primarily along its southern and western margins. Two large extensions were added to the Maesgeirchen housing estate in 1953-58 and 1967-68, and the council's Coed Mawr scheme (1955-67) and private developments at Eithinog (1955-70) and Trefonwys (1965-66) have used up much of what remained of land suitable for building within the borough. More spectacular perhaps were the numerous buildings raised for a variety of purposes by the university and college authorities nearer the core of the city and those built as a result of the redevelopment of existing sites in the core itself.

THE PERIOD 1974-1983

The period since local government reorganization in 1974 has not been a particularly happy one for the nation. World oil price rises dating from 1973, dangerously high inflation rates, labour unrest, deep, world-wide recession, strict economies in the public services and high rates of unemployment have left unfulfilled many of the promises and expectations of the prosperous 1960s and early 1970s. While Bangor has not escaped the trauma of these events it has succeeded in weathering the adversities of the past decade remarkably well. This may be attributed to two principal reasons. The first is the fact that people were still moving into the area to live. While the population of England and Wales was practically static between 1971 and 1981 (it rose 0.6 per cent), that of Bangor and its tributary area increased by 9.4 per cent, a rate greater even than in the previous decade (9.1 per cent).[34] Population growth on the attractive northern shore of the Strait between Llanfairpwll and Llandegfan and within easy commuting distance of Bangor increased by 35 per cent. Secondly, statistical evidence for the country as a whole shows that real consumers' expenditure, after allowing for inflation, rose by 14 per cent between 1972 and 1982. Over 70 per cent of households in 1982 now had a vacuum cleaner, refrigerator, washing machine and colour television; 60 per cent had a car and central heating and the number of people taking holidays increased by 15 per cent in the decade.[35] There is no reason to doubt that the population in the Bangor area shared to the same degree in this increasing prosperity.

Population growth and increased affluence have led to a greater demand for goods and services which Bangor, as the local regional centre, has provided in large measure. Employment in the service sector of the local economy increased by 30 per cent between 1971 and 1978,[36] many city centre premises have been enlarged and a number of commercial firms have established themselves at the new Britannia Shopping Centre near the western boundary of the city.

Despite reductions in public expenditure, the hospital and health services have had to cope with the steadily increasing demands which have been placed upon them. The number of admissions, operations and outpatients at the C. and A. Infirmary increased by 10, 15 and 5 per cent respectively between 1972 and 1982.[37] Ever since the Second World War a new hospital had been planned for Bangor but it was not until 1976 that work began on building a regional hospital at Penrhosgarnedd. Plagued by faulty design and planning problems the hospital, Ysbyty Gwynedd, was not officially opened until 1984. Regional headquarters of the Welsh Water Authority were established at Penrhosgarnedd in 1978.

Few in the expansionary days of the 1960s would have predicted the contraction which has occurred in higher education over the past decade. Declining birth rates after 1964, dropping very sharply between 1970 and 1977, forced the government to drastically reduce the number of teachers in training and to use the opportunity to restructure and rationalize the higher education system. St Mary's College lost its separate identity in 1976 when it was merged with the University College and the number of full-time students at the Normal College fell rapidly from around 850 in 1975-76 to 329 in 1981-82. The turn of the University to contract came in the 1980s; the 1983-84 session opened with 2,673 students, compared twith 2,962 in 1980-81, the number of academic staff had been reduced and the sale of the St Mary's campus was being considered.

The brunt of the recession of the past few years has been borne principally by manufacturing industry, which is a relatively minor component of Bangor's economy (12 per cent of those employed in 1978).[38] Although a number of firms have left the industrial estates in the district, others have been established and on aggregate there has been a small increase in the number employed in this sector. In addition, several major public works projects such as the Dinorwic pumped storage electricity scheme (opened in May 1984), the reconstruction of the Britannia Bridge and the construction of new approach roads (opened 1979), and the Llanfairpwll and Bangor by-passes (opened 1983) have provided employment opportunities for local labour. Even so, the rate of unemployment in the Bangor area has risen in line with national trends from 5.5 per cent in 1973 to over 16 per cent in 1982.[39]

In the year which marked the centenary of the city council, Bangor stood out as the principal regional centre in north-west Wales. Pre-eminently a shopping and service centre for the area astride the Menai Strait it has in addition a wide range of functions and institutions which serve an area well beyond its immediate hinterland and in this respect, and considering its size, it is probably unique in the United Kingdom. Despite the changes which the passing of time has inevitably wrought, there are certain strands in its fabric which can be traced to the medieval period and beyond, notably its function as a diocesan, market, educational and route centre commanding an important crossing of the Menai Strait. The cathedral, around which the city grew, remains a living witness to the Christian faith which led Deiniol to found his cell on the banks of the River Adda over fourteen centuries ago.

*Notes*

1. Sir J. E. Lloyd, Presidential Address, *Archeologica Cambrensis*, 92(1937), p. 201.
2. L. T. Smith (ed), John Leland, *Itinerary in Wales . . . 1536-39* (London, 1906), pp. 80-81.
3. Browne Willis, *A Survey of the Cathedral Church . . . of Bangor* (London, 1721), p. 49.
4. U(niversity) C(ollege) of N(orth) W(ales) MSS, 2943 and 2944 and G(wynedd) A(rchives) S(ervice), Vaynol MS. 245.
5. Browne Willis, p. 50.
6. W. Hutton, *A Tour of North Wales* (Birmingham, 1799).
7. J. Evans, *A Tour through a part of North Wales in the year 1798* (London, 1800), pp. 229-30.
8. UCNW, Penrhyn MSS. 812 and 815.
9. A. H. Dodd, p. 232.
10. GAS, Penrhyn Port Books, XM/1998.
11. E. Hyde Hall, *A Description of Caernarvonshire, 1809-11*, edited by E. Gwynne Jones, (Caernarfon, 1952) p. 146.
12. W. Bingley, North Wales delineated from two excursions, second edition (London, 1814), p. 112.
13. GAS, Penrhyn Port Books, XM/1998.
14. N(orth) W(ales) G(azette), 28 July 1808.
15. NWG, 13 June 1822.
16. NWG, 29 July 1824.
17. NWG, 26 August 1824.
18. NWG, 2 June 1808.
19. P. E. Jones (1973), p. 186.
20. Inscription on plaque erected at the entrance to the Dispensary, now Tan-y-Coed.
21. N(orth) W(ales) C(hronicle), 22 March 1851.
22. Worrall's Directory of North Wales, (Oldham, 1874).
23. NWC, 26 June 1851.
24. See P. E. Jones (1975), pp. 124-35.
25. NWC, 31 May 1851.
26. Calculated from data in Enumerators Schedules for the City of Bangor for the censuses of 1851 and 1871.
27. UCNW, Belmont MS 67, 'A statement of the advantages that commend Bangor as the best site for the University College in North Wales'.
28. Enumerators Schedules, 1881 Census.
29. For a detailed analysis of the chronological growth of the city see P. E. Jones (1973).
30. P. E. Jones (1973) p. 337.
31. NWC, 14 May 1937.
32. Royal Commission on Local Government in England, 1966-69, Report, Cmnd. 4040, 3, p. 31.
33. Ibid., p. 35.
34. The census was taken when the city's colleges were on vacation whereas the 1971 census occurred during term time. Since comparisons between the 1971 and 1981 population would be misleading, the Gwynedd County Planning Department obtained an estimate of students away on census night 1981. On the basis of this information the Department has amended the 1981 population figures in order to enable comparison with the 1971 census data. It is the amended figures that are

used as the basis for these figures. See 'Gwynedd 1981, Information Sheet 1, Population Change' published by Gwynedd County Planning Department.
35. Central Statistical Office, Social Trends 14 (1983).
36. Census of Employment, 1971 and 1978. The figures relate to the Employment Exchange Areas of Bangor, Beaumaris and Bethesda.
37. From data supplied by Gwynedd Health Authority.

| C. & A. General Hospital | 1972 | 1982 |
|---|---|---|
| Admissions | 8,896 | 9,798 |
| No. of operations | 5,104 | 5,987 |
| No. of out-patients | 15,811 | 16,570 |

38. Census of Employment, 1978.
39. The figures relate to the numbers unemployed in June 1973 and June 1982 at the Bangor, Bethesda and Beaumaris Job Centre areas. Data obtained from the Manpower Intelligence Unit, Wales, Manpower Services Commission, Cardiff.

# CHAPTER 2

## LOCAL GOVERNMENT BEFORE 1883

FOR CENTURIES the small settlement clustering around the cathedral was an integral part of the manor of the bishop of Bangor. The bishop's title to the manor was confirmed by Edward I following the defeat of Llywelyn, the last Prince of Wales, in 1282. Certain privileges, such as the right to hold fairs and to operate a ferry across the Strait, were granted to the bishop by the monarch in the next century.

The bishop exercised supreme authority within his manor but in practice delegated his powers to his steward and court leet and baron over which the steward presided. The court had both judicial and administrative functions and the bishop's tenants were obliged to attend when summoned. Twelve of its number were elected jurors to settle judicial matters brought before it. Others assisted the steward in the administration of the manor, e.g. as constables, whose duty was to maintain law and order.

Early in the fourteenth century the bishop granted a charter to sixteen named burgesses conferring upon them certain privileges with respect to the court and to trade, but at the same time he imposed upon them certain obligations.[1] Their prerogatives were very limited, however, when compared with the rights enjoyed by the burgesses of the neighbouring castle dominated boroughs of Beaumaris, Caernarfon and Conwy, each of which had been granted a royal charter. The embryonic borough, possibly stifled by medieval autocracy, failed to evolve and acquire the status of its neighbours. When the Caernarvon Boroughs Parliamentary Constituency was created by the Act of Union 1536 Bangor was not designated one of the contributory boroughs.

Throughout the fifteenth and early sixteenth century changes taking place in the fabric of medieval society led gradually but inexorably to the disintegration of the manorial system. A new class of landowning gentry arose and to this class the Tudors entrusted the administration of the county. As justices of the peace they became responsible for maintaining order, dispensing justice and, indeed, for most activities which fell within the ambit of local government at that time. Yet, the Act of Union allowed the perpetuation of manorial courts and although most of them became practically effete, there is evidence that the bishop's court at Bangor was active up to 1818;[2] constables were being appointed each year and in 1805 the jury of the manor court, who managed the surviving common lands of the manor and the pound, were consulted in connection with the granting of a building lease on a portion of the commons.[3]

The relationship between the manor court and the parish vestry is not clear. Originally a meeting of the parishioners, called together to discuss matters pertaining to the church, the vestry had acquired responsibility for keeping the roads in a state of repair, and, under the Poor Law Act of 1601, for the care of the poor. To this latter end the Act empowered the vestry to levy a rate on property and to appoint an overseer to collect the rate and dispense assistance to the poor. The Act, however, being permissive, was not adopted in Caernarvonshire until the end of the eighteenth century; that the parish of Bangor had adopted the Act is evident from the decision of the churchwardens and overseers in 1803 to build twenty-four cottages to house the paupers of the parish.[4] No more was heard of the bishop's court after 1818. In that year the Vestries Act, followed in 1819 by the Poor Relief Act, strengthened the powers of vestries in the management of parochial affairs. It is safe to assume, therefore, that parochial administration superseded episcopal management from that time.

The vestry, however, with its limited powers and responsibilities, was grossly ill equipped to manage the affairs of the rapidly growing city. Part-time, unpaid constables appointed by the vestry could not possibly cope with the rising level of crime committed in the burgeoning community. In a desperate attempt to protect their properties the well heeled gentlemen of the city got together in 1808 to form an Association for the Apprehension of Felons, but it was not particularly successful in combating crime. Having adopted the permissive Lighting and Watching Act of 1833, the vestry appointed three or four part-time but paid constables to keep order; judging from correspondence in the *North Wales Chronicle* they again were not very effective. In the 1840s money from county rates paid for a police station and new lock-up which replaced the existing filthy and insecure one. A county police force, under the control of the county justices, was set up in 1856 following the passing of the County Police

Act of that year and for the first time Bangor was served by a disciplined and well organized police force.

Another function removed from the jurisdiction of the vestry was the relief of the poor. The Poor Law Amendment Act, 1834, authorized the grouping together of parishes for the purpose of poor law administration and the erection of a workhouse in the market town which acted as the natural focus for a group of parishes. The workhouse for the Bangor and Beaumaris Poor Law Union was erected in Bangor in 1845 on the site in Glanadda from which the twenty-four cottages built for the poor of the parish of Bangor had been cleared.

Turnpike Trusts took over responsibility for the main roads through Bangor at the end of the eighteenth century. The other roads continued to be inadequately maintained by the parish even though the vestry appointed a part-time paid surveyor, whose office was sanctioned by the Highway Act, 1835. Roads supposedly maintained by the trusts and the parish were in a deplorable state; the condition of unadopted streets leading off these roads must defy imagination.

In response to a call from the inhabitants of Bangor for the lighting of streets a public meeting was held in 1829 to concert measures for that purpose, but there is no evidence that a lighting system was installed. Some fourteen years later an Irishman, James Smyth Scott, purchased a plot of land at the bottom of Well Street for the erection of a gas making plant and gasometer. In 1845 Scott constituted the Bangor Gas and Coke Company with a capital of £2,500 comprised of 250 £10 shares, half of which were taken by Scott himself and the remainder by nine local tradesmen. An *ad hoc* lighting committee was appointed by the parish vestry, in accordance with the Lighting and Watching Act 1833, to administer a street lighting system using gas. By 1849 forty street lamps had been erected along High Street.

In the same year that he built the gas works Scott constructed a reservoir at Cae Ffynnon Deiniol, above Glanadda (120 feet above sea level), and piped water into town through a three inch diameter pipe. Two years later he sold to Hugh Roberts, Draper, of High Street, a half share of his interest in the waterworks and agreed that Roberts should become manager. In 1846 Roberts bought Scott's share in the enterprise, built a new reservoir a little higher up the hillside at Nant (210 feet above sea level) and extended the distribution system.[5]

Innovations such as a rudimentary gas and water supply system did little to mitigate the intolerable pressures on the inhabitants, especially in the field of public health. Inadequate supplies of well water, a polluted River Adda, an almost complete absence of a drainage and sewerage system, filthy streets and tightly packed, poorly built houses, lacking basic amenities and invariably overcrowded, were the recipe for miserable living conditions, the persistence of endemic and epidemic diseases and excessively high mortality rates. Problems such as these could only be relieved by concerted action entailing enormous capital expenditure, yet neither local entrepreneurs nor the feeble public bodies which then existed were capable of addressing themselves to the solution of these problems. The Poor Law Guardians, for example, who were saddled with the responsibility of carrying out the provisions of the Nuisances Removal and Diseases Prevention Act, 1846, reported 'without extended powers we can do nothing effectively in the way of sanitary reform'.[6]

The threat of another cholera epidemic in 1848 focused the minds of sanitary reformers on unified measures of sanitary control. The government rushed through parliament the Public Health Act, the first national legislation in the field of public health charged with undertaking measures of sanitary reform and the abatement of nuisances injurious to health. In accord with the ethos of the time, the Act was a permissive one yet mandatory in towns where the death rate exceeded 23 per thousand. Initiative for its application rested upon the inhabitants of a town who were instructed to petition the General Board of Health in London.

Public discussion in Bangor culminated in the calling of a vestry meeting in November 1848 at which it was resolved to petition the General Board of Health '. . . praying that the town may be brought under the operation of the Public Health Act'.[7] The petition was forwarded by Col. Pennant of Penrhyn Castle, the M.P. for the County of Caernarvon, and in June the following year, George Clark, a General Board Inspector, visited Bangor to report upon its sanitary state. His investigations revealed that the mean mortality rate of the Bangor sub-district of the Bangor and Beaumaris Union was 23.1 per thousand and that the rate in the town itself was even greater. Clark therefore had no hesitation in recommending that Bangor be placed under the operation of the Public Health Act. He recommended that the Local Board of Health which would be established under the Act should be composed of nine members, one third of whom should retire each year, and that its area of jurisdiction should include not only the parliamentary borough but also an extension to the west to the line of Hendrewen – Ainon and Belmont Road.[8] The Board, once established, should undertake to extend a piped water supply to all houses, construct a comprehensive sewerage and drainage system, instal privies or water closets where they did not exist and make these facilities mandatory in all new houses. In addition, the Board was empowered to make by-laws to limit nuisances, particularly those arising from slaughter houses, low lodging houses and the state of the streets. Improvements recommended by Clark were to be paid for by the community; three rates, a water rate, a sewerage or general district rate and a private improvement rate would be levied on owners or occupiers of property.[9]

The Public Health Act was made applicable to the city by an Order in Council dated 14 August 1850 and after elections the Board held its first meeting in October 1850. There are a number of reasons why the inhabitants of Bangor petitioned for the application of the Act to the city. Fear of an imminent outbreak of cholera was the immediate one. Hundreds of sailors arrived each week from ports around the coast and mingled with the local populace in their homes and public houses, especially in Hirael, where sanitary conditions were notoriously bad. The editor of the *North Wales Chronicle* warned his readers in October 1848 of 'the presence of Asiatic cholera within our immediate confines'[10] and three weeks later there appeared in the same paper a long letter headed 'The Cholera' in which advice was proffered for the prevention of the disease.[11] There is no evidence that an epidemic broke out in the autumn of 1848 but one was reported in the local papers in July and August 1849.

Another reason for seeking an administrative structure which would create a cleaner and healthier city was the fact that Bangor derived some of its prosperity from visitors; a growth in their number was eagerly anticipated now that the railway had been extended to Bangor and another masterpiece of engineering skill had been erected across the Menai Strait. A third reason was that ratepayers accepted the argument that preventative measures were justified on economic grounds. By reducing sickness and preventing the early death of the breadwinner of a family the burden on the parish poor rates would be eased.

However, the fundamental reason for Bangor's initiative was the wretched sanitary state of the city and the relationship which was then perceived, though not properly understood, between filth and disease. An insight into the insalubrious state of the town at mid-century may be gleaned from the local press and from Clark's report.

A Leader in the *North Wales Chronicle* in 1850 lamented the fact that:

Although a more delightfully situated spot is not to be found . . . the people seem to have been very careless about those arrangements by which health and comfort can alone be secured . . . and the vilest nuisances have been tolerated and encouraged until it may be said that every inhabitant has set himself down in the midst of filth.[12]

The absence of an effective drainage and sewerage system was the subject of frequent censure:

Public sewers there are none: and the drains which were constructed by the Shrewsbury and Holyhead road authorities . . . are, with few exceptions, the only outlets into which the contents of privies and offal from the houses can be discharged . . . they serve as receptacles for filth, and act as conduits to distribute offensive effluvia, which become a perfect nuisance and a prolific source of diseases.

In Hirael there was a large open ditch '. . . into which whatever filth passes from the houses on the south side of the main street, and to the eastward of Dean Street, finds a vent. This ditch, or rather general reservoir for animal and vegetable putridities, becomes in dry weather extremely offensive'. Dr Pring, informed Clark that 'Fevers of a typhoid form are constantly generated at Kyffin Square, Glan-yr-Afon, . . . Drum Street and Hirael, owing to the constant miasmata arising from the decomposition of animal and vegetable matter accumulating in open drains'.[13]

Many houses had no privies at all, and Dr Owen Owen Roberts regarded the 'absence of proper accommodations, such as ought to be attached to every house . . . a source of great discomfort and . . . a direct tendency to produce disease'.[14] A correspondent writing in the *North Wales Chronicle* complained 'that occupiers of houses having no back yards necessarily commit all sorts of nuisances and trespasses on the public thoroughfares'.[15] Mary Pritchard, living in Glan-yr-Afon, had no back premises at all and no privy. 'The (night) soil', she affirmed, 'is thrown into the brook (River Adda)'.[16] Even the King's Arms Tavern on High Street had '. . . no privy at all. The soil is collected in a box and carried to the brook, just above where it enters the Deanery garden'.[17] The River Adda had become a running sewer, since '. . . all the drains from the streets, the offal of slaughter houses and skinners' yards and wastes from the gas works are discharged into it'. It also received '. . . a part of the filth and much of the (night) soil and refuse of the adjoining houses'.[18]

Water had customarily been drawn from the river for domestic purposes, but because of its polluted state it was no longer fit for those purposes. Wells and springs provided supplies of potable water, but they were not capable of supplying the needs of a greatly enlarged population. Wells were sometimes dry in summer, and Clark states 'At present there are only four or five scantily supplied springs upon which so many hundreds of poor people have to depend for a supply of water'.[19] The piped water system pioneered by Scott and Roberts supplied only a fifth of the city's houses in 1849 and these naturally were the higher class houses flanking High Street.

Streets were unmetalled and unpaved, and the accumulation of filthy matter on them was regarded as a hazard to health. Conditions along High Street are summed up in a letter which appeared in the *North Wales Chronicle* in 1848:

> I doubt whether a single person can be found in Bangor who does not lament the deplorable state of our streets . . . Let anyone walk from Pendre to the Penrhyn Arms Hotel (before starting I would advise his putting on a pair of stilts if he wished to avoid getting ankle deep in mud) he will find that there is a parapet here and there, in most places not paved; that the parapet is never cleaned; the mud scraped by the scavenger is heaped in the gutter and there it remains for a considerable period. If our principal street is in this state what shall I say of Hirael, Glan-yr-Afon and other parts of the city where a scavenger never enters, where impurities of all kinds are ever stagnating and spreading over the neighbouring localities the pestilential miasma laden with diseases generated in these localities. It is well known that disease is, as it were, fed and kept up by all manner of filth and dirt.[20]

Other nuisances injurious to public health were the state of slaughter-houses, the presence of pigs in confined yards close to houses, and the overcrowding which occurred in common lodging-houses. Slaughter-houses were located close to houses in several districts. Dr Richards, in his evidence to Clark, claimed that 'The slaughter-houses . . . are highly prejudicial to the health of the poor people who reside in their vicinity' and he had '. . . not the least hesitation in averring, that the health of the people residing in . . . (Glan-yr-Afon) . . . is seriously injured by the decomposing animal matter which is allowed to accumulate near (them)'.[21] Clark inspected the slaughter-house at Glan-yr-Afon and found it to be 'ill built, ill-paved and very dirty. In the yard was a sort of pit filled with putrid blood and animal refuse in a state of fermentation, and so offensive that I could not remain in the yard'.[22]

Pigs had been kept in the town for generations. In the early decades of the century they freely roamed the streets. An order from the magistrates to householders to confine their pigs to their own premises was greeted with approval by a correspondent of the *North*

*Wales Chronicle*, who thought it would have the effect of 'restoring cleanliness to our streets, besides removing the obstacles which these animals lying across the lanes presented in the way of passage'.[23] Their continued presence, however, in small back yards in the densely built-up districts of the town constituted an intolerable nuisance.

In common with the situation in most expanding towns, house construction in Bangor had failed to keep abreast with the demographic explosion and young migrants were forced to seek accommodation for variable periods of time in the homes of other families. Analysis of the Enumeration Schedules of the 1851 Census reveals the presence of about 620 lodgers in the town on census night, representing 9.1 per cent of the population. Nearly 300 households (20.6 per cent of the total) included at least one lodger.[24] Respectable conditions were probably enjoyed by most lodgers. There were, however, the common lodging-houses whose cheap accommodation attracted the casualties of the economic and social upheavals of Victorian society. Conditions of gross overcrowding invariably prevailed in them and they were the breeding grounds for disease and vice. A report in the *North Wales Chronicle* in 1847 alluded to the holding of a public meeting '. . . to adopt some expurgatory measures with regard to the low lodging houses in the back slums of the city . . . in a word, receptacles of impurities of all sorts, fever and vagrancy. Imagine twenty to thirty persons of both sexes, old and young, parent and offspring, huddled together for the night in one small apartment. Disease is engendered inevitably and the sick become chargeable to the parish'.[25]

The following statement, made in 1847 to the Board of Guardians of the Bangor Union by Mr Richards, medical officer to the Bangor District, is quoted by Clark:

'. . . on the night of the 18th October I requested the police to visit these (lodging) houses, and furnish me with the number of persons sleeping in each of them . . . in the nine houses visited there were no less than 111 persons, men, women and children huddled indiscriminately together in the same room. I myself can speak of the filthy, unwholesome, crowded state of these houses, and that they are seldom free from contagious and infectious diseases. The class of people who generally frequent them are organ and hurdy-gurdy players, street singers, match-vendors, vagrants of all descriptions, who wander about the country begging and committing all manner of depredations'.[26]

Clark exemplifies conditions in the lodging-houses with reference to a house in Hugh Street, Hirael: '. . . a low lodging house of three floors crowded to excess and throughout in a most filthy condition.

There were ten beds in three rooms and the back premises are nearly as bad as those in any other part of the town. Fatal fever has prevailed here, and as many as forty-seven lodgers have been counted in the house'.[27] Common lodging-houses were also found in Drum Street (off Dean Street) and Kyffin Square; they were, in the main, kept by Irishmen and were frequented by Irish and other vagrants.

Another of the sanitary needs of the city was a burial ground outside the town. The cathedral ground was almost full and the new cemetery, Tan-y-Fynwent, was 'exceedingly wet'. A drain from the High Street passed through the cemetery, '. . . the water from which percolates the side of the sewer, and when the wind is from the eastward, the smell is intolerable'.[28]

Clark sums up the situation in the lower class districts by reference to Hirael: 'It is difficult to convey in words any correct idea of the dreadful conditions of this quarter of the town. It is far worse than anything I have seen in crowded cities'.[29]

The principal task facing the Local Board when it assumed its duties was the draining and sewering of the city.[30] It appointed Capt. Edward Johnston R.N., a civil engineer, to undertake the work. His scheme, estimated to cost £4,600, was approved by the General Board of Health in June 1852 yet the work was not completed until the early months of 1854. There were immediate complaints. Dr Owen Owen Roberts wrote to the General Board deploring the fact that the outlet of the system was '. . . closed for ten out of twenty-four hours by tidal waters. At extraordinary spring tides, sea water rushed up the pipes and overflowed into the streets and houses in Hirael'.[31] The problem was exacerbated by a consequence of the Lighting and Watching Act 1854 which forbade the discharge of gas wastes into a running stream. Such wastes, which hitherto had been discharged into the River Adda, were now conveyed into the main drain and at high tide noxious effluvia were carried via the drains into houses. Such was the dissatisfaction with the system that when it was planned to extend it to Upper Bangor the ratepayers there forwarded a petition to the General Board of Health earnestly entreating it to remove Upper Bangor from the jurisdiction of the Local Board. They objected to the extension there of works which were '. . . evidently calculated to create so much discomfort in private families and to produce so much public mischief'. They also objected to the laying of a water supply system since Upper Bangor was already '. . . abounding with pure spring water'.[32] A General Board inspector reported favourably on the system, so in July 1855 the Local Board proceeded with its plans to extend the mains to Upper Bangor. Mains drainage was not extended to West End or Glanadda until 1883.

Once the mains system was laid, property owners could undertake the connection of their house drains to it and the installation of water closets at their own expense, or they could request the Local Board to undertake the work for them, agreeing to reimburse the Board over a nominated period of years. If they were not inclined to incur this expense, however, the Board had no power under the Public Health Act to make these improvements mandatory unless the existing arrangements created a nuisance and were specifically complained about to the Board. Predictably, the minutes of the Local Board are a catalogue of complaints about foul smelling ash-pits, privies and drains and of the Board's directions to householders to abate the nuisance, preferably by connecting the drains to the mains and installing water closets. In his Report to the Board in 1856, the Surveyor complained that 'Several owners (in Upper Bangor) continue in objecting to drain their houses in any shape whatever'.[33] In 1861 he stated that 'the majority of tenements (in Kyffin Square) have no privy or closet whatever and no gulley or drains for the effective carrying away of the surface and domestic water'.[34] Dr John Richards in his report on the sanitary state of Kyffin Square in 1870 condemned the use of common privies and recommended that tenants of Miss Jones's property in the Square '. . . should have one water closet made for the use of the whole'.[35]

Dr F. W. Barry, a Local Government Board Inspector, in his report on the sewerage and drainage of Bangor at the time of the typhoid epidemic in 1882, considered that house drainage, where it had been introduced, was very defective: 'The house drains are connected directly with the sewers, a trap between the two being regarded as a useless superfluity'. In some houses he 'found a strong current of sewer air passing directly through the slopstone pipe into the kitchen and living rooms', and 'in several instances the house drains were found to be choked with sewage'.[36] Dr E. O. Price, in the same year, stated: 'In one block of buildings . . . I found cisterns but rarely a water supply. Here, at intervals, the privies would become choked with sewage matter from the drain. The only flushing in these cases the closets obtained was from the slops and dirty water at times thrown down'.[37] Both doctors were highly critical of the mains system as well: 'The ventilation of the sewers is highly defective, as are the means for inspecting them', states Barry, 'neither lamp holes nor man-holes being placed at the points of change of direction in the sewers'.[38]

Barry was also concerned about the polluted state of the River Adda and the condition of the beach below high water adjacent to the sewer outfall. 'The river', he observed, 'is unquestionably a source of great nuisance to all the houses in its immediate neighbourhood . . . it acts as a receptacle for all kinds of solid filth wherever houses abut upon it'. Most of the houses in Glanadda drained directly into the river. Below the outfall of the river 'a large expanse of most offensive matter (was) exposed every low tide all along the shore between Garth and Hirael', because the sewer had not been laid far enough out into the bay.[39] The system of drainage and sewerage, for which the Local Board was responsible, evidently left much to be desired.

An efficient drainage and sanitary system naturally depended upon a satisfactory supply of water and it was the intention of the Local Board to purchase and extend the system established by Scott and Roberts. A General Board Inspector advised them that the purchase would not be desirable since the undertaking was too small to supply the whole town, and considerable alteration would be required in the system of distribution. In any event the estimated cost of purchasing the works and their extension, together with the cost of draining and sewering the city, would exceed by £5,000 the assessed value of the Local Board district. Any expenditure beyond this sum was prohibited under the Act. Consequently the provision of a water supply was left to the initiative of private enterprise. An Act 'for the better supplying of the inhabitants of Bangor with water' was passed in 1854 and this provided for the formation of a limited company called the Bangor Waterworks Company.[40] Later that year, the Directors of the Waterworks Company and the Gas and Coke Company agreed to amalgamate the two companies and an Act of Parliament authorized the formation of the Bangor Gas and Water Company. The new company negotiated with Col. Pennant for the extraction of water from the River Caseg which drains the northern slopes of the Carneddau mountains, for the laying of pipes through parts of the Penrhyn Estate and for the construction of a service reservoir at Twrgwyn on Bangor Mountain. Complaints in the 1870s about the unreliable supply of water to Upper Bangor in particular led to pressure being exerted on the Board to purchase the Company and run the gas and water undertaking as a public utility. The Board bowed to this pressure in 1878.

The streets of the city came under the aegis of the Board, a high proportion of whose funds was allocated to the repair, cleaning and lighting of the streets. The Board purchased a road sweeping machine and its water cart plied the main streets in dry weather. High Street, the principal thoroughfare, however, was the responsibility of the Commissioners of the London to Holyhead Turnpike Road. Naturally, the Local Board desired to have the road properly cleaned, flagged and channelled, but under the Public Health Act it could not compel the owners of the road to do this work. An agreement was reached in 1852 whereby the Commissioners paid the Board £15 per annum for cleaning the road. In 1853 the Commissioners agreed to the flagging of the road from the station to the Penrhyn Arms Hotel, but evidently this was not accomplished since, in 1862, the Board served notices on individual householders '. . . to level, flag and channel the footways in the High Street co-extensive with their respective properties'. Further notices to this effect were issued in 1867. In 1881 the Local Board, as urban sanitary authority, took over responsibility for that section of the turnpike road which ran through its district. Progress in constructing pavements and in metalling the other streets was exceedingly slow. Twenty years after the establishment of the Board the Surveyor reported that only three streets were completely flagged in Lower Bangor and four in Upper Bangor were partly flagged. 'The remainder of the streets . . .' he stated 'are without paths at all or have simply pebbled paths'.[41]

The Local Board took over responsibility for lighting the streets; it purchased gas from the Gas and Water Company until 1878, when it took over the company. The Lighting Committee was a standing committee of the Board, and its Chairman claimed in 1872 that 'the lighting of the streets was in a very satisfactory condition . . . they were better off in this respect than the inhabitants of the metropolis, the light in Bangor being far more bright than in London'.[42]

By-laws made by the Local Board in 1861 strengthened its control over the construction of new streets, pavements and houses and the draining and sewering of new houses. The alignment, width and mode of construction of every new street was made subject to the approval of the Board, and a plan for each new building had to be submitted for scrutiny. Building materials, fire-places and chimneys, the height of rooms, the number and size of windows, the construction and ventilation of house drains and the situation, dimensions, etc., of privies and water closets were all subject to the approval of the Board. The object of these by-laws was the raising of housing standards, the reduction of housing densities and the minimizing of health hazards, but it is doubtful whether they were strictly enforced.

Other by-laws were passed to control major nuisances such as those generated by slaughter-houses which had to be registered. Dr E. O. Price, commenting on the state of slaughter-houses in 1882, said that they were '. . . still generally in a highly unsatisfactory state. They are all situated amidst a dense population and much of the blood and offal is . . . allowed to pass into the drains, in defiance of existing by-laws'.[43]

A by-law enacted by the Local Board in 1851 prohibited the keeping of pigs within thirty feet of a dwelling house. It was blatantly ignored and the Board, apparently, was reluctant to enforce it strictly because of the economic benefits which members of the lower income groups derived from keeping pigs. Minutes of the Board record a succession of complaints concerning the keeping of pigs within proscribed limits: at a Board meeting in 1871, a member revealed that 'A man kept a pig . . . within a yard of the back door in Summer Hill Terrace (later College Road) and another kept "piggie" under difficulties . . . in the water closet'.[44] The Surveyor investigated these allegations and at the next meeting he reported that at No. 10 Summer Hill Terrace he found 'piggie ensconced against a wall in the yard right under the kitchen window; and at No. 3 . . . his swineship was accommodated in a passage used by other houses'.[45] Within twelve months of this episode a member of the Board exposed the case of a person living in Mountain Street '. . . who keeps a pig in the back garden in the daytime and allows it to sleep in the back kitchen at night time'.[46] Dr E. O. Price stated in 1882 that pigs were to be found in all parts of the town and the Local Board was lax in insisting on their removal.[47] At the height of the typhoid epidemic the Board insisted upon the removal of all pigs from within the proscribed limits. Once the epidemic abated the practice was resumed, for in October 1883 it was reported to the Board that pigs were kept in several of the small yards at the back of houses in Well Street, and that pigsties at the rear of the Red Lion Inn were in '. . . a very foul and offensive state'.[48] It is evident that the Board proved to be quite incompetent in dealing with this nuisance.

Early steps were taken to exercise control over lodging-houses and the Surveyor was authorized to determine the number of lodgers who could be accommodated in a house and to ensure that the house was connected to the mains water and drainage systems. Powers of inspection were also given to the Surveyor. It proved difficult, however, to check on the number of lodgers taken in on a particular night and to prevent holders of unregistered houses from taking in lodgers. After a spot check on the night of Saturday, 14 April 1855 the Surveyor stated:

'At Common Lodging House No. 3 . . . in Kyffin Square, in a room where only four persons are allowed, I found nine, as follows: seven men and a woman and one child – the room was disgustingly close and filthy. At No. 9 Hughes Street, Hirael, I found a small room containing three filthy beds and nine persons as follows: a man and wife, four boys, two men and one young women. Application was made some time since to register this house but was refused. I have frequently warned them not to take lodgers'.[49]

The problem had not diminished by the 1870s and the effectiveness of the Surveyor's monthly visit was questioned. A Board member thought that 'The present system was little less than a farce although the Surveyor could not be expected to go round oftener, and besides it was rather disagreeable work that could be best done by the police'.[50] It transpired that the Surveyor had always been accompanied by a policeman during his tour of inspection! The Clerk said that visiting was useless unless it took place between midnight and one o'clock in the morning. An application was made to the Chief Constable of the County requesting the police to undertake the inspection of lodging-houses and this came about in 1872.

In addition to its responsibilities in the field of public health the Board took positive steps to improve the general environment by providing facilities for the benefit of both the local public and visitors. Water fountains, urinals and seats were erected at several points. In July 1867 the Board resolved that 'In order to give every inducement possible to visitors to stop in Bangor and to be protected as well as amused' a field should be acquired for a pleasure ground.[51] Lord Penrhyn agreed to lease a section of Bangor Mountain at a nominal rent and to make a donation towards the cost of making proper footpaths thereon. Permission was granted for the levelling of two sites, one for a bowling green and the other for a croquet ground. A part of the ground was set apart for quoiting and archery but no provision was made for cricket. Supervision was exercised by a park ranger. Endeavours to acquire a recreation ground in Upper Bangor were frustrated, so too were the Board's intentions to improve the appeal of the city as a sea-bathing place. Plans for new bathing pools and a marine drive along the Strait were drawn up but nothing came of them.

Success, on the other hand, attended the Board's resolve to acquire a library and reading room. Capt. John Jones, a native of Bangor, established a museum in 1851 to exhibit his unique collection of curios, which he had acquired from many lands in the course of a long career at sea. He offered his collection in 1870 to the Local Board, entreating it to act as trustee for the citizens of Bangor, so that the collection might be preserved and enlarged. Unfortunately the Board was not able to accept the gift since it had no authority to levy a rate for the running and maintenance of the establishment. The Board viewed the gift as a foundation for its broader vision of a library, reading room and exhibition hall complex and determined not to let this opportunity pass. A petition was presented to the Secretary of State for the Home Department entreating him to draft a Bill which would enable Local Boards to adopt the Public Libraries Act, 1855. An Act was subsequently passed which embodied this request and at a meeting of ratepayers held in November 1870 the proposed adoption of the Public Libraries Act by the Local Board was approved. Lord Penrhyn granted a lease of the museum premises for thirty years at a nominal rent, a committee of management was set up and a penny in the £ was added to the General District Rate for its upkeep. The museum was opened free to the public on 1 March 1871 and the library and reading room were opened on 1 January 1873. The institution proved extremely popular: the annual report for 1881 records the issue of 4,620 books and a daily average use by 105 persons. A Working Men's Improvement Society met in the library and was the means whereby scores of young men extended their elementary education. 'Thus we conclude', says the 1881 Report, 'the reading room, in conjunction with the library is discharging no unimportant function to the community. We are quite prepared to contest the number of our daily visitors with any other public house in the town'.[52]

In 1880 the Departmental Committee set up by the Government to enquire into the state of intermediate and higher education in Wales recommended the establishment of a University College in south Wales and another in north Wales. At a meeting of the Local Board in February of that year, a resolution was passed '. . . that a memorial be prepared and forwarded to the President of the Committee of the Council on Education calling (his) attention to the advantages offered by Bangor for the proposed College for north Wales and a high class school for girls and praying that Bangor may be selected for that purpose'.[53] A committee was set up to prepare a case for the selection of Bangor for the consideration of the arbitrators who were appointed to select the site for the new University College in North Wales.

The Local Board of Health accomplished much in the period it discharged its responsibilities. Bangor was certainly a cleaner, healthier and more agreeable place in which to live in the early 1880s than it had been thirty years previously. Furthermore, in accepting a wider definition of urban welfare, it undertook duties which were never conceived by the architects of the Public Health Act 1848 and thereby created the framework for a comprehensive system of local government.

Even so the Board's sanitary administration left much to be desired and censure was frequently directed at it for its indecisive and ambivalent attitude towards sanitary reforms. Both the water supply and sewerage systems were defective and offensive smells were prevalent; householders were slow to connect their houses to the sewerage system; by-laws relating to slaughter and lodging-houses, pigsties, house construction and streets were not strictly enforced and were often completely ignored. The character of government legislation was partly to blame for this state of affairs. Before the Public Health Act 1875 much of the legislation in the sphere of public health was permissive and it was left to the initiative of local authorities to interpret and administer the acts; in addition there was no provision for regular control and oversight by government inspectors. Boards had no powers of compulsion and depended in large measure on the willing co-operation of house owners. If house owners refused to comply with the Board's instructions to abate nuisances the ultimate sanction of taking legal action was costly and time consuming and frequently deterred the Board from exercising its powers. Of course the Board was aware of its shortcomings: an exasperated member in 1868 implored the Board to adopt measures which would '. . . secure a more punctual and careful attention to the general orders of the Board',[54] and the Chairman, Lord Penrhyn, agreed 'It is no use making by-laws to be set in defiance'.[55]

Another reason for the Board's reluctance to undertake essential improvements and adequately service the drainage and water systems was the parsimony of ratepayers. Members of the Board were drawn from a small group who contributed most to the rates and their view reflected the antipathy of the property owning electorate to the payment of rates.

Criticism was also levelled at the Board for its lack of resolution in promoting Bangor as a tourist centre. This view was frequently articulated in meetings of the Bangor Parliamentary Debating Society which was founded in 1871 to debate local and national issues. The Society recognized that Bangor had found it difficult to compete with the new holiday resorts which had sprung up along the north Wales coast after the coming of the railway and had superior stretches of sand and safe bathing. It was of the opinion, however, that Bangor could re-establish its primacy if certain improvements were carried out such as the construction of a landing stage to facilitate the landing of people and goods from steamers which plied between Liverpool and the Menai Strait, the building of two swimming pools at Siliwen and the making of High Street a more attractive place to shoppers. These proposals were embodied in a petition which the Society presented to the Local Board in January 1882, entreating it to act in the matter. Little positive response was forthcoming from the Board.

It was the outbreak of typhoid fever in the summer of 1882, however, which really exposed the weaknesses in the Board's administration.[56] Between the last week in May and the end of September, 548 cases were reported and forty-two died of the fever. Its simultaneous appearance in Bangor and Bethesda and locations in-between suggested a common medium of infection and the only possible link was the water supply.

A case of typhoid was identified in a house in Llwynrhandir, a short distance above the Bangor reservoir on 22 May. On a visit to the house on 13 June, Dr Rees, the Bangor M.O.H., found that the slops and washing water from the house were thrown into a sink emptying via a short drain into a stream which discharged into the River Caseg about 350 yards above the intake of the city's water supply. Rees informed the Local Board on 8 July of the extent of the epidemic and of its probable cause. He recommended the cutting of an intercepting trench between the stream and the River Caseg and the renewal of the filtering material. In response the Local Board rejected the opinion of its M.O.H. and clung to their belief that the cause of the infection lay in the drains.

Dr F. W. Barry, who examined the water works in early August, found that the filter beds were defective and that a third of the water was passing directly into the water main without any filtration. This situation was exacerbated on 29 June by a burst in the main between Bangor and Bethesda. After repair work, water was allowed to pass into the mains in considerable quantities without first being filtered. Just at this time there was a further outbreak of typhoid at Llwynrhandir.

The cutting of the intercepting trench and the renewal of the filtering materials, remedies proposed by Dr Rees in July and confirmed as necessary by Dr Barry on 12 August, were not commenced until 17 August; the work was completed on

5 September. Dr Barry was of the opinion that had the trench been dug in July the most serious stage of the outbreak, which occurred in August, might have been avoided and the whole epidemic cleared up in a shorter time with less suffering. Dr Barry attributed the spread of the fever '. . . almost if not entirely owing to causes directly under the control of the Sanitary Authority, viz., the liability of the water supply to contamination, the defective ventilation of the sewers and house drains, and the foul accumulations of excrement and refuse in the town. These latter, even where not actually the critical causes of the disease, undoubtedly favoured its spread'.[57]

This was a devastating indictment of the Local Board. After taking over the Gas and Water Company in 1878 it had not thoroughly inspected the water intake or filtration systems both of which were patently defective. However, the Board had responded positively and energetically in the crisis. Defects in the drainage system were immediately attended to, sewers were flushed daily and disinfected, cesspool privies were abolished and nuisances abated with determination. Arrangements were made for the use of isolation wards in the Workhouse Infirmary and in the C. and A. Infirmary. Fairview, an eight-bedroom house in Hirael, was fitted out as a hospital and two tent hospitals were erected in the Bishop's Park. Houses in Albert Place, Upper Bangor, were converted into a convalescent home. Voluntary aid was mobilized: nurses were recruited and a Ladies Committee superintended the making and distribution of beef tea. Additional staff, including a deputy medical officer of health, were employed. It was unfortunate that the Board's aetiology of the disease was a mistaken one.

Besides being distressing to the local populace the epidemic gave wider cause for concern. Firstly, persisting as it did throughout the summer season of 1882, it had a disastrous effect on the trade normally derived from summer visitors and it was years before Bangor regained its popularity. Secondly, it caused the city acute embarrassment since at the time it was petitioning to be selected as the site for the new University College in North Wales. The claim made by the college committee that Bangor 'compared with other towns is exceptionally healthy' suddenly sounded unconvincing but in its final statement to the arbitrators the committee emphasized that the epidemic had been '. . . induced by accidental and purely temporary causes', which had since been removed. It went on to predict that if Bangor were granted a charter of incorporation a more efficient management of the health services would ensue and Bangor's 'reputation as one of the healthiest cities in the Principality (would) stand higher than ever'.[58]

The outbreak of typhoid fever sealed the fate of the Local Board of Health. When the city returned to normality support for the view that Bangor should actively seek an alternative form of city government gathered momentum. A more prestigious and potent model had been established by the Municipal Corporations Act 1835 and this commended itself to local activists. The Act applied only to existing boroughs whose charters of incorporation in most cases dated back to the Middle Ages. It confirmed the charters of all but the smallest boroughs and imposed on them a representative form of government. Over the centuries borough councils, the governing bodies of boroughs, had been taken over by corrupt and exclusive oligarchies of privileged citizens who invariably perpetuated their own power by a system of self election and by confining the electorate largely to their own nominees. Strong support for representative institutions in the 1830s led first to the reform of Parliament in 1832 and then inevitably to the reform of borough government in 1835. Boroughs were henceforth to be divided into wards so that all parts of the borough would be represented on the council; a prescribed number of councillors was assigned to each ward based on the population and rateable value of the ward; councillors were to elect aldermen, who were to comprise a quarter of the council, and the mayor who was to have precedence in the borough. A councillor was to hold office for three years, alderman for six and the mayor for one year, although each was eligible for re-election. One third of the councillors were to retire each year and half the aldermen every three years. The franchise was extended to all ratepayers resident in the borough for three years. Certain people were ineligible to become members of the council under the Act: for example, persons occupying property valued below a certain sum, women, clergy and ministers of religion. Subsequently this constraint was removed.[59] Meetings of councils were to be open to the public and their accounts were to be publicly audited.

There was deep concern too in the 1830s about the high level of crime committed in the expanding industrial towns in particular. In an attempt to protect life and property and to raise moral standards the statutory duties imposed on borough councils by the Act were the appointment of a watch committee to be responsible for lighting and policing and the appointment of magistrates to administer justice.

Urban squalor, insanitary living conditions, the prevalence of disease and high mortality rates were yet another area of concern, so the Act authorized councils, if they so desired, to concert measures designed to improve the environmental welfare of the community. Their duties in this field became mandatory under the Public Health Act 1875, which was designed to impose national standards of public health in towns and country districts alike.

One of the most important clauses in the 1835 Act was the one which laid down procedures which unchartered towns might follow if they decided to seek a charter of incorporation. Rather than central government imposing a uniform system of town government through-out the country, the Act left it to individual towns to decide where their constitutional futures lay. Soon after the passing of the Act the growing industrial towns of the Midlands and the North, such as Birmingham, Wolverhampton, Manchester and Sheffield, petitioned for chartered status and within forty years over a hundred charters had been granted.

The idea of a charter for Bangor was first mooted by John Roberts, Draper, of Bradford House, a member of the Local Board of Health. In a letter to the *North Wales Chronicle* in August 1877 he set out the advantages possessed by a chartered town over one governed by a Local Board of Health.[60] The timing of Roberts's initiative is significant: it came just a year after Conwy had received a reformed charter of incorporation and at a time when the controversy surrounding the Local Board's reluctance to purchase the Gas and Water Company was at its height. Furthermore, the Municipal Corporations Act 1877 transferred to the prospective ratepayers of a chartered borough the costs of the petition to the Privy Council which previously had fallen on the individuals who had petitioned for a charter.

Roberts' letter aroused considerable interest in the city; a public meeting was held in September 1877 to discuss the matter and a resolution was passed that Bangor should petition for a charter of incorporation. The resolution was presented to the Local Board requesting it to take the appropriate action but the Board declined to act and the matter fell into abeyance.

The next initiative came in 1881 when the Parliamentary Debating Society presented a petition to the Local Board of Health requesting it to respond positively to suggestions the Society had made with regard to town improvements and the incorporation of the borough. Once again there was no response from the Board.

Finally in November 1882, in the wake of the typhoid epidemic, several prominent citizens sympathetic to the idea of incorporation

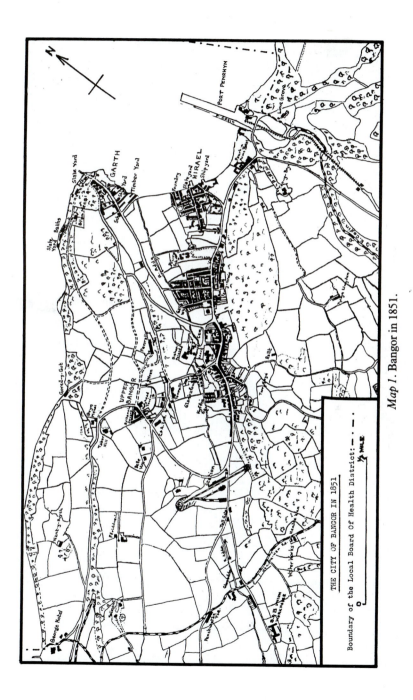

Map 1. Bangor in 1851.

*Plate 1.* The scene outside 'The Old Bank' immediately after the reading of the Charter of Incorporation, 25 August 1883.

met at the Old Bank to discuss the proposition. The meeting, under the chairmanship of Major Henry Platt of Gorddinog, Llanfairfechan, unanimously agreed to proceed in the matter and to remove any obstacles which might have hindered its progress. They agreed, for example, that a collection should be raised to defray the costs of the petition so that there would be no charge on ratepayers. To ascertain the response of ratepayers to the idea of incorporation it was decided to call a public meeting. This meeting unanimously passed a resolution calling on the Local Board to commence proceedings with a view to obtaining a charter. The Board once again declined to act so the parish churchwardens were asked to call a vestry meeting to settle the issue.[61]

The meeting held on 3 January 1883 was described as '. . . one of the largest and most enthusiastic ever witnessed in Bangor'. A resolution to petition Her Majesty's Privy Council for the application of the Municipal Corporations Act to the city was passed and an incorporation committee was elected to pilot the petition through its various stages. The petition, signed by nearly a thousand ratepayers, was soon despatched to London and on 30 April a commissioner appointed by the Privy Council held a public enquiry in Bangor. No dissenting opinions were voiced and the commissioner, having satisfied himself that it was a popular and viable proposition, submitted a favourable report to the Privy Council, which advised the Queen to grant a charter of incorporation.

After passing through its Parliamentary stages the charter arrived in Bangor on Friday, 17 August. News of its arrival, proclaimed by the bells of the cathedral and St James's church '. . . ringing merry peals' spread like wildfire through the city.[62] The incorporation committee planned a day of celebration for Saturday, 25 August which was to take the form of a procession through the streets culminating in the reading of the charter in front of the Old Bank.

During the afternoon preceding the appointed day, news was received that the city had been selected out of thirteen competing towns as the site for the University College in North Wales. Another wave of excitement spread through the city and was accompanied by the ringing of bells. The college committee, in consultation with the incorporation committee, hurriedly decided that the celebration next day should mark both events and the display of even more support for the arranged programme was encouraged.

Saturday 25 August turned out to be a warm sunny day which was entirely propitious for the occasion. Hardly a house failed to show its colours, indeed, some of the lower classes had hung out bedsheets decorated with calico of various shades, evergreens and flowers. The procession, led by the band of the Artillery Volunteers, comprised representatives of uniformed bodies and friendly societies, a contingent of Bethesda quarrymen, clergy and ministers of religion, members of the incorporation committee and the college committee, the fire brigade and hundreds of citizens. It wound its way through the principal districts of the city, cheered by thousands of onlookers, and returned to the Old Bank in front of which a platform had been erected. First of all, members of the college committee ascended the platform and several speeches were delivered congratulating Bangor on its good fortune and reminding it of its new responsibilities to the Welsh nation. At five o'clock a small procession composed of members of the incorporation committee escorted R. H. Pritchard, who bore the charter, onto the platform. The large crowd which had assembled was silenced by a fanfare of trumpets and Pritchard proceeded to read the text of the charter which filled four skins of parchment [Plate 1]. Having done so, there were loud cheers, further fanfares and a photograph of the incorporation committee was taken. When the principals retired '. . . the crowd lingered for some time around the scene' before dispersing to reflect upon and celebrate in their several ways this momentous day in the history of Bangor.

*Notes*
1. N(ational) L(ibrary of) W(ales), Welsh Church MSS 243669/9.
2. UCNW, Bangor MS 22796 Folio 6/22.
3. NLW, Welsh Church MSS B/DL/661.
4. UCNW, Carter Vincent MSS 751 and 1857. The houses were built on the site now occupied by the Kwik Save supermarket.
5. UCNW, Bangor MS 10068.
6. P(ublic) R(ecord) O(ffice), MH 13/13 8689/49.
7. NWC 7 November 1848.
8. Bangor joined Caernarvon, Conwy, Cricieth, Nefyn and Pwllheli as Contributory Boroughs of the Caernarvon Boroughs Parliamentary Constituency in 1832. See Appendix, Table 11, Note 1 (b) and (c).
9. G. T. Clark, Report p. 15.
10. NWC 10 October 1848.
11. NWC 31 October 1848.
12. NWC 15 June 1850.
13. G. T. Clark, Report pp. 7-8.
14. G. T. Clark, Report p.5.
15. NWC 10 October 1848.
16. G. T. Clark, Report p.9.
17. G. T. Clark, Report p.10. The King's Arms, 208 High Street, is still a public house.
18. G. T. Clark, Report p.8.

19. G. T. Clark, Report p.6.
20. NWC 31 October 1848. See also Dr Richards's evidence in G. T. Clark, Report p.7.
21. G. T. Clark, Report p.7.
22. G. T. Clark, Report p.8.
23. NWC 26 November 1829.
24. P. E. Jones, (1973) pp.206-09.
25. NWC 19 October 1847.
26. G. T. Clark, Report p.14.
27. G. T. Clark, Report p.11.
28. G. T. Clark, Report p.7. The Tan-y-Fynwent cemetery was opened in 1841 and the Glanadda cemetery in 1862.
29. G. T. Clark, Report p.11.
30. See P. E. Jones (1976) for improvements undertaken by the Board and an analysis of its membership.
31. PRO MH 13/13 333/1854.
32. PRO MH 13/13 3680/1854. Petition dated 21 August 1854.
33. GAS B2/1151, 21 August 1856.
34. GAS B2/115/2, 5 December 1861.
35. GAS B2/115/2, 6 January 1870.
36. F. W. Barry, Report, pp.73-74.
37. Gwen Owen, p.159.
38. F. W. Barry, Report p.73.
39. F. W. Barry, Report p.73.
40. UCNW, Carter Vincent MS 1917.
41. NWC 4 February 1871.
42. C(aernarvon and) D(enbigh) H(erald), 6 January 1872.
43. Gwen Owen, p. 160.
44. NWC 4 March 1871. Meshach Roberts lived in 341 High Street.
45. NWC 18 March 1871.
46. NWC 13 April 1872.
47. Gwen Owen, p.160.
48. GAS B2/115/3, 11 and 25 October 1883.
49. NWC 21 April 1855.
50. CDH 13 May 1871.
51. GAS B2/115/2, 11 July 1867.
52. NWC 7 January 1882.
53. GAS B2/115/3, 16 February 1882.
54. GAS B2/115/2, 28 May 1868.
55. NWC 16 December 1876.
56. Gwen Owen, p.159.
57. F. W. Barry, Report p.81.
58. UCNW, Belmont MS 67.
59. Property Qualification by the Town Councils and Local Boards Act 1880; women by the Qualification of Women (County and Borough Councils) Act 1907 and clergy and ministers of religion by the Representation of the People Act 1918.
60. NWC 4 August 1877.
61. Vestry meetings were still held to ascertain public opinion. The Vestry transferred its civil functions to Bangor City Council in May 1916, but retained its ecclesiastical functions.
62. NWC 27 August 1883.

# CHAPTER 3

## 1883 — 1914

### 'The city of light and learning, the Athens of Wales.'[1]

THE READING of the charter outside the Old Bank was doubtless something of an anticlimax to the high spirited crowd which had assembled there after the rousing procession through the streets of the city. Comparatively few could have come within earshot of the narrator and to many the precise terminology of the charter must have been barely comprehensible.

The charter recited the authority of the Privy Council to grant charters and to extend to an unincorporated town the provisions of the Municipal Corporations Acts; it confirmed that since the prescribed procedures for the granting of a charter had been complied with a municipal borough in the name of the Borough of Bangor was created; it fixed the boundaries of the Borough; it declared the inhabitants and their successors to be a corporate body entitled to act in all legal matters as an individual, having, therefore, certain rights and duties, including the right to hold property, to make contracts and to sue in a court of law; it granted the corporation a common seal which would authenticate its acts and decisions; it gave it the privilege of assuming armorial bearings; it constituted a council of twenty-four members, eighteen of whom were to be councillors and six to be aldermen; it divided the borough into four wards and delineated their boundaries; it prescribed that north and west wards should elect six councillors each and east and south wards three each; it specified the dates on which the first mayor, aldermen and councillors were to retire. Finally, the charter outlined the procedures which were to be followed leading to the constitution of the first council: it appointed Thomas Lewis, Chairman of the Local Board of Health, to be mayor *pro tem.* and Richard H. Pritchard town clerk *pro tem.* and charged them with the responsibility of producing a burgess list and a list of persons qualified to be councillors and making arrangements for the first election; it appointed Thomas Lewis Returning Officer for the first election and convenor of and chairman at the first meeting of the council; it fixed the date of the first election for 1 November and of the first meeting of the council for 9 November, at which the mayor and aldermen were to be elected.

No specific functions were assigned to the council in the charter and it should be noted that Bangor was neither granted a separate bench of magistrates nor the right to raise its own police force. The mayor, however, became *ex officio* a member of the county bench of magistrates which met in the city. In assuming from the Local Board of Health the functions of an urban sanitary authority the council immediately became responsible for all matters relating to public health and it was given authority to make by-laws for the suppression of nuisances and the creation of a healthy environment. The council also took over functions which the Local Board had assumed over the years such as the manufacture and supply of gas, street lighting, maintenance of the library, reading room, museum and fire brigade and various licensing functions. Since one of the areas of disenchantment with the Local Board of Health was the sluggish approach it had shown to town improvements and the attraction of tourists it would have been surprising if the council had not given priority to these issues. One of its tasks at its first meeting was to set up an improvement committee to initiate measures which would make the city more attractive. Economic prosperity was seen as a keystone to the city's development; not only would it benefit citizens directly but by raising the rateable value of the city the council would derive more income from rates to carry out necessary improvements. These major functions of the council are closely interwoven and it is difficult to separate them for discrete analysis.

However, with the typhoid epidemic fresh in the minds of members it is obvious that the first priority of the council was public health and the safety of the water supply in particular. A sanitary and health committee was set up under the chairmanship of Dr John Richards and it pursued a more active and positive approach to sanitary reform than did the Local Board of Health.

To avoid further risk of contamination it was decided to extract water from the River Llafar, a parallel stream to the Caseg. Problems caused by the conflicting interests of the Penrhyn Estate, the Bethesda Improvement Commissioners, who obtained water from the same source, and the council were not speedily resolved and it was 1889 before work was commenced on the construction of a weir and a new water intake. Abnormally heavy rainfall on 23 and 24 March led to the breaching of the uncompleted weir by flood water and the site had to be abandoned for one higher upstream. When completed, water from the new intake was led for nearly a mile in stoneware pipes to the old screening plant and then through cast iron pipes to connect with the existing system. The improvement cost over £2,800 (£96,000) and to mark its completion a 'brilliant little ceremony' took place at Castle Square on Saturday, 13 July 1889. John Gill, the surveyor, improvised a spray fountain rising out of a miniature rockery in which were embedded ferns and evergreens. With due civic pomp the mayor, Charles Pierce, turned a handle and jets of water began to play. So great was the force of water that many onlookers were drenched and others stumbled over pipes in retreating from the spray. A reassuring display of the force of the new supply was given by the fire brigade and the Volunteer Band played a selection of music.[2] The ceremony affords a fitting illustration of the pride and interest which the small community took in town improvement at that time.

Contrary to expectations the undertaking did not solve Bangor's water supply problems. Demand for water steadily increased as the population, swollen by students, grew and more houses were built. The railway company's need for water increased as its services multiplied and, after the opening of the pier in 1896, the council contracted to supply visiting steamers with their water requirements. Furthermore, with rising living standards, baths were being installed in more houses. John Gill reported in 1907 that there were 700 baths in the city whereas thirty years previously when he first came there were very few. Complaints concerning the low pressure and erratic nature of the supply came from Upper Bangor which was the highest sector of the city and housed the more articulate and influential ratepayers.

On the supply side there was considerable seepage of water from old and defective pipes, large lengths of which had been laid in the 1850s and 1860s by the Water and Gas Company. Frequently the pipes had been laid at a shallow depth and were often ruptured by the movement of heavy waggons over them. Very severe wintry weather in the early months of 1895 exposed the weaknesses of the system; even the mains froze and when the thaw set in scores of major bursts had to be attended to.

Besides improving the distribution system the surveyor convinced the council of the need for supplementing Twrgwyn Reservoir on Bangor Mountain by another reservoir capable of storing half a million gallons of water. A new reservoir adjacent to the existing one was built in 1897, yet complaints of shortages and the unreliability of the supply in Upper Bangor were heard for many years thereafter. The surveyor reported in 1908 that the problems connected with the supply of water to Upper Bangor might be remedied by the construction of yet another reservoir but the council would not sanction it, claiming that there was already sufficient water in the system to supply a town far greater in size than Bangor. In 1913 a consulting water engineer was called in and his diagnosis confirmed the council's belief that the fault lay in the distribution system. Sections of the mains were corroded and the bore of the pipes was generally too small to ensure a constant supply. He rejected the need for another reservoir and suggested that houses in Upper Bangor should have storage cisterns installed.

Problems with the supply of water soon beset the infectious diseases hospital which was built in 1895 on an elevated site on Bangor Mountain and sixty-two feet above the Twrgwyn Reservoir. The surveyor won approval for the erection of a windmill on the exposed summit to pump water up into a small reservoir to be built at Bryniau. This reservoir came to supply not only the hospital but also the nearby village of Minffordd.

Household refuse normally accumulated in ashpits in the back yards of houses from whence it was removed, sooner or later, by scavengers working under contract to the council. During warm weather these accumulations gave off offensive smells. Scavengers collected and dumped the refuse on the foreshore between Hirael and the mouth of the Adda and in the course of time extended the land there into the bay, later, in the 1930s, to be levelled and turned into playing fields. The council became increasingly aware of the health hazard posed by this tip so near built up areas but attempts to find alternative sites did not succeed because of the opposition of ratepayers living near to them. To overcome the problem the council in 1898 considered erecting a rubbish destructor. In essence a destructor was a chamber into which household rubbish was fed by gravity and burnt at high temperature. Only if operated in conjunction with an electricity generating plant, however, was this device a viable alternative, for the heat generated in the destructor, when converted into steam, could contribute to the energy needed to operate the electric generators. Once the council decided in 1899 to proceed with the installation of an electric generator the way was clear to build a destructor on a site adjacent to the electricity station in Dean

Street. The idea of a destructor was *avant-garde* since it was a means of converting rubbish, including offal from slaughter houses, into energy which could be used to help generate electricity, and it practically eliminated the need to dump rubbish, thereby removing a hazard to health. On the other hand the plant emitted large quantities of smoke and when it needed servicing and repairing, rubbish tended to accumulate.

The River Adda constituted another health hazard. Nightsoil and household rubbish from the poorer class houses in its vicinity continued to be dumped into the river. On several occasions the council had been advised to culvert the river but it was slow to act and only short sections of it below St Paul's school had been culverted by 1914.

Flooding, particularly in the low lying district of Hirael, was another hazard posed by the river. It frequently occurred after periods of unusually heavy rainfall or during high tides when the outlet of the river was impeded for long periods. Flood water often got mixed with sewage and caused acute distress to people in Hirael. Despite a number of attempts to remedy the problem none was entirely satisfactory.

Insanitary and overcrowded houses were a constant threat to the health and well-being of large numbers of people. Since such a high proportion of the city's housing stock dated from the period of its most active growth in the early decades of the century it is inevitable that there were large numbers of small, ill-ventilated, tightly packed, inferior houses without indoor sanitation, water supply, food storage and preparation facilities. Initially the Inspector of Nuisances and, after 1894, the Sanitary Inspector, were empowered to inspect dwellings thought to be insanitary and to report to the council. Based on these reports the council consistently urged houseowners to install water closets linked to the mains water supply and the sewers. When persuasion failed, the council frequently used its powers to compel owners to keep their properties in a habitable state.

Houses in which members of the working classes lived were invariably overcrowded. A survey of 2,427 houses conducted by the Sanitary Inspector in 1898 revealed that thirty-three of them were overcrowded according to his criterion for measuring this aspect; between them they had forty-four bedrooms which were occupied by 207 persons, an average of nearly five persons per bedroom.[3] These were clearly the extreme cases. If the present day criterion for determining overcrowding, *viz.* over 1.5 persons per room (i.e. more than six persons in a two-bedroom house), is applied to the housing data for the 1911 Census, then 237 families or 15.2 per cent of the population living in private accommodation were living in overcrowded conditions.

A government initiative, the Housing of the Working Classes Act 1890, strengthened the hand of local authorities in dealing with insanitary houses and in providing decent houses for the working classes. Parts I and II of the Act clarified and extended the powers of a local authority with regard to insanitary dwellings. Part III was innovative in that it empowered municipal authorities to acquire land and to erect houses for the working classes and also, if necessary, to furnish them. The council was slow to respond to the new powers it was given and it was January 1897 before the provisions of the Act were first discussed. Some members were strongly opposed to the implementation of Part III on the grounds that the council had already overstretched itself on town improvements since 1883 with a result that rates were very high and they considered that there was no shortage of houses in Bangor at that time. Other members were of the opinion that it was the council's duty to see that its poorer citizens were decently housed since they perceived insanitary and overcrowded housing conditions to be a principal cause of misery, disease and crime. The decision to implement this part of the Act was taken on the casting vote of the mayor and a committee was set up to look for a site on which the council might build houses. Councillors who supported the motion were probably influenced by reports which were then circulating of the model village Messrs. Lever Bros. had built for their employees at Port Sunlight. Here, working class people were housed in spacious, well ventilated, attractively designed houses in a semi-rural setting and the concept fired the imagination of many philanthropically minded persons in north Wales. Members of local authorities nationwide were invited to Port Sunlight to view the estate. Henry Lewis represented the Bangor council at one of these open days and in a speech he delivered at the banquet for the guests he expressed the delight and appreciation of the visitors for the pioneer work done for the working man by the firm.[4]

After considering several sites the council in 1899 approved the purchase of a plot of land, barely an acre in extent, bordering on Sackville Road. Ten houses which stood on a portion of the site had been declared unfit for human habitation and it was the council's intention to demolish them and build new ones. The decision was reached by a slender majority since many councillors were loath to enter a field which traditionally had been the domain of the private investor and building speculator. They argued, moreover, that the situation had changed since the council first committed itself to the venture in 1897 by the fact that the Friars School Estate had come onto the market. A syndicate of local businessmen, including several councillors, had purchased the land for the specific purpose of building houses for the working man. Indeed, several houses had already been built on recently laid down Orme Road and Friars Avenue.

Early in the new century the council was deeply involved in its quest for a new site for the University College and with the prospect of yet another financial commitment it was in no mood to proceed with its controversial housing programme. However, an Act of 1903 extended the period of the repayment of loans for the erection of workingmen's houses from forty to fifty-five years and made borrowing for this purpose independent of all other sums which a local authority might want to borrow. These concessions induced the council to proceed with its house building programme. Designs submitted by Owen Roberts, a Liverpool architect, for the erection of forty-three houses on the site were approved and the Local Government Board made a loan of £7,700. Before the end of 1905 the construction had begun of nine superior 'A' class houses fronting onto Sackville Road and thirty-four 'B' class houses fronting onto two new streets, Treflan and Minafon [Plate 8(i)]. No bathrooms were incorporated into the houses and the water-closets were built outside.

A long discussion ensued over the terms of tenancy and the rents to be charged. It was decided that rents should be paid a week in advance, that tenants be given one week's notice to quit if the rent was unpaid, that no lodgers might be kept, that the premises might not be used as a shop, store, warehouse or laundry, that no shed, greenhouse or fowlhouse could be erected in the back yard and no fowls, pigeons or domestic animals, apart from cats, could be kept. These rather harsh conditions, laid down in an attempt to create a high quality residential area, did not meet the unqualified approval of Cllr. Vincent who did not want to deny a working man the pleasure of keeping a pet canary in a cage! A decision had to be taken as to whether the houses were to yield a profit to the council like its other revenue raising enterprises, or whether the working classes should derive some advantages which they would not obtain if they were tenants of private landlords. It was resolved that rents should cover only the principal sum and the interest charges thereon. Weekly rents for the Sackville Road houses were fixed at seven shillings and those for the others at either four shillings and nine pence or four shillings.

Even rents fixed on a non-profit basis proved far too high for the majority of working class families; the first tenants included two commercial travellers and a church organist. Cllr. David Owen enquired whether the council was really meeting the needs of the working man and thought it was contravening the spirit of the 1890 Act. The Mayor, Cllr. Bayne, who lived in some style and comfort in Menai View Terrace and who had consistently opposed the erection of the houses, was not at all sure whether one could accurately define a working man. He considered himself to be one!

Building forty-three houses did little to alleviate Bangor's housing problems. Concern about insanitary and overcrowded houses prevailed to the end of the period under discussion. In 1908, for example, the Sanitary Inspector reported that there were '. . . a number of insanitary houses in the city scarcely fit for human habitation'.[5] Cllr. Joseph Davies, reacting to the report in highly emotive and exaggerated terms, stated that the smell in a house he had visited 'was sufficient to kill anybody'. From this particular instance he generalized about houses 'in which some people are compelled to live (as being) enough to make sober men drunkards'.[6]

The council's powers with respect to insanitary dwellings were strengthened by the Housing and Town Planning Act, 1909. Rather than as hitherto, the council bringing recalcitrant owners before the magistrates to enforce orders to abate serious nuisances, the Act empowered it to put the matter right and charge the expense to the owners. It also made it easier for it to close insanitary property and to acquire land compulsorily for the erection of working class houses. Even when armed with these powers the council proceeded very cautiously, for example, in November 1913 the Sanitary Committee advised it to serve notice on the owners of seventeen back to back houses in Kyffin Square to prohibit them letting the houses. The Council refused to act, however, as it did not wish to appear dictatorial. Cllr. Jones-Roberts claimed that the health record of Kyffin Square compared favourably with any other part of the city and to prove his point he said that fifty men from the fifty-two houses in Kyffin Square had seen active service in the South African War. With such entrenched negative attitudes among members of the council towards involvement in the housing field it was difficult to make progress. However, nudged by the Welsh Housing Association, which mounted a crusade against insanitary houses and tuberculosis in Wales, the council in 1914 did serve closing orders on the Kyffin Square houses and its decision was upheld at a subsequent public enquiry. By a majority of one it also decided to build fourteen houses on the cleared site and twenty-four on another plot of land fronting onto Sackville Road. When it came to apply for a loan to construct the houses the Great War was into its second year and the application was rejected.

The problem of overcrowding and its ever present hazard to health was acute in those houses into which lodgers were taken. Although the council demanded registration and regular inspection of lodging houses it would appear from the number of transgressions reported that little had changed since the council had taken over these functions from the Local Board of Health. In 1905, for example, the Sanitary Inspector reported Catherine Williams of Dean Street for keeping an unregistered lodging house in which he found twenty persons occupying five rooms: in the front room on the ground floor there was a man and three youths, in the wash-house there were two men 'having the appearance of militiamen', in the backroom on the first floor there were three women who were very drunk, in one of the rooms on the second floor there were six men occupying three beds and in the other there were five men occupying three beds. In the same report he charged Mary Jones of 47 Dean Street, a registered lodging house keeper, with overcrowding (there were sixteen persons in the four roomed house) and with allowing more than one married couple to occupy a room which had no screen to separate them, as was required in the by-laws.[7]

Despite the closer supervision of slaughter yards cases of diseased animals being prepared for slaughter and of unfit meat being offered for sale were frequently reported. There were demands after 1900 for the council to build a public abattoir but whenever it earmarked a site, residents in the area would vehemently object. In 1914 a public meeting called for the establishment of an abattoir but before a decision could be taken the Great War broke out. The council took steps to ensure that cows supplying the city with milk were healthy and that the dairies were kept in hygienic conditions by appointing in 1901 a part time veterinary inspector who was required to present a monthly report to the council. Stricter enforcement of the by-laws relating to the keeping of pigs in small back yards led to the suppression of that nuisance soon after incorporation.

Step by step the council was laying the foundations for disease prevention and the general improvement of the health of the community. The death rate fell steadily from twenty per thousand in the period 1884-87 to thirteen per thousand in 1905-10. On adopting the Compulsory Notifications of Infectious Diseases Act 1889, it undertook the obligation of providing an institution where patients who had contracted an infectious disease might be isolated from the rest of the community while undergoing treatment. The first positive step towards the building of a hospital came when Ald. Charles Pierce, at the termination of his mayoralty in 1890 donated £500 towards the cost. It was the custom of mayors in the early days, on completing their term, to donate a gift to the city. Lord Penrhyn made the gift of a site on Bangor Mountain and the sum of £200 and Dr J. Richards gave £100. The surveyor, John Gill, drew up plans for the building which cost £2,249 (£85,000); it was opened by the Mayoress, Mrs Langford Jones on 23 January 1895.

Councillors carefully scrutinized the running of the hospital. In 1897 they wanted to know why £15 had been spent there the previous year on brandy; in 1898 they dismissed a nurse who was caught smoking and in 1900 they were astonished to learn that £720 (£23,000) had been spent at the hospital although only seventeen patients had been treated. The probity of four doctors who were also councillors was called into question. In their latter capacity they were members of the management body and therefore had sanctioned their own fee. At the same time, however, their influence succeeded in defeating a motion which aimed at the appointment of a medical superintendent at the hospital on a part-time basis. Such an arrangement would have saved the council a considerable sum of money and placed the hospital under stricter control.

The first call for a mortuary was heard in 1895. A councillor pointed out that if an accident occurred in the city and the body could not be conveyed home, it had to be deposited in the cellar of the police station, 'a transgression of the dignity of the dead',[8] he claimed. Soon afterwards a building at the gas works was equipped for the purpose but this equally unpropitious location was abandoned in 1913 when one of the stables in the former Bishop's Palace, by now the town hall, was converted.

Responsibility for the city's cemetery at Glanadda had rested since 1859 with the Burial Board. This Board was dissolved by Act of Parliament in March 1899 and its duties were transferred to the council which immediately set up a cemetery committee. New burial fees were introduced in 1913: for a plot nearest the paths the fee was raised to forty shillings, for a second row plot, thirty-seven shillings and sixpence, and for a third row plot, thirty-five shillings. Was it that councillors felt that those who had attained material success in life should have the opportunity to display this fact when they were laid down to face their Maker?

Allied to the perceived need to provide and maintain a healthy environment were the steps taken by the council to provide open spaces, gardens and leisure facilities for people to enjoy themselves in the open air. Such amenities also enhanced the attractiveness of the city to visitors. In 1885 the lease of Bangor Mountain, the city's main recreational area, was re-negotiated and seven and a half acres of Menai Woods between Upper Bangor and the George Hotel were leased from the Vaynol Estate. At Garth headland, near the ferry terminus, a garden was attractively laid out on land leased from the Penrhyn Estate.

An important function of the council was the construction, maintenance, draining and cleaning of streets and footpaths and, at night, the lighting of streets. Although the Board of Health had done much in this connection scarcely a start had been made on draining, kerbing and creating footpaths on streets other than High Street and some of the other principal streets. This enormous task was undertaken street by street over the years and by the turn of the century most of it had been accomplished.

Surfacing material was commonly broken stone, obtained from the Brynllwyd Quarry, mixed with mud. This readily broke up under wheeled vehicles and became very muddy in wet weather and very dusty in dry weather. A steam roller compacted the surface materials and a water cart helped to keep down the dust. Tar was sprayed on the surface in 1912 but there were instant complaints that linoleum flooring in shops was ruined by customers carrying in tar on their shoes. Complaints about the condition of the footpaths led the surveyor in 1895 to advise the laying of concrete slabs in place of the asphalt which had proved to be an unsatisfactory material. Care and maintenance of the main roads, including the London to Holyhead road and the road to Caernarfon, passed to the County Council in 1889, but the normal procedure was for the local council to undertake the work and the County Council to refund the cost.

In 1899 the council revised its by-laws for the good government of the city. With reference to the streets the by-laws forbade the playing of any musical or noisy instrument or singing without prior consent of the council; indecent shows, betting, the erection of shooting galleries or roundabouts; the throwing of orange peel, glass, pottery and other dangerous substances; the carrying of manure after 8 a.m. and the leading of bears for the purpose of exhibition.

Whether or not the prohibition on bear leading inconvenienced anyone is not known, but the one on the carrying of manure certainly did. Farmers customarily cleaned out town stables but they found it impossible to do so before 8 a.m. The council's dust carts, they contended, constituted a far greater nuisance but they were not so proscribed. Soon complaints were received about the smells emanating from accumulations of manure in stables since farmers no longer collected it.

The passing of by-laws was one thing, their observance was quite another as the Local Board had been acutely aware. Frequent complaints were voiced in council about the noise created by organ grinders and the ringing of hand bells by coal vendors. In 1904, the council specifically enacted that 'no coal vendor shall proclaim the advent of his cart along the street by the sound of a bell'. At the same time it prohibited the playing of football in the streets as it was 'positively dangerous to passers by'.[9]

By-laws such as these help to convey some impression of the vibrant nature of town life at the turn of the century. The narrow, winding High Street echoed to the calls and bells of vendors of various descriptions, to the voices and musical chords of itinerant musicians, the clatter of iron clad hoofs and wheels on the stony surface and the cries of children playing marbles and youths kicking footballs. Many such activities would continue well into the evening for the often congested, rubbish strewn High Street was the hub of the community's life.

Onto this chaotic scene there appeared one damp morning in November 1897 a very curious and noisy intruder. A motor car belonging to Messrs. Lever Bros. of Port Sunlight passed hesitatingly along the High Street and the *North Wales Chronicle* informs us that 'its progress . . . was watched with interest by large crowds of people'.[10] It was the forerunner of a new age. Not even members of the council appreciated at the time the impact that the new technology would have upon their domain; they were more concerned with the leading of bears through the streets than with the driving of motor cars. However, the motor age soon made an impact, for at a meeting of the council in September 1901 a member said that he had had a narrow escape in High Street when a motor car almost knocked him down. Another councillor volunteered the information that he had seen a car being driven through Upper Bangor at 25 m.p.h. Members generally agreed that motor cars were being driven and bicycles ridden in a very dangerous manner and decided to refer the matter to the police and to consider enacting a by-law to restrict the speed of cars. Four months later councillors again complained of the 'furious way motor cars were being driven through the streets, . . . it was a public nuisance and it was high time a stop was put to the practice'.[11] Accidents inevitably happened and one of the earliest victims was Dr H. Grey Edwards, Mayor 1896-97; while riding his bicycle down High Street he was struck by a car being driven in the opposite direction and was thrown down. He died some months later from injuries he received.

The number of vehicles on the roads increased steadily and so did the time that the council had to spend dealing with the menace. Hundreds of cars were reported travelling along the Holyhead road over the Easter weekend, 1907, and the clouds of dust they raised was the subject of general complaint. The council asked the government to provide a contribution to the increased expenditure which wear and tear on the highways and the abatement of the dust nuisance incurred. It applied to the Local Government Board for regulations to control 'the excessive speed at which motor cars were being driven along High Street'.[12] Councillors considered motor cars to be 'the greatest evil of the day'[13] and suggested that motor car owners should be compelled to pay more for making up the roads.

While councillors condemned the evil machines local entrepreneurs perceived their business potential. By 1910, John Owen of the City Livery Stables was advertising motor cars for hire with capable chauffeurs to drive them. The following year two cycle dealers, E. W. Elias of 347 High Street and W. Evans opened up garages for the repair of motor cars, as did D. Fletcher, proprietor of the Castle Hotel. Evans, an early market researcher, made a census of traffic passing his premises on High Street between 7.30 a.m. and 7.30 p.m. on Whit Monday, 1911; he counted 106 motor cars (nine per hour, on average!), forty-five motor cycles and 346 bicycles.[14]

By 1914, the council was coming to terms with the motor car and was intent on controlling its presence. Ten m.p.h. speed limits were posted on all roads leading into town and an *ad hoc* committee was set up to consider traffic congestion in High Street. Among its recommendations were the limitation of parking on High Street to twenty minutes, the diversion of through traffic from the east down Garth Road to Deiniol Road, the provision of a parking ground for those car owners who had to spend some time on business and the application to the Road Board for a grant of £100,000 to widen High

Street. Not one of these measures was implemented due to the intervention of the Great War but some did form a basis for relieving the traffic problem in the inter-war years. Meanwhile, over the August Bank Holiday weekend, 1914, there was 'a continuous procession of motor cars and motor bikes through the city'.[15]

One of the principal reasons for establishing gas works in Bangor in 1843 was to supply gas for street lighting. The council inherited this public utility from the Local Board and soon realized that the Board had struck a very poor bargain when it bought it in 1878. Payments made to annuitants were a heavy burden to shoulder and not surprisingly heavy losses were incurred in its operation. In a dramatic bid to encourage householders to consume more gas, thereby reducing unit costs of production, the council in 1889 reduced the price of gas from five shillings to three shillings and sixpence per 1,000 cubic feet. Subsequent events justified this gamble: the quantity of gas sold between 1889-90 and 1899-1900 increased from 18.2 to 39.2 million cubic feet. Such a welcome response brought its problems, however. Gas sold at the lower price resulted in even greater deficits for several years and as demand increased the plant proved incapable of meeting it. Complaints were rife about the pressure and the quality of the gas produced. In 1891, twenty additional retorts were installed but it was not possible to store all the gas produced during the day for use in the evening since the holder was too small. By 1895, 185,000 cubic feet were being manufactured daily but there was storage for only 100,000 cubic feet.

Early in 1895 a consultant gas engineer was called in to advise the council; he recommended the closure of the existing works and the erection of a new plant and storage facility on a site removed from the densely built up areas. Excluding the cost of land he estimated the cost in the region of £10,000 (£380,000).

The engineer's report was an untimely blow to the council since it had only just committed itself to the expenditure of £35,000 on the pier and ferry enterprise. Out of the ashes of despair, however, there arose a phoenix of light. Cllr. Grey Edwards urged the council to examine the feasibility of installing an electricity generating plant before it decided on the future of the gas undertaking. He argued that an electricity plant would supply the growing demand for energy which would inevitably occur so that the output from the gas works might be stabilized at, or a little below, its existing level. He was confident that electricity was the energy of the future and feared that if a large sum of money was spent on new gas works the advent of

electricity would be delayed for a very long time. He persuaded the
council to engage an electrical engineer to report on the practicability
of an electricity plant. An engineer reported that the idea was a
feasible one and estimated the cost of an installation capable of
supplying 7,500 eight-candle power lamps to be in the region of
£9,500, a lower figure than the one quoted to build new gas works.

   Heartened by this favourable report the council decided in October
1895 to proceed with its electricity generating scheme. Although the
scheme was not an issue at the November elections a group of
councillors at the first meeting of the new council determined to
persuade the council to rescind its earlier decision. They argued that
gas was very popular and a new and efficient plant would return a
substantial profit; they feared that the gas undertaking would be
neglected if electricity works were established, and they reckoned that
electricity would be more expensive than gas and that only the well-to-
do would be able to afford it. Why then, they argued, should working
men pay dearly for a facility which would benefit only the rich? Cllr.
Henry Lewis countered this argument by pointing out that 'gas was
more expensive than tallow candles yet people were prepared to pay
for greater advantages'.[16] Those opposed to the electricity project
were defeated by thirteen votes to eight.

   Within a fortnight of this decision a public meeting was held at the
Penrhyn Hall to enable ratepayers to express their views. By a very
large majority the meeting rejected the electricity scheme, but this
decision did not influence the council in its resolve to proceed. Even
so, the controversy split the council into two factions and the
municipal election of 1896 was fought on the issue. As a result of the
election the pro-electricity faction on the council was strengthened.
Dr Grey Edwards, the main proponent of electricity was elected
mayor and by August 1897 the council had obtained a provisional
order under the Electricity Lighting Acts 1882 and 1888 to supply
electricity within the borough of Bangor.

   After several more months of desultory wrangling an *ad hoc*
committee was set up comprising three members from each faction to
find a formula which would satisfy both sides of the argument.
Circumstances forced the issue. The gas works were in need of
immediate attention; their storage capacity was woefully inadequate
for the demands placed upon them, accidents occurred and all
attempts to find a site for new works had failed. Under the terms of the
compromise reached in April 1898 several matters were agreed upon:
a new two-lift gasholder with a capacity of 108,000 cubic feet was to be

erected on an adjacent site to supplement the existing holder; a scrubber-washer capable of purifying one million cubic feet of gas daily was to be built and electricity works to supply High Street, Garth Road and Upper Bangor were to be constructed. In view of the state of the city's finances it would have been improper to have called upon ratepayers to bear the burden if there had been a loss on the electricity undertaking. It was therefore suggested that a number of prominent ratepayers should sign a bond undertaking to be responsible for a sum of £500 annually for a period of five years in the event of there being a deficit.

Having given its assent to this compromise the council proceeded to implement its terms. For a sum of £650 it bought a plot of land at the bottom of Dean Street on which to build the electricity works. In order to reduce the fuel costs incurred in raising steam to operate the generator it was decided to erect a rubbish destructor. There was no difficulty in obtaining signatures in support of the bond and in no time a sum of £650 was guaranteed. Finally, it applied to the Local Government Board for permission to borrow the following sums of money: £13,500 for improvements at the gas works; £15,900 for the electricity works and land and £5,480 for the destructor. After a public enquiry the Board declined to grant permission due to the dubious legality of the bond, so the council had to reconsider the matter. Early in 1899 it approved of a scheme whereby prominent ratepayers were to be invited to enter into a binding agreement with the council for the purchase of a total of 40,000 units of electricity per annum for five years. Actually, seventy-three ratepayers promised to purchase 47,000 units, thereby assuring the financial viability of the enterprise. At a subsequent enquiry the Local Government Board approved the revised scheme and the council went ahead with its plans. The electricity plant comprised two steam dynamos of sixty kilowatt capacity capable of lighting 6,000 eight-candle power lamps. A young electrical engineer, Price Foulkes White, was appointed to take charge of the plant and in October 1900 a supply of electricity was inaugurated. Three months later the refuse destructor was commissioned.

Electricity proved an instant success. Householders clamoured to be connected to the supply and within twelve months, demand exceeded the capacity of the plant. A new generator which doubled the generating capacity of the plant was installed in 1903. Since demand outstripped the capacity of even this new generator a diesel driven machine was installed in 1910. After 1906 the large institutions, the cathedral, university, teacher training colleges and schools converted to electricity for lighting. The rise in the consumption of electricity during the period is shown in Table 1.

TABLE 1
*Sale of Electricity, 1902-14*

| Year ending 31 March | Quantity sold to private consumers ('000 B.T.U.'s) | No. of 8-candle-power lamps connected |
|---|---|---|
| 1902 | 115.0 | 6,000 |
| 1906 | 145.9 | 13,233 |
| 1910 | 176.1 | 18,653 |
| 1914 | 194.7 | 21,880 |

Despite the success of the venture and an annual trading surplus of about £1,600, when repayment of the capital sum borrowed and the interest charges on it were taken into consideration, there was a deficit on the electricity account. After 1909 profits slumped as carbon filament lamps were replaced by metal filament lamps; these lamps were more efficient in that they took less energy to produce a given candle power of light, resulting in a lowering in the demand for electricity for a while.

The advent of electricity did not, as many feared, curtail the demand for gas (Table 2); in fact in the first ten years of competition with electricity, the amount of gas sold increased by 17 per cent. Although the amount of gas used for lighting decreased by 9 per cent in this period there was an increase of 50 per cent in the amount sold

TABLE 2
*Consumption of gas 1883-1913*

| Year ending 31 March | Gas sold (million cu.ft.) | Meters in use | Stoves installed | Public lamps |
|---|---|---|---|---|
| 1883 | 12.8 | 504 | — | 166 |
| 1893 | 25.9 | 677 | 62 | 247 |
| 1903 | 40.5 | 1,401 | 582 | 326 |
| 1913 | 44.0 | 2,173 | 1,498 | 379 |

for cooking and for heating water. The first gas stove was installed in 1883; by 1914 over half the households had a stove and the council had the monopoly for their sale and installation. The number of gas lamps used for lighting the streets increased from 306 in 1901 to 380 in 1914 and gas retained its monopoly until 1926. In contrast to the deficit on the electric undertaking the gas enterprise returned a handsome profit; between 1904 and 1913 it amounted to £6,662 and helped to offset deficits incurred by other municipal enterprises.

Another responsibility taken over from the Local Board was the maintenance of the library and museum. The rented building on High Street was too cramped, books were old and in poor condition and valuable pictures were deteriorating under the attack of mould and moths. Fewer than a thousand books were issued in the early years of the century and a councillor averred in 1904 that the library 'was a disgrace to a town which lays claim to the title of the Athens of Wales'.[17]

As the council was considering the future of the institution, whose lease was due to expire, it came to hear of the gifts of money that Mr Andrew Carnegie, the wealthy American steel magnate and philanthropist, was making for the purpose of establishing libraries. On application to Carnegie the council was granted a sum of £2,500 to which it added £300 from Capt. John Jones's legacy (see p.45-6). With these sums in mind architects were invited to submit designs for a new library which was to be 'worthy of the place'.[18] A site was chosen on a portion of the former Bishop's Park Estate fronting onto a proposed new road, Ffordd Gwynedd and the successful architects were Messrs. Dixon and Potter of Manchester. The library is built of plastic red Ruabon brick with dressings of stone from the Stancliffe Quarries, Darley Dale, Derbyshire and roofed with Penrhyn Quarry slates. A notable feature is the octagonal hall 16´6´´ x 16´6´´ which is covered with a dome. A penny rate which the council was allowed to raise for its upkeep yielded £600 a year and this sum was considered a sufficient amount. When the wording of the title to be inscribed on the stone ornament above the main entrance was discussed it was suggested that it should be in English and Welsh. Ald. Henry Lewis thought the lettering would be too cramped and his suggestion that 'Llyfrgell Rhydd 1907' only should be inscribed was carried. Rather than lay the conventional foundation stone the council decided to erect a brass tablet in the entrance hall on which a suitable inscription was engraved. The library was opened by the third Lord Penrhyn on 8 November 1907.

The council, still encumbered with the museum on High Street, decided in August 1908 to build a new one at the rear of the library; it was unwilling, however, to spend another £500 in order that it might be on the same level as the library. The museum was opened in 1910. The city's fire brigade, transferred to the council on incorporation, was the responsibility of the Museum and General Purposes Committee. The fire engine was horse drawn, manually operated and inadequately equipped; pipes were frequently withdrawn for flushing out the drains and ladders had to be borrowed from builders and painters. A fire in the almshouses on 5 May 1889 exposed all the physical and human weaknesses of the brigade. A leader in the *North Wales Observer and Express* condemned the domineering conduct of the captain, John Gill, and his inability to organize voluntary help and the inefficiency of the men who 'did not possess that tact and courage which ought to characterize men in their position'.[19]

Stimulation of the local economy was a major objective of the council. It recognized that the financial foundation for town improvements, the rating system, rested in the long term on the prosperity of the wide variety of commercial enterprises which functioned in the city and which provided a livelihood for its citizens. Steps taken to make the city an attractive place for residents and holidaymakers have been noted. Not so apparent were the strenuous efforts the council made to popularize the city through the advertising media of the period and the constant dialogue it had with the railway company with a view to improving train services and access to the station. More tangible was the support it gave and the initiatives it took in consolidating the role of Bangor as a shopping, commercial and entertainment centre and as a centre for higher education.

Even before 1883, much of south east Anglesey and the Bethesda slate quarrying district looked to Bangor as their natural centre for higher order goods and services. Its economic hegemony over these areas was strengthened by the improvement after 1896 in the ferry service across the Strait in the case of the first area, and by the construction in 1884 of a branch railway line to Bethesda in the case of the second. Bangor's nearest trading rival was Caernarfon and attempts were made in two directions to encroach upon its tributary area. Between 1883 and 1885 the council promoted the construction of a branch railway line from Bangor to Llandinorwic in order to tap the custom of the slate quarrying communities in that region. Some years later it urged the Railway Company to open a station at Llangaffo in south west Anglesey in order to attract to Bangor the people of the farming communities of that area who had traditionally crossed to Caernarfon via the ferry. Both these initiatives were unsuccessful.

It was, however, the advent of a motor transport system which really wedded the city more closely to its tributary area. Among the responsibilities the council inherited from the Local Board of Health was the licensing of cabs and horse drawn omnibuses. Operators of motor buses too had to apply to the council for a licence and to arrange with it where to pick up and let down passengers and where to park. The first licence was granted in November 1912 to the Llandudno Motor Company to operate a service between the railway station, Upper Bangor and the pier and between Bangor and surrounding villages. Licences to run buses in and out of Bangor were granted to another three bus companies in 1913 and enquiries were made at that time as to whether it was possible to run buses to Clwt-y-Bont, Ebenezer and other villages within Caernarfon's tributary area.

Anxious to enhance the status of Bangor as a seaside resort the council purchased the Siliwen bathing ground in June 1887 with the intention of improving it. Tons of sand were conveyed to the site by barge and the changing huts were renovated. Problems remained, however, in spite of these improvements; it was only possible to bathe at high tide so bathing was limited to a few hours each day and these varied with the state of the tide. In addition, there were so few huts that bathers had to wait such a long time for a hut to become vacant that the tide in the meantime had receded! A severe storm in December 1899 wrecked the huts so the council was forced to make a decision on the ground's future.

Most councillors saw the connection between sea bathing and a healthy body and realized also that a bathing facility was necessary to attract visitors. Cllr. Dr E. O. Price considered it 'would be well for the health of the town if the habit of bathing could be cultivated' and he championed the case for a purpose built swimming pool. Cllr. T. J. Williams thought sea bathing 'directly concerned the sanitation of the town' but Cllr. Huw Rowland saw it only 'in the nature of amusement, and what they (the people) needed to cultivate was the habit of washing'.[20] He advocated the building of baths near the city centre for people who did not have a bath in their home.

Dr Price's proposition found favour with the council. John Gill's plans were accepted for a concrete lined swimming pool having a surface area of 2,200 square yards and a depth of eighteen feet; two outlets enabled the pool to be renewed with water at every tide. The cost of building the pool and erecting new bathing huts was £2,343 (£80,000). They were opened on 25 June 1902 and the *North Wales Observer and Express* reported a week or so later that 'hundreds of bathers have availed themselves of the improved facilities'.[21] Reduced terms were granted to schoolchildren and students and as the years went by the pool proved popular with the youth of the city, successive generations of students and visitors. An average of about 8,000 persons a year patronized the pool up to the summer of 1914.

TABLE 3

*Number of persons using Siliwen Baths, 1903-13*

| Season | Open baths | Indoor baths | Enclosure | Total |
|--------|-----------|--------------|-----------|-------|
| 1903   | 5,899     | 145          | 902       | 6,945 |
| 1908   | 6,739     | 113          | 1,023     | 7,975 |
| 1913   | 8,714     | 76           | 1,153     | 9,943 |

An interesting innovation was the permitting of mixed bathing at the pool between 8 a.m. and midday daily. Some councillors wanted the pool to be divided into a ladies' and gentlemen's section but it was pointed out that ladies could still use the adjacent old bathing ground if they objected to sharing the pool. Mixed bathing proved to be very popular and in 1903 the concession was extended to 5 p.m. Sunday bathing was allowed in 1911 and in that year new changing huts were added. In spite of its popularity, 'Dr Price's tank'[22] was a financial liability to the council from the outset.

One of the many reasons why the council decided in 1892 to construct a pier at Garth Point was the desire to attract more visitors to the city. The idea of building a pier was first mooted by Col. Platt during his first term as mayor and a consultant engineer, J. J. Webster of London, was invited to submit plans. Seven years later the idea had become an attractive proposition. Its proponents saw it fulfilling four necessary functions, each one of which would yield revenue to the council, and, by greatly enhancing the popularity of the city with visitors, would boost the local economy. The functions were those of providing improved landing facilites for passenger steamers plying along the North Wales coast between Liverpool and the Menai Strait, improved landing facilities for the ferry which crossed the Strait between Garth and Llandegfan, landing facilities for freight, and promenading and entertainment facilities on the pier itself.

A regular passenger service between Liverpool and Bangor was inaugurated by the *Albion* in 1822. Later, piers were constructed at Llandudno, Beaumaris and Menai Bridge to accommodate the large paddle steamers which were brought into service towards the end of the century. To embark and disembark at Bangor passengers had to be transferred from and to smaller vessels which plied from the jetty at Garth. This was a time-consuming and hazardous operation and would only be undertaken when sea and wind conditions were propitious. Bangor was therefore at a considerable disadvantage compared with Beaumaris and Menai Bridge in exploiting the growing excursion traffic which the Strait, with its two fine bridges, was attracting. The secretary of the Liverpool and North Wales Steamship Co. said that whilst about 10,000 passengers had embarked and disembarked at Bangor in 1892, 70,000 had done so at Menai Bridge; he was confident that if a pier were erected in Bangor 35,000 steamship passengers a year would use it.[23]

The relationship between the proposed pier and the existing ferry had to be resolved before any progress could be made. The right to run a ferry between Garth and Llandegfan on the Anglesey shore of the Strait had been granted to the Bishop of Bangor in medieval times; the bishop also owned the land at the Garth terminus. If a new terminus were to be established at the head of the projected pier both the length of journey across the Strait and the time of crossing would be considerably reduced. Such a facility might also be used to accommodate larger steam ferries which could operate a scheduled service to Beaumaris. These advantages would not accrue to the lessee of the ferry if he continued to ply from Garth Point and it was not likely that the council would allow him to use the new facility to enhance his own financial gain. A solution would be for the council to buy out the operator's lease of the ferry, negotiate with the Ecclesiastical Commissioners for the transfer of the ferry rights and land at Garth and operate and extend the whole business as a municipal enterprise. That it would be a successful one there could be little doubt since numbers crossing on the Garth ferry alone were estimated to be 160,000 annually.[24]

Apart from Port Penrhyn which was a private port and used almost entirely for the transport of slate and coal there was no suitable facility in Bangor for loading and unloading freight carried by sea. Businessmen considered such a facility might break the monopoly which the railway company then held and force down its high charges. The first steps were taken in August 1891 when the council bought the disused slate yard at Garth and improved the jetty there.[25] The jetty came to be known as the 'Ja Ja jetty' after the name of the steamer *Prince Ja Ja* which then began to run a twice weekly service between Liverpool and the ports on the Strait. Eventually the council was persuaded that the unloading of freight and promenading were incompatible activities so it dropped the idea of the pier as a freight terminal. Promenading and entertainment, therefore, were seen to be an important function of the pier. Although the sea washed nearly half the length of the borough's boundaries access to it was not easy and not even a sea-side promenade had been constructed.

The decision to proceed with the ferry and pier package was taken in mid 1892. Permission to construct a pier one third of a mile out into the navigable waters of the Strait was obtained from the Board of Trade. The council then negotiated successfully with the Ecclesiastical Commissioners for the purchase of the ferry rights and the land at Garth, with John Morgan for the transfer of the lease of the ferry and with Mrs Salis Schwabe of Glyngarth for the purchase of the jetty and Gazelle Inn at the Anglesey terminal. It then petitioned the Local Government Board for the loan of £25,000 (£875,000)[26] to be apportioned as follows:

|  | £ |
|---|---|
| Pier and approach .. .. .. .. .. | 16,000 |
| Purchase of Garth ferry and appurtenances .. .. | 5,500 |
| Extending Garth wharf and jetty .. .. .. | 500 |
| Improving of landing stage at Llandegfan .. .. | 300 |
| Purchase of freehold of Gazelle Inn, improving and enlarging same; purchase of new ferry boats, steam launches, etc. .. .. .. .. .. .. | 2,700 |
|  | 25,000 |

The realization that the cost of the project would now be £25,000 instead of the £13,000, which was the initial estimate, unleashed a hostile reaction which was manifest at the Local Government Board enquiry on 15 March 1893. Among the grounds for opposition was, firstly, the cost of the project. The city was already in debt to the tune of £100,000 and £25,000 was more than the city could afford. Interest charges on the loan itself at 3½% per annum would amount to £875 per annum to which sum could be added £450 a year to cover the cost of repairs, painting, salaries of officials, lighting, insurance, etc. An annual outlay of £1,325 would be incurred and there would be the repayment of the loan in addition. Assuming a penny toll was levied, the standard charge for admittance to piers at that time, it would need over 300,000 people a year to patronize the pier to make it a viable proposition, clearly an unrealistic figure based on the most optimistic estimates of future use. If the pier were proceeded with, the burden on the rates would be intolerable. Secondly, at low tide dirty mud and the outflow from two nearby sewers would be exposed. Promenading in these circumstances would be neither agreeable nor conducive to health. Lastly, Bangor had little to attract visitors who might sail on the Liverpool steamers. Menai Bridge was the obvious place to disembark to view the bridges and there were castles at Beaumaris and Caernarfon.[27]

Despite objections at the enquiry the Local Government Board sanctioned the borrowing of the necessary sum of money subject to Parliamentary approval for the venture. A Parliamentary Bill would involve additional expenditure and by mid June pressure was mounting to abandon the scheme, especially since a number of its early supporters began to have second thoughts. The mayor, W. A. Dew, his deputy, Donald Cameron, and Cllr. Henry Lewis insisted that the council should ascertain the views of ratepayers before they proceeded any further.[28] A meeting of tradesmen in September gave overwhelming support to the project. A public meeting at the skating rink on 12 October carried with acclamation a motion supporting the acquisition of the ferry and the construction of the pier. Cllr. Henry Lewis presented the case against the project 'but the meeting was in no mood to listen (to him)'.[29]

Having obtained this clear mandate the council proceeded to draft the Parliamentary Bill undeterred, the objectors continued in their opposition to the project. Amidst growing unease due to the claim that the public meeting on 12 October did not reflect the true opinion of ratepayers, since everyone at the meeting voted whether a ratepayer or not, the new mayor, Donald Cameron, called a public meeting at the Penrhyn Hall in December. After a lively debate the mayor requested those who were not ratepauyers to refrain from voting on the motion that the council should proceed with the ferry and pier venture. The motion was carried by an overwhelming majority whereupon the council authorized the mayor to affix the seal of the council to the Bangor Corporation (Pier etc.) Bill 1894.[30]

Opposition to the project continued, however, and in response to requests from a number of influential ratepayers the mayor called yet another public meeting, on 16 January 1894. The Penrhyn Hall was packed for the occasion. Ald. Thomas Lewis, who remained a loyal supporter of the venture, was greeted with 'ringing cheers' when he rose to present the council's case. David Owen, solicitor, who led the opposition to it was 'heartily hooted' on the other hand. Owen asserted that supporters of the ferry and pier project were drawn from the ranks of those who would derive most benefit from it, namely the merchants, lodging house keepers, publicans and cab owners and that the majority of ratepayers would pay very dearly for the facility. Ratepayers still clamoured for the pier, however.[31]

In a final bid to frustrate the designers of the Parliamentary Bill the objectors demanded a poll of ratepayers on the matter. A leader in the *North Wales Chronicle* the week before the poll urged ratepayers to vote decisively in favour of the pier. 'If a pier is vetoed the door to municipal progress will be closed . . . (and) men who have been entrusted with the work of pushing the town on will feel that they have lost the confidence of the constituents. This is really the question at issue. Shall Bangor for all time be content with a primitive and dangerous approach to the sea, shall the city deny itself the advantage of being in connection with the great centres of trade and commerce, shall no improvements of any kind be carried out, for fear, forsooth, the rates may go up a few pence in the pound . . .? It is certain that the pier, in any event, will not be a heavy burden on the rates. Shall we not take a very small risk for the purpose of securing a valuable property and greatly improve the town of Bangor?'[32] The result of the poll echoed these sentiments for 1,342 voted in favour and 545 against the pier. The size of the dissident vote must have surprised the promoters of the scheme and in some measure vindicated David Owen and his fellow objectors who all along claimed that there was considerable opposition to the pier among ratepayers.

The poll was the *coup de grâce* of the opposition and the Parliamentary Bill received the Royal Assent at the end of August 1894. From early confidence based on not very reliable statistics and entrepreneural hunches, the council had wavered as opposition to it hardened but nevertheless held its ground, always believing that even if the venture did not itself show a profit, the benefits which would accrue to the city from increased trade would fully justify the construction of the pier. Much credit for the persistence of the council in pursuing its goal throughout these anxious years must be given to Cllr. Richard Davies,[33] chairman, and the members of the Pier and Ferry Committee, whose undivided and passionate support for the venture strengthened the resolve of other council members.

Once it obtained Parliamentary authority, the council moved

quickly. Negotiations with the Ecclesiastical Commissioners, John Morgan and Mrs. Schwabe were finalized and the ferry was handed over at the end of September 1894. The official ceremony at Garth Point was preceded by a procession of various organizations through the city.[34]

Meanwhile J. J. Webster, who had designed the pier was appointed engineer of the pier project and Alfred Thorne was contracted to build it. The pier was 1,550 feet long and consisted of cast iron screw piles and pillars supporting a superstructure of steel girders and joists which carried the pitchpine deck planks. The width of the pier was twenty-four feet except at four places where it opened out to fifty-five feet to incorporate eight ornamental kiosks. At its head it was wider still and its two extreme corners were circular to accommodate covered wind shields or shelters. Beyond the fixed portion of the landing stages was a floating stage, eighty feet by eighteen feet, which was kept in position by greenheart timber dolphins and was approached from the pier by a bow string girder bridge with a span of 120 feet and a width of 7.5 feet. Landing steps for pleasure boats were fixed at each side of the pier head and at two thirds of the length of the pier. Ornamental cast iron railings with seats at convenient intervals were fixed at the sides of the pier and were surmounted by ornamental gas lamps. Elegant gates were erected at the entrance on either side of the decorative paybooths and worked into the design of the gates were the arms of the city. Tramlines of three foot gauge used to run the whole length of the pier onto the landing stage for the purpose of carrying light merchandise.

The pier was opened on 14 May 1896 [Plate 3]. It was a warm sunny day and since it was Ascension Day the Penrhyn Quarry, according to a long standing custom, was closed and hundreds of workmen and their families travelled to Bangor to join the crowds of Bangor people who converged on the pier to witness the opening ceremony. The town was gaily decorated and a procession was assembled at the town clock; it comprised the brass band of the local Volunteers, various friendly societies, the football club and fire brigade, pier officials, members of the public, the mayors of Beaumaris, Caernarfon and Conwy and the chairman of Llandudno Urban Council, the mayor, aldermen and councillors of the Borough and Lord Penrhyn and his daughter. After a rousing march through the streets the procession arrived at the pier and Lord Penrhyn performed the opening ceremony. In his address he aptly said that Bangor, in building the pier was 'extending its hand, as it were, as a token of welcome to

*Plate 2.* The First Council, 1883.

*Back row, left to right:* K. W. Douglas, J. R. Brown, Hugh Jones, Edward Jones (Coachbuilder), John Evans, Edward Jones (Brynmeirion), J. Willmann.

*Middle row:* Richard Rowlands, T. J. Humphreys, T. Hathaway, Col. Savage, W. A. Dew, R. Roberts (Mace Bearer), R. H. Pritchard (Town Clerk), J. Glynne Jones, J. Evan Roberts, Josiah Hughes, William Rowlands.

*Front row:* John Pritchard, W. Francis Williams, Charles Pierce, Dr Richards, Col. Platt (Mayor), Thomas Lewis, Meshach Roberts, Robert Roberts.

*Plate 3.* The opening of the pier, 14 May 1896.

visitors, who would, he trusted, not be slow to reciprocate the cordiality of the invitation'. While Lord Penrhyn sat down that evening as one of the many honoured guests of the Mayor and Corporation at a sumptuous banquet at the George Hotel, the *hoi polloi* were treated to a number of spectacles at the pier. Here a confetti fête and a grand display of fireworks were arranged and to round off the evening's entertainment an impressive procession of beautifully illuminated boats sailed past the pier head in the still darkness.[35]

It was a memorable day, more so, probably, than the one thirteen years previously when the city had turned out to celebrate the granting of the Charter and the selection of Bangor as the site for the University College, for the pier was a proud and tangible proof of the city's enterprising spirit, a facility which could be enjoyed by all, and a herald of hope for a brighter and more prosperous future. One ingredient was absent from the celebrations that day, however: there were no visitors to be welcomed at the pier head. Once the landing stage was in place, it was discovered that the water there was too shallow to take the large pleasure steamers which had been scheduled to visit. A channel had to be dredged causing considerable additional expense and an ominous delay. When the work was completed it was too late in the season for the steamship companies to alter their schedules and so a summer season passed without revenue originating from this source. Thus began, at the very outset of its life, the spate of misfortunes which were to plague the pier almost up to the present day.

As a novelty the pier proved an immediate attraction for the steamship companies and their passengers, and for promenading and entertainments. The ferry side of the enterprise too benefited from the shorter crossing to Llandegfan and the inauguration of a ferry service, first to Beaumaris and later to Caernarfon. Three types of boat were used to convey passengers to and from Llandegfan: a rowing boat for eighteen passengers, a sailing boat and a small steamer called the *Mona*. Not one of them had any shelter for passengers so journeys were frequently cold, wet and miserable and neither the rowing boat nor the sailing boat had any room for bicycles. The steamer was more comfortable and had space for passengers' belongings but since it was costly to run it was seldom used. Originally there were no lights on the pier head and one had to be very careful in negotiating the steep iron steps at night; the stone landing stage at Llandegfan was positively dangerous because of its uneven and slippery surface and there was no lighting there either. In 1897 £300 (£11,400) was spent on erecting a wooden jetty at Llandegfan. The Gazelle Inn was renovated and extended and licensed to sell beer, wines and spirits. Despite its shortcomings the ferry retained its popularity up to 1914, carrying, incredible though it may seem today, an average of 140,000 passengers a year. In addition it was carrying about 5,000 bicycles a year and in 1914 over 1,600 parcels.[36] Bangor was obviously the major employment, market, shopping and service centre for the people of south-east Anglesey; Bangorians also made the ferry terminus at Llandegfan their starting point for cycling trips into the coutryside and to the beaches of that quarter of the island.

Soon after taking over the ferry in 1894 the council inaugurated a ferry service to the pier at Beaumaris. A second-hand steamer capable of carrying 150 passengers and called the *Torbay* was acquired for the purpose. At first it operated during summer months only but it soon maintained a skeleton service throughout the winter months too. A recommendation of the Pier and Ferry Committee in 1897 that the *Torbay* should run on Sundays was passed in the council by eight votes to five. Some of those in favour argued that Sunday was the only day that large numbers of working class families could make the trip across the Strait and enjoy the fresh air and sea breezes; others argued, somewhat unconvincingly perhaps, that many people from Beaumaris wished to attend church services in Bangor. The decision was greeted with immediate and loud protests from Nonconformist congregations both in Bangor and Beaumaris. The issue was settled by the Beaumaris pier authority refusing to allow the *Torbay* to land there on Sundays.[37] More frequent schedules led the council in 1904 to buy another steamer capable of carrying 300 passengers which it called the *Lady Magdalen* (after the wife of the proprietor of Baron Hill, Beaumaris) and in 1906 it was able to inaugurate a regular service to Caernarfon during the summer months. Throughout the period from 1898 to 1914 the Beaumaris service attracted an average of 50,000 passengers a year while an average of 4,500 used the Caernarfon service.

One of the main reasons for the construction of the pier was to provide a safe anchorage for pleasure steamers which plied between Liverpool and the Menai Strait. Both the Liverpool and North Wales Steamship Company and the Blackpool and Isle of Man Steamship Company agreed in 1897 to use the pier as a regular port of call for their scheduled services to the Strait. The Liverpool company's ships, the *Snowdon* and *St Elvies*, called twice a week at first, but when the company commissioned in 1904 the new 'palatial saloon paddle steamer' *La Marguerite*, capable of carrying 2,000 passengers, it was able to maintain a daily service. In that year it replaced the *Snowdon* with a steamer with the familiar sounding name, *St Tudno*, and the *St Elvies* ran a service around the Isle of Anglesey. A pleasant little custom was established: when the first of the season's steamers arrived in May and the last one departed at the end of September, the boats, decked with flags, would fire a cannon to which blast the cannon sited on the pier would respond. Many spectators were present at the pier head to witness these seasonal exchanges.

The Blackpool and Isle of Man steamers called less frequently. On 5 July 1899 the Blackpool steamer landed between 500 and 600 passengers among whom were the mayor, town clerk and members of Blackpool Corporation; they were met by the Mayor of Bangor and his reception party.[38] Other companies ran occasional excursions, for example, after a pleasant run from Liverpool in August 1897, the Cunard tender, *Skirmisher*, landed about 600 employees of the company's Cargo Department and their families. They were accompanied by the Department's brass band and immediately filled the pier with a great throng which elicited from the Borough Accountant the fervent exclamation, 'I wish this crowd would come every day'.[39] They paid a subsequent visit in 1899. The prediction of the Secretary of the Liverpool and North Wales Steamship Company in 1892 that 35,000 passengers a year would use the pier was not wide of the mark since between 1897 and 1914 the pier was used by 34,000 passengers a year on average.

As a facility for promenading, the pier was greatly appreciated by townsfolk and visitors alike. On the Saturday after its opening 1,600 paid for admission and on the Sunday, another 1,800. The number of promenaders varied with the season, but during the period May 1896 to March 1914 nearly 442,000 paid to enter the pier and another 296,000 bought contract tickets.[40]

The pier offered scope for a wide range of activities and entertainments and the focus of these was the pier head where a stage and bandstand had been erected. Popular attractions included fancy dress carnivals, best decorated pram competitions, brass band contests, walking competitions along a measured two mile course, and swimming races across the Strait. On Strait Regatta Day hundreds of people came to view the sleek white sailed cutters speeding up and down the Strait and the side entertainments such as swimming races, duck hunts and climbing the greasy pole. Stunt divers would exhibit their bravado by diving off the top rail of the pier and as darkness fell processions of illuminated boats would sail past the pier head.

More formal entertainment was provided by brass bands and choirs and the opening of the pier undoubtedly stimulated the formation of local music groups. Dr Rowland Rogers, organist at the cathedral, formed a town band which played on the pier for many seasons, alternating with the bands of the local Artillery Volunteers, the Anglesey Engineers and the *Clio*.[41] New choirs were formed and sacred concerts were given on Sunday evenings.

The most popular form of entertainment was the seaside vaudeville typical of the late Victorian and Edwardian era. Entertainment troupes were hired by the council to perform for the season. The golden years of vaudeville were during the Edwardian era when Will Summerson was contracted to provide the entertainment. He had a basic company of five or six performers but he engaged artistes for varying periods through the season to add variety to the programme. Under the name of firstly the Bangor Operatic Pierrots and later the Merry Musical Middies his repertoire comprised solos and duets, comic songs, coon songs, ballads, lullabies and recitations; there were piano and violin items, banjo and mandolin numbers, dances and sketches. Usually members of the troupe would dress up in costume. Among the specially hired artistes were ventriloquists, conjurors, trick cyclists, Japanese jugglers and ornamental swimmers.

Yet, into this world of amateur and professional live entertainment the technical age was beginning to intrude; in August 1903 the first electrograph show was screened and was followed twelve months later by the projection of Jules Vernes's 'The Wonders of the Deep' which drew large crowds. Gramophone concerts began there in 1908 and soon there was dancing to the music of gramophone records.

Between the summer seasons of 1897 and 1914 inclusive the number of people who patronized pier entertainments was nearly 400,000, an average of about 23,500 a year. The peak year was 1906 with nearly 40,000 spectators; by 1909 the number had dropped by half and in 1913 it was only 5,370.[42] Such a sharp decline in popularity may be explained by a number of related factors. The immediate one was the weather. The summers of 1909 and 1910 were damp and cool and they revealed the patent unsuitability of the pier head site as a venue for entertainment. Lying half way across the Strait it was exposed to the vagaries of the weather and, although canvas wind shields had been erected, councillors complained of people being 'starved to death' listening to the Merry Middies.[43] In inclement weather the show was transferred to the Penrhyn Hall, but the decision had often to be taken at short notice and this confused patrons. With hindsight it is difficult to understand why a pavilion was not incorporated into the design of the pier, preferably at its landward end; one can only assume that the additional costs would have been unacceptable.

Depressed by dwindling audiences, harassed by the weather and seeing a promising future for films, Will Summerson opened a pavilion in January 1910 on the site of the present day Plaza cinema. Here he blended the old and the new in a mixture of variety entertainment and a film show on premises which could remain open whatever the state of the weather and which were heated in winter. His Cosy Corner Pavilion proved an immediate success for the attraction of the film was magnetic. Films made in America appeared early in 1912 and on 17 March 'Cowboy films – full of stirring scenes' were advertised in the local press. A new form of entertainment had arrived; people enjoyed it and wanted more of it. Local entrepreneurs responded. The old Tabernacl chapel in Dean Street was converted into a variety and picture theatre to seat 1,200 people and opened its doors in September 1912 as the New County Theatre. In March 1914 an electric theatre called the New Palace Theatre (now the City Cinema), with seating for 650 persons was opened on High Street. Matinées were scheduled and late trains arranged.

Summerson's troupe performed for one last and shortened season on the pier in 1910. Councillors, during a discussion on entertainment on the pier in May 1911 agreed that 'pierrots are played out in Bangor' and that visitors had become 'tired of them'.[44] They were reluctant to see an end to this particular municipal enterprise, however. They continued to engage various troupes and brass bands, albeit for very much shorter periods, and held occasional picture shows; they even went so far as to build a small changing room, board the sides, back and roof of the stage and call the structure the Pier Pavilion in a desperate bid to win back the audiences of yesteryear. However it was too little and too late and in August 1914 more powerful forces than the weather and the celluloid strip forced the curtains to close for good on seaside vaudeville on the pier.

Looking out before renovation started at the forlorn, deserted and decaying structure protruding into the Strait at Garth it was difficult to realize that in its heyday the pier was a major focus of activity in the city, for in the region of 700,000 people a year, on average, converged upon it for one reason or another. Yet, despite all the activity, neither the pier nor the ferries yielded the council any financial profit during those thriving years. Receipts from the various activities balanced the working, maintenance and repair costs of the enterprise and yielded a surplus most years, but when the payment of loan charges and the repayment by instalments of the loan itself are taken into consideration there was a regular deficit of about £1,500 (£50,000) a year. Few ratepayers would begrudge this subsidy towards the enjoyment of townspeople and there were other incalculable benefits besides. Running the pier and ferries created employment and cabmen and traders on High Street benefited from the crowds of visitors and day trippers from the steamers who invariably made their way into town to visit shops and eating places in typical tourist fashion. The presence of the pier also spurred the council to improve access to it; the main road from the town clock to Garth was widened, resurfaced, and provided with footpaths and seats in 1902. The council's dream of a road running direct from the station to the pier was realized in 1905 when Deiniol Road was opened; in planning a road forty-eight feet wide the council envisaged the running of electric trams between the two facilities but this project never materialized. Up to 1914, then, the council could congratulate itself on providing a facility which benefited the city in a number of ways.

The outstanding illustration of the council's commitment to enhancing the prosperity and status of Bangor is its endeavour to acquire a permanent site for the University College of North Wales. The College opened in the Michaelmas Term 1884 in temporary premises at the Penrhyn Arms Hotel, which with its extensive outbuildings had been substantially remodelled to serve educational needs. Fifty-eight students enrolled in the first session; within fourteen years the number had risen to 312 and many new departments had been added, including education, agriculture and electrical engineering. With the supply of students from the recently established Welsh intermediate school system steadily increasing it was becoming clear by the end of the century that the temporary buildings and the constricted site would seriously militate against the growth and efficiency of the institution. Principal Reichel drew the College Council's attention to this fact in February 1899 and invited it to consider in what manner permanent provision could best be made. As a preliminary step the College Council suggested that the Principal, together with its Chairman, should appear before the city council in order to invite their co-operation in the securing of a permanent site. At the meeting held in May, Principal Reichel reminded the council that the history of the University was contemporaneous with that of the municipality; so far they had prospered together and he expressed the hope that they would continue to do so. He pointed out that the municipal authorities in Aberystwyth and Cardiff had co-operated handsomely with the College authorities in both towns and at Cardiff, in particular, the city council had presented to the College an admirable site in Cathays Park near the city centre. The Bangor council was invited to appoint representatives on the College Building Committee.[45]

The Penrhyn Arms site was located in the least desirable quarter of the city and the Building Committee soon concluded that it was too small for permanent buildings. Upper Bangor, where already most of the University staff lived and large numbers of students lodged, presented a more salubrious alternative. All the land there, however, belonged to Lord Penrhyn, who, wanting the College to remain in the Penrhyn Arms vicinity, declined to sell any land in Upper Bangor.

A remarkable turn of events pointed a way out of the impasse. In August 1899 the Bishop of Bangor died and his successor refused to live in the Palace because of its delapidated and damp state. He petitioned the Ecclesiastical Commissioners to sell the Palace, together with the estate of sixteen acres, and use the proceeds to build a more agreeable episcopal residence. The coming of the estate onto the market in March 1900 opened up the possibility of building the college on a site in the Bishop's Park.

The city council had for many years yearned for possession of this valuable estate near the heart of the city for other reasons. It wanted to build a road from the railway station to Garth Road to establish a direct line of communication between the station and the pier, but the Bishop's Park lay astride the proposed road. It also wished to lay a new sewer along the whole length of the road to collect sewage and drain water from Upper Bangor which, having grown rapidly, had rendered the existing sewer totally inadequate. Possession of the estate would enable the council to raise public buildings thereon, especially civic offices and a hall, which were urgently needed.

However, it was not the council but a syndicate of local gentlemen under the chairmanship of Col. Platt who bought the estate in March 1900. Anticipating that the council would be slow in responding to the opportunity, it decided to act quickly in order to forestall any outside property speculators buying the estate and developing it insensitively. The syndicate's intention all along was to offer it eventually to the council to dispose of it in the best interests of the city. It duly offered the estate to the council in April and the price of £15,500 was accepted.[46]

As a gesture of good will the council resolved in June 1900 to offer a six acre plot lying between the Palace and Penrallt as a gift to the college.[47] Having inspected the site a Board of Education architect declared in October of that year that the site was 'in every way unsuitable for the erection of the college'.[48] Meanwhile the College Buildings Committee had been considering eight sites in Upper Bangor and concluded that the Penrallt site of four acres was the most suitable. The Board's architect, however, would not consider the site as it was too small. Persisting in its view that the Penrallt site was the best, the Building Committee decided that if it were to accept the city's gift of the adjacent Bishop's Park site, the combined site might meet the Board's requirements. In December the Committee succeeded in persuading Lord Penrhyn to sell the Penrallt site for £8,000 and invited the Board of Education's architect to inspect the combined Penrallt-Bishop's Park site of ten acres.[49] The architect reported that 'it is by far the finest site in Bangor for the purpose and almost unmatchable in North Wales'.[50]

With this seal of approval the council applied to the Local Government Board for permission to borrow £20,000, the sum required to buy the Bishop's Park Estate, and implement its designs upon it. The application was, however, turned down by the Board on the grounds that it was not empowered under the Municipal Corporations Act 1882 to allow a council to dispose of land by way of a gift. To do so it would have to seek parliamentary approval.

This was a blow to the expectations of both the College Building Committee and the council. It was compounded by the action of a group of councillors, notably David Owen, Owen Owen and Jones-Roberts, who discovered that the syndicate had only paid £12,500 for the Bishop's Park Estate but had sold it for £15,500 making thereby a handsome profit; they charged Col. Platt and his associates with profiteering at the expense of the city. They persuaded the council to rescind the provisional agreement to buy the estate and enter into fresh negotiations with the syndicate for the purchase of only those parts of the estate needed for roads, municipal buildings and the new College buildings. Thereupon Col. Platt withdrew his offer to sell any part of the estate.

In view of the total breakdown in attempts to find a site for the Bangor college, a special meeting of the Court of Governors of the University College was held on 4 December 1901. Objections were raised about the price asked for the Penrallt site and doubts were expressed whether the combined site was the best procurable. Details were given of the offer of free sites made by Caernarfon, Denbigh, Rhyl and Wrexham and the Governors made it known that they were not tied to a site in Bangor. A number of important resolutions were passed at the meeting. Bangor was given twelve months to sort out the provision of a site; in view of the free offers of sites from other towns, a free site would have to be provided in Bangor if the college was to be retained there. The decision by the College Council to purchase the Penrallt site was therefore rescinded.

When the council met in February 1902 to consider the resolutions of the College Governors it was in sombre mood. Henry Lewis, the mayor, caught the mood of the occasion when he said they were witnessing 'one of the most important crises in the history of the town'.[51] The financial stakes were high: the purchase of the Penrallt site and the Bishop's Park, together with the development of the latter, would amount to an expenditure of about £25,000, a sum of money almost equal to that spent on the pier and ferry undertaking only six years previously. Henry Lewis acknowledged the burden that this would impose upon the city but spelt out in no uncertain terms the consequences of the removal of the college from Bangor: four hundred members of staff and students would depart, ancillary workers and lodging house keepers would lose their livelihood, the Baptist and Independent Colleges might be transferred elsewhere, there would be a diminution of from £12,000 to £15,000 a year in commercial turnover and there would be an appreciable loss in rate revenue. And what of the more intangible costs to Bangor in terms of status and its proud claim to be the 'Athens of Wales'? Henry Lewis successfully prevailed upon the council to work together for the future of the city and to be generous in its gift of the whole ten acre combined site.

The council once more negotiated with the Bishop's Park syndicate and agreed to buy 12.4 acres of the Park for £11,000. At its March meeting it formally agreed 'to enter into a provisional agreement with Lord Penrhyn for the purchase of Penrallt (for £8,000), and that we present Penrallt together with six acres of the Bishop's Park Estate to the College'.[52] If the offer proved acceptable to the Court of Governors of the College, the council undertook to obtain parliamentary powers to give effect to its decision. The resolution was passed by fourteen votes to six.

At a special meeting of the Court of Governors of the College held on 30 April 1902 the offer of the site was accepted. The city council was thanked for its 'munificent gift' and for its 'great and public spirit' in making it.[53] Particular tribute was paid to the mayor, Henry Lewis, for his herculean efforts in bringing the matter to a successful conclusion.

In the knowledge that parliamentary powers were being sought, the Local Government Board sanctioned the borrowing of the requisite sum of money. The Bangor Corporation Bill was presented in the 1903 session of Parliament and received the royal assent on 14 August 1903. Included in the Bill were clauses empowering the Corporation to purchase the Penrhyn Hall and the market building. The Penrhyn Hall had been presented to the city by the first Lord Penrhyn in 1857 on the occasion of his son attaining his majority; it was administered by trustees but the council wished to gain control of it for the greater benefit of the citizens. It was vested in the Corporation on 1 January 1911.[54] An attempt had been made by the council to purchase the market hall in 1884 but no agreement had been reached; the council eventually bought the hall in 1935.

The two plots of land designated for the new University College buildings were formally handed over in April 1904 and on 11 July 1907 King Edward VII visited Bangor to lay the foundation stone of the building. His son, King George V, opened the building on 14 July 1911, thereby consummating the combined endeavours of the city council and the college authorities. It was a proud moment for the city of Bangor and a most significant step in its development.

Having purchased the Bishop's Park the council went ahead with its plans for the development of the estate. A road was constructed from the railway station to Garth Road and a main sewer was laid from the station to the sea. In naming the road the council honoured Deiniol, the Celtic saint who founded the monastic cell around which the city had grown, though one councillor facetiously suggested that the road should be called 'Golden Avenue' in view of the money spent in purchasing the land! An interesting innovation was that road nameplates were printed in English and Welsh – probably the first bilingual nameplates in the Principality.[55] Another road, across the park was called Ffordd Gwynedd, the council thereby establishing the tradition of giving Welsh names to new streets in Bangor. Seven hundred pounds were earmarked for the conversion of the Bishop's Palace into municipal offices and for furnishing them. Since incorporation the council had met in various rented premises and office accommodation for its officials was dispersed and totally inadequate. The town hall was opened in May 1904, only a few months before the council's coming of age; the renovated building was a symbol both of the city's genesis and early growth and of its recently enhanced status as one of the most progressive towns in North Wales. An attempt to identify the building more closely with its Welsh roots by naming it 'Cynghordy Dinas Bangor', however, did not succeed.[56]

The extensive outbuildings belonging to the old Palace were a valuable acquisition and they were converted into storage facilities, accommodation for the fire engine and ambulance and eventually a mortuary. Finally, the grounds around the palace were developed for the erection of public buildings and for recreation facilities. A post office and government office block were built on a plot of land fronting onto Deiniol Road in 1909, and the free library (1907) and museum (1910) were built adjacent to this plot.

The council in the period 1883-1914 operated the community services, bequeathed to it by the Local Board of Health, in a more efficient and effective manner. It also continually widened its functions and responsibilities in an attempt to mitigate urban environmental problems and in so doing progressively adopted interventionist policies. The process of municipal collectivism which began with the laying down of the sewerage and drainage system in 1851 was extended to a widening range of activities in the sphere of public health and to aspects of the recreational and cultural needs of the citizens. The council was active too in laying down certain foundations for the continued economic growth of the city. Powers to undertake these measures were derived from a number of sources: Acts of Parliament, some of which, particularly in the field of public health, had become mandatory by the early years of the twentieth century; by-laws which the council itself ordained for the good government and welfare of the community, and private Parliamentary Bills by means of which Parliamentary approval was sought for major projects such as the construction of the pier and the presentation of land to the University College. Thus, progress in this period was in large measure the outcome of local knowledge, pride and initiative rather than national directives from central government.

Although the council laid down an effective framework of municipal government in Bangor, it did not succeed in finding a solution to certain chronic problems, notably the Upper Bangor water supply and the flooding of the River Adda. Financial viability eluded practically every one of its municipal enterprises: 'Everything in our hands seems to fail', the mayor confessed in despair in 1913,[57] and the council was not without its critics. Neither was there unanimity in the council's purposes; nearly all its major initiatives, the establishment of an electricity supply, the building of houses, the erection of the pier and the presentation of a permanent site to the University College of North Wales were fiercely contested.

*Notes*

1. The first reference the author can find to Bangor being called 'the Athens of Wales' appears in the leading column of the North Wales Observer and Express dated 9 November 1888, '. . . Bangor, now admitted to be the city of light and learning, the Athens of Wales'. It is interesting to note that the King of the Hellenes accepted an invitation to become a patron of the National Eisteddfod held in Bangor in 1902. See NWC, 2 August 1902.
2. N(orth) W(ales) O(bserver and) E(xpress), 19 July 1889.
3. Quoted in NWC, 26 October 1901.
4. NWOE, 30 July 1897.
5. NWC, 5 February 1908.
6. Ibid.
7. NWC, 11 August 1905.
8. NWOE, 9 July 1897.
9. NWC, 10 December 1904.
10. NWOE, 26 November 1897.
11. NWC, 11 January 1902.
12. NWC, 7 June 1907.
13. NWC, 9 August 1907.
14. NWC, 9 June 1911.
15. NWC, 7 August 1914.
16. NWOE, 15 November 1895.
17. NWC, 9 July 1904.
18. NWC, 8 April 1905.
19. NWOE, 17 May 1889.
20. NWOE, 9 December 1899.
21. NWOE, 4 July 1902.
22. So called by the locals since it was Cllr. Dr E. O. Price who championed the building of the swimming pool.
23. CDH, 17 March 1893.
24. NWOE, 31 March 1893.
25. Council Minutes, 5 August 1891.
26. The final bill for the project came to £34,911 (£1,222,000). Additional costs included: dredging, £3,850; kiosks, £1,700 and Gazelle Inn and steamers, £4,873.
27. The arguments against the pier are set out in NWOE, 2 December 1892. For advantages, see NWOE, 3 March 1893.
28. NWOE, 9 June 1893.
29. NWOE, 20 October 1893.
30. NWOE, 8 December 1893.
31. CDH, 20 January 1894.
32. CDH, 20 January 1894.

33. Richard Davies was born in Llanfairfechan in 1843 and trained to be a joiner. About 1875 he commenced business as an architect and surveyor and specialized in the designing of Nonconformist chapels. So extensive was his work in this field that he might justly be called the foremost chapel builder of North Wales. He was a deacon at Parkhill C.M. Chapel, Lon-y-Popty and was working on plans for a new chapel there when he died in 1906.
34. CDH, 5 October 1894.
35. NWOE, 15 May 1896.
36. City of Bangor, Abstract of the Treasurer's Accounts, 1914.
37. NWOE, 11 and 18 June and 9 July 1897.
38. NWOE, 8 July 1899.
39. NWOE, 23 August 1897.
40. City of Bangor, Abstract, 1914.
41. The *Clio*, a former wooden warship, was anchored off Garth Point and functioned as an industrial training school for about 250 boys. The *Clio* Silver Band often took part in civic processions (as did the band of H.M.S. *Conway* in the third quarter of the twentieth century). The ship was sold in 1919 and broken up on the beach at Garth.
42. City of Bangor, Abstract, 1913.
43. NWC, 28 May 1904.
44. NWC, 5 May 1911.
45. Council Minutes 3 May 1899 and NWC, 6 May 1899.
46. NWC, 7 April 1900.
47. Council Minutes, 21 June 1900.
48. UCNW Belmont MS 67. Report of Mr Tatham dated 24 October 1900.
49. Ibid., entry for 9 December 1900.
50. NWC, 12 April 1902.
51. NWC, 22 February 1902.
52. Council Minutes, 15 March 1902.
53. Ibid., 11 June 1902.
54. NWC, 6 January 1911.
55. Deiniol Road was opened by the Mayor, Cllr. Mathews on 1 July 1904.
56. NWC, 22 August 1903.
57. NWC, 9 May 1913.

# CHAPTER 4

## 1883 — 1914

'Meetings of the Bangor City Council are invariably interesting, sometimes amusing and occasionally, also, ridiculous.'[1]

THE PREVIOUS chapter focused on the main functions of the council and on some of the initiatives it took to improve the quality of the environment and promote the development of the borough. Policies adopted by the council were the result of myriads of decisions taken by those who had been elected to undertake these responsibilities. Since members were drawn from the local community and answerable to it, their decisions were bound to reflect not only the ethos of the community itself but also their own position within it, their attitudes towards it and their perception of its needs.

What were the characteristics of the community which the council was established to serve? Its economic and physical characteristics have already been outlined in the first chapter; socially its life was a tangled web of influences, inherited and acquired, in constant symbiosis. A sense of belonging to the place and the sharing of common traditions and basic values gave it a feeling of unity. This feeling was fortified by the reality of its being relatively isolated from the mainstream of modernizing influences and ideas which were emanating from the urban centres of Britain. Although Bangor was on the main railway line with speedy connections to all parts of the country and its business and professional élite was frequently in touch with the civilizing influences of the new urban culture of Victorian Britain and countries further afield, the horizons of the vast majority of its citizens did not extend beyond the boundaries of the borough. Neither would the majority be able to read any of the locally published newspapers, the only source of national and international news. People were preoccupied with the events of their immediate neighbourhood since there was little else to distract them. An active interest was thus taken in the new governing body and in the personalities who formed its membership. The council itself helped to foster unity; pride was taken in the improvements it initiated – as we have seen in connection with the opening of the new water supply and the pier, for example. The council, and the mayor in particular, personified the city on public occasions and the town hall (when established) became the focus of the city's identity.

Never was the display of unity greater that at times of national celebrations or on royal occasions. Perhaps the most unanimous and spontaneous celebration occurred when the news of the relief of Mafeking was received on Friday, 18 May 1900. There were scenes of wild excitement, crowds thronged High Street cheering and singing patriotic songs, fireworks were lit and the Artillery Volunteers fired their cannons. Next day flags and bunting appeared all over the city and the mayor declared Monday a general holiday. A procession, accompanied by three bands, assembled at the town clock and paraded through the streets and money was collected for the relief of the citizens of Mafeking. That evening a torchlight procession, headed by the Menai Bridge Brass Band, wound its way through the streets and bonfires were lit on prominent sites. The hero of Mafeking, Major-General Baden-Powell, was invited to become the first honorary freeman of the city (Appendix, Table 14).

There were on the other hand a number of forces which fractured this unity. Disunity arises and feeds upon the inequalities which occur in society and on the different attitudes and perceptions which persons have about the community. Divisions were primarily the outcome of a person's occupation and the life style usually associated with it, of political outlook, which at the time had a much deeper meaning than it does today, and of religious denominationalism which in the nineteenth and early twentieth centuries was a powerful divisive agency. While all members of the council would subscribe to the view that their function was to further the health and well-being of the citizens, how far they would go to achieve this end and what paths they would follow were governed by perceptions moulded by their position in the social hierarchy and by their politico-religious affiliations.

Let us now examine in greater detail the principal dimensions along which society in Bangor in late Victorian and Edwardian times was divided. One of the most prominent of these was social class, a concept which has been widely used in the social sciences to describe members of social groups with certain shared and closely related characteristics such as occupation, income, house type, lifestyle, education and aspirations. Possibly the most widely accepted and easily recognised defining characteristic is occupation, since people frequently evaluate one another in terms of what they do for a living, and occupation is used by the Registrar General as a standard classification for identifying social groups.

Henry Lewis, a young grain and flour merchant and native of Bangor was meticulous in recording his views on a range of social, political, religious, civic and educational issues. Writing in the early 1880s he committed to posterity his perception of the social structure of Bangor. From the viewpoint of a middle class businessman he identified a hierarchial structure based on four orders. Firstly,

'the aristocrats who lived about us in the country lived in little worlds of their own. On all public occasions they claimed the front seats. Clinging to them were the smaller county families and others who wriggled their way to Quarter Sessions and the County Magisterial Bench. These all bore the hall marks of the higher order. Next to them are the professional men, with very few exceptions all of them Conservatives and churchmen . . . (and comprising) lawyers, medical men and clergy of the Church of England. Then came the tradesmen and ministers of other denominations. . . . Finally, the labouring classes.'[2]

By the aristocrats, Lewis clearly identified the Penrhyn family who resided in Penrhyn Castle just outside the city. In Chapter One we recorded how the intervention of the first Lord Penrhyn in the last quarter of the eighteenth century dramatically changed the whole economy of the district. The estate provided employment for hundreds of men in the city itself, it owned scores of houses and was the largest landowner. Col. Douglas Pennant, the first Baron Penrhyn of Llandegai (1800-86) took a paternalistic interest in the borough; he gave decisive support to the establishment of a Board of Health in 1850 and was its chairman, with one brief interlude, for thirty years from its formation. His devotion to the Board was unremitting: he ensured that all the houses he owned were connected to the mains drainage and water systems and hardly a year went by but that he contributed a sum of money to offset some necessary improvement or leased land and property for some civic use. He allowed the Gas and Water Company to abstract water from his land and to lay pipes across it. As an M.P. (1841-66), Lord Lieutenant, magistrate, chairman of several important bodies, particularly those connected with the church and agriculture, he wielded tremendous influence and power. The pseudo-castle at Penrhyn was as much the symbol and reality of power in nineteenth century Caernarvonshire as were the fortified castles in medieval times. The community recognized his standing and the council was pleased to offer him the mayoralty at its inception. He declined the invitation because of his advanced years. His son, the second baron, was not held in such high esteem because of the confrontational policies he adopted towards the employees at his quarry which resulted in bitter strikes in 1876, 1892 and 1901-3. Nevertheless, he was in many respects the uncrowned king of the borough; he opened the pier, he welcomed members of the Royal Family and was invited to become mayor on more than one occasion. Qualifying as one of Henry Lewis' county families were the Platts of Bryn-y-Neuadd and Gorddinog, Llanfairfechan. The Platts were successful industrial entrepreneurs and relatively newcomers to the district.

Lewis' next two classes, the professionals and tradesmen, together formed the upwardly mobile and expanding middle class. Its members fell into two broad categories: there were those who had been born into well-to-do families, who had had grammar school and possibly university education and had entered the professions or their fathers' flourishing businesses, and there were the self made men who had started life in humble circumstances but had prospered by applying their native intelligence, skills and business acumen with success or who had capitalized on their share of good luck. Lewis made a distinction between the professionals, who were in the main Conservative and churchmen and whom he placed a little higher up the social hierarchy than the traders, the majority of whom were Liberal in politics and nonconformist in religion. 'Some professional men', he observed 'condescended to associate with tradesmen in public and business affairs and there the line was drawn', suggesting that their social lives did not impinge on one another. He cynically asserted that 'a few professional men and tradesmen who had done well and enjoyed the patronage of the castle and on Sundays patronized the cathedral, affected to be genteel'. Business and social success, he implied, was enhanced by deference to the castle and worship at the cathedral.

The broad base of the social pyramid was occupied by the 'labouring classes'. Sharing common ties as wage earners and a commitment to manual work, they were nevertheless differentiated according to the skills they possessed and their place in the organization of the local econony. In Chapter One it was shown that the majority of workers were employed in various kinds of service and craft occupations; the slate manufacturing works were small scale enterprises and only the Penrhyn enterprise and the railway company employed large numbers of workers. Apart from the railway company, all employment was in family enterprises where the relationship between employer and worker was often direct and highly personal. Workers, recognizing their masters as superiors, deferred to them both socially and politically; masters, for their part, exercised their leadership in a paternalistic manner. The railway company, employing by far the largest workforce was a category apart, for its workers were subject to a distant and unknown authority. Yet the railway company was paternalistic too; it built houses for its workmen and an institute (1898) which became the focus of their leisure activities. There developed among the railway workers, who lived in closely knit communities bordering the railway station in Upper Bangor, West End, the Belmont estate and Glanadda, a strong occupational culture based on shared work and leisure time experiences and on feelings of togetherness, charac- teristics typical of a working class community.

Social position was to a large degree the corollary of accumulated wealth but before it could carry status and authority it had to be translated into personal possessions for all to see; dress, education, travel and above all houses. The aristocracy and 'county families' lived in large mansions out in the country and their estates were surrounded by intimidating high walls. The middle classes occupied the large three and four storey houses which lined High Street and some of the more fashionable streets in Upper Bangor. Increasingly, however, they had been building for themselves in Upper Bangor spacious detached and semi-detached villas sited on large plots of land and displaying in a variety of building materials and designs the architectural taste of the time. Small, plain, two storey cottages built in terraces at high densities housed the labouring classes. Despite these distinguishing features, the homes of the middle and labouring classes were often built cheek by jowl, for immediately behind and in the shadow of the substantial houses which lined the main roads stood the terraces of cottages which dressed the back streets. The contrast was stark but there was a mutual dependence of one class upon the other which generated social control and harmony. Close associations gave people knowledge of each other's personal attributes enabling them to place individuals into particular social and status groups. The ranking of these groups was well known and accepted and individuals knew their place in the hierarchy of prestige, consciously acknowledging the rights and dignities of those above and below them. Henry Lewis observed that 'tradesmen and working men were happy in their general contentment with their lot and in their freedom from envy of those above them. 'Bangor', he writes, 'was a socially democratic town' and although 'a great gulf (existed) between the first and the other classes (there was) much confraternity between the second, third and fourth – until a (parliamentary) election came to rouse the old Adam in each of them'.

Parliamentary elections were keenly fought in the highly charged political atmosphere of Wales in the last quarter of the nineteenth century. After generations of political and social control by the Conservative land-owning class and the established church there was an awakening of political consciousness among those classes who at various stages since 1832 had been given the franchise. Although reluctant to vote according to their consciences before the concept of the secret ballot was enshrined in the Act of 1872, they eventually lent their power and influence to the cause of dissent from the prevailing social order and contributed to the groundswell of support for the Liberal Party which, in the parliamentary election of 1880, gained twenty-nine of the thirty-three seats in Wales. For the next forty years Liberalism was to dominate the political scene in Wales.

With the patronage of the castle and the cathedral the Conservatives had more support in Bangor than in any of the other contributory boroughs which constituted the Caernarvon Boroughs parliamentary constituency. They had a clubroom in the Masonic Hall (built in 1882) and they sponsored Workingmen's Clubs at Hirael and Glanadda, which were a focus of recreation and the indoctrination of deferential working men. However, the Conservatives' monopoly in the constituency ended in 1859 and apart from a brief interlude between 1886 and 1890, they lost their hegemony for eighty-six years; for over half these years the most astute politician Wales has produced, David Lloyd George, represented the constituency in Parliament. The election of 1880 ended Conservative representation of the county constituency also, a seat which was held by Col. Douglas Pennant from 1841 to 1866 and from 1866 to 1868, and again from 1874 to 1880 by his son. The Liberal Party in Bangor, however, was neither as cohesive nor as well organized as the Conservative; it had neither a headquarters nor a clubroom before 1885 and it was frequently censured in the Liberal press for its lack of zeal.

As the party of protest against economic and social inequalities, the Liberal Party, particularly its more radical wing as personified by David Lloyd George, championed causes aimed at bringing about an improvement in the conditions of the working man. In its early years the Labour movement had allied itself to the Liberal Party but by the end of the nineteenth century it had developed its own exclusive ideology and had established its own platform to express it. Two main strands featured in the early labour movement both of which found a fertile environment in which to germinate in the Bangor area. The first was the trade union movement which was primarily concerned with improving working conditions and in protecting members' rights rather than in political ideology. The slate quarrying districts were the birthplace of trade unionism in Caernarvonshire with the formation of the North Wales Quarrymen's Union in 1874. Its first president was a leading Bangor radical Liberal, Morgan Richards. The union figured prominently in the bitter disputes which affected the Penrhyn Quarry in the 1890s and the early years of the twentieth century. In Bangor itself the large, cohesive labour force employed by the railway company, some of whose members were in daily contact with their fellows further east along the railway network, was the first to be unionized.

The second element in the labour movement was ideological and socialist in character and, in its Fabian form, spread among the intelligentsia. It is not surprising therefore that a Fabian society was formed at the University College in November 1900 with a view to propogating its ideas among the new Welsh educated élite. The growth of an independent Labour Party in the early years of the present century introduced a new dimension into the political scene and although its impact was minimal in the period up to 1914 it was a force to contend with thereafter.

Enshrined in the political ideology of the Liberal Party in Wales and giving it a distinctive Welsh dimension were strong nonconformist influences. Disestablishment of the church in Wales and the role of church schools in the new national educational system received major priority in the party's programme alongside reform of the ownership of land, which was firmly in the hand of the alienated, predominantly Anglican, squirearchy. Liberalism and nonconformity became synonymous. The Welsh model of Liberal-nonconformity was highly puritanical in character, often intolerant and frequently bigoted, and being predominantly Welsh in language imposed its ethos on Welsh cultural and social life. Subscribing to the world-rejecting ethic it laid stress on the sanctity of the Sabbath and on teetotalism. The Sunday Closing Act 1881, the outcome of pressure exerted by Welsh Liberal M.P.s, was a victory for the sabbatarian-temperance alliance and it helped to keep the Sabbath holy. Recreation on Sundays, particularly in the form of organised activities and in public places, was anathema to them.

In the politico-religious atmosphere of the time it was the spirit of nonconformity which constituted the driving force in society. Chapels built for Christian worship and Sunday schools for religious instruction became also centres of social life and fellowship, where members involved themselves in choral, dramatic, debating and eisteddfodic activities. Nonconformists set up their first chapels in the early years of the century and as the city grew so did their number and size. By the mid 1880s there were seventeen chapels with 7,650 sittings and some mission halls to boot. The strongest denomination was the Methodist: the Calvinistic variety had a complement of nearly 3,000 sittings (including mission halls) and the Wesleyan, 1,830. Then followed the older denominations, the Congregationalists (2,100 sittings) and the Baptists (1,120). The process of church and chapel building or extending continued into the twentieth century; more people were drawn into places of worship following the religious revival of 1904-6 and a steady increase in the number of communicants continued beyond 1914. There was little unity among the denominations, however, and jealousies between them were as pronounced as the divisions between them and the established church. Long before the 1880s the cathedral city had been overwhelmed in numbers by the nonconformists, only 3,000 or 27 per cent of total sitttings were in the Anglican churches in 1885. Henry Lewis described the clergy as a 'small, quiet and unobstrusive class apart', yet in alliance with the castle it was still an influence to contend with. The church was not idle during the period it was overtaken by the nonconformists. It carried its mission to the new neighbourhoods which developed during the century and built churches there – St Mary's (1864), St James', Upper Bangor (1866) and St David's, Glanadda (1884).

Social unity was further fractured by a language division although at the time language was not the divisive and emotive issue it became in the 1960s and 1970s. Throughout the period of the city's rapid growth, migration was on a short distance basis and an analysis of the census data for 1851 reveals that migrants came predominantly from the surrounding Welsh speaking districts (Table 4).

During the second half of the century, however, anglicizing influences steadily increased: the railway company and post office brought in skilled workmen for a range of duties, and a majority of the academic staffs at the University College and teacher training colleges and of the staff at regional government offices were Englishmen. So, too, were those who chose Bangor as a centre for retirement. At the time of the first language census 1901, about 20 per cent of the population over three years of age was unable to speak Welsh.

TABLE 4

*Birthplace of Household Heads, 1851*

|  | Parish of Bangor | Parishes within 10m. radius | Remainder of Anglesey and Caernarvonshire | Merionethshire and Denbighshire | Remainder of country |
|---|---|---|---|---|---|
| Number | 372 | 334 | 376 | 142 | 178 |
| Per cent | 26.2 | 23.5 | 26.4 | 10.1 | 13.8 |

*Source: P. E. Jones (1973), Table 3.9, p.200*

Divisions such as these in the local community came to light as the city prepared for its first municipal election. There was a general feeling abroad that the new organ of government was a microcosm of the one at Westminster and that membership of it should be decided on political party lines. This feeling had been nurtured by the presence of the Parliamentary Debating Society supported by political activists who debated national and local issues on the Westminster model, with Mr Speaker presiding and members standing for chosen constituencies and holding portfolios of office. The incorporation committee however, conscious of the deep political-sectarian feeling which pervaded the city at election times and of its divisive effect, advised the electorate to nominate only those persons who, irrespective of their political and religious affiliations, had given service to the community and had proven expertise and success in business. In order to defuse the situation it went so far as to promote ward meetings to nominate only the required number of candidates for each ward so that an election might be avoided. This well-meant paternalism failed in its intention and when nominations closed all candidates stood on a party label, there being sixteen Conservatives and twenty Liberals.

Polling day passed off quietly and the result was a decisive victory for the Conservatives who won twelve seats In terms of votes cast for each party, however, it was a closer run contest: 2,585 to 2,353. Henry Lewis, commenting on the result, stated

'of course Conservatives are much more numerous than Liberals because so many of our middle class are Conservative owing to Penrhyn rather than

Church influence. Our best candidates failed through over confidence and neglect of canvassing and because we had too many candidates. Our strength became our weakness'.[3]

The first task of the newly formed council at its meeting on 9 November was to elect a mayor. The mayoralty was offered to Major (later Colonel) Henry Platt who accepted the honour. It will be recalled that Platt had played a leading role in the incorporation movement and being a prominent Conservative, Anglican and Freemason he represented the council majority. His social standing as a wealthy landowner and gentleman of position and influence was considered to be an invaluable asset for the leader of the fledgling council.

Henry Platt, J.P., C.B. [1842-1914 Plate 4(i)] was the eldest son of John Platt, J.P., D.L., of Bryn-y-Neuadd, Llanfairfechan and of Oldham, Lancs., an eminently successful manufacturer of textile machinery.[4] Henry was educated at Cheltenham College, in an institution in Berlin and at St John's College, Cambridge. Besides his contribution to the civic affairs of Bangor he gave long and devoted service to several organizations: the Conservative Party – he was President of the Caernarvonshire County Conservative Organization and stood as a Parliamentary candidate for the Arfon division (1885 and 1886) and for the Caernarvon Boroughs (1900); the Church of England, to whom he was a generous benefactor; the Militia – he commanded for twenty years until 1899 the 4th Battalion, Royal Welsh Fusiliers (Caernarvon and Merioneth Militia); the Freemasons – he founded the Royal Leek Lodge in Bangor, was a member also of the St David's Lodge and held high office in the movement at provincial and national level; the Welsh Black Cattle Society, which he helped to establish in 1880 and was its President for many years. From the time he took over the Gorddinog estate he devoted himself to the improvement of agriculture in Caernarvonshire, in particular the breeding of cattle, and his home farm, Madryn, was a model of good husbandry.

After the election of a mayor came the election of aldermen. Major Platt and Thomas Lewis, who was appointed acting mayor under the Charter and was therefore disqualified from standing in the election, were obvious choices. Two successful businessmen, Charles Pierce (L), shipowner, and William Francis Williams (C), ironmonger, were elected for their business expertise and two councillors, John Richards (C), physician, and Meshach Roberts (L), chemist, were elevated to the aldermanic bench. By-elections were held to fill the vacancies created by Richards' and Roberts' elevation and these resulted in the return of Edward Jones (L), grain and general merchant, and John Glynne Jones (L), solicitor. The first council when finally constituted, comprised fourteen Conservatives and ten Liberals [Appendix, Table 18 and Plate 2].

Richard Hughes Pritchard was appointed town clerk, a part-time appointment, and John Gill, Surveyor and Water Engineer to the Local Board of Health, was appointed to a similar position with the new council. The post of Treasurer went to W. Pughe, J.P., Manager of the National Provincial Bank; this was an honorary position, the finances of the borough being administered by E. Smith Owen, the Borough Accountant.

At the end of the first year two members, Josiah Hughes (L) and William Rowlands (C), retired and in the ensuing election two Liberals, Don Cameron, draper, and Hugh Williams, accountant, were elected, resulting in the reduction of the Conservative majority to two. Liberals further strengthened their position in the election of 1885 by gaining a seat from the Conservatives. The municipal elections of that year coincided more or less with the parliamentary election which heightened public interest. By now a Liberal Reform Club, under the chairmanship of Thomas Charles Lewis, President of the Caernarvonshire Liberal Association and son of Thomas Lewis, had been established in Bangor and the Liberal organization was greatly strengthened. The organ of the Liberal Party in the district, the *North Wales Observer and Express*, in the run up to the municipal election expressed the view that politics could not be excluded from municipal affairs and ventured to claim that never could politics 'be of more ability than at the present time'.[5] The year 1885 was a memorable one for the Liberal Party: it gained thirty out of the thirty-four parliamentary seats in Wales; it gained equal representation with the Conservatives on the city council; and Col. Sackville-West, Lord Penrhyn's Land Agent, the leading spirit of Conservatism in Bangor was eased out of the Chairmanship of the Bangor and Beaumaris Board of Guardians, a Tory preserve since it was first established in 1835.

With equal representation of both parties on the council the election of mayor was bound to be a crucial issue since the mayor had a casting vote in addition to his own vote as member. Although Col. Platt had told the council on his re-election for a second term in 1884 that it was not desirable for one person to hold the office for a long period and that he would definitely retire at the end of that year, in view of the knife-edged situation he was persuaded by Conservative members to stand for a third term. Platt was reminded in no uncertain terms, however, of the views he had expressed twelve months previously and he gracefully withdrew his candidature. In the event Thomas Lewis was elected mayor by a majority of one and the Liberal ascendancy on the council was assured.

Thomas Lewis (1830-1922) was a native of Pentraeth, Anglesey, and attended Beaumaris Grammar School. At the age of thirteen he was apprenticed to Meshach Roberts, chemist, and four years later went to Dublin to complete his studies. He returned to Bangor in 1850 and set up in business at 315 High Street. His business interests broadened to the selling of groceries and flour and in the 1870s he converted and extended the Assembly Rooms near the bottom of Dean Street into a flour mill, known as the Snowdon Flake Flour Mill, which was one of the first steam driven mills in the district. Success attended this enterprise and he had a jetty built at Garth, known today as Lewis's jetty, to facilitate the unloading of ships carrying grain from Liverpool. Lewis took an active interest in community affairs. He became a deacon at Horeb Welsh Methodist Chapel and was a circuit steward for fifty years. He was elected onto the Board of Guardians, the Burial Board, the School Board and the Local Board of Health (1867). When Lord Penrhyn retired from the Chairmanship of the Local Board in 1880, Lewis was elected to the post; he held that office at the time of the typhoid epidemic and the dissolution of the Board. He obtained honours in other fields besides: he was appointed a J.P. and was chairman of the Bangor Bench of Magistrates for many years; he was an active member of Caernarvonshire County Council and held the office of High Sheriff. For his long and devoted services to the community in many spheres he was made an honorary freeman of the borough in 1907.

Great interest was shown in the election of 1886 and all four wards were contested. It was the year of Gladstone's defeat on the Irish Home Rule issue and in the ensuing parliamentary election the Liberals lost some ground in Wales. One of the seats lost was the Caernarvon Boroughs where Edmund Swetenham, Q.C., the Conservative candidate, won by a narrow majority. Col. Platt was again defeated in the Arfon division but Thomas 'Palestina' Lewis, a local trader who had been active in local politics for many years, and who was the father of Henry Lewis, was elected the Gladstonian Liberal member for Anglesey.[6] It was the year too of the first aldermanic elections. Three aldermen were due to retire: Francis Williams (C),

Charles Pierce (L) and Meshach Roberts (L). Should the Conservatives increase their representation on the council they made no secret of the fact that they would use their majority to elect three Conservative aldermen.

In a desperate bid to frustrate their intentions, Meshach Roberts decided to stand as a candidate in South Ward.[7] The Liberal Party considered that this much loved character, who had given a lifetime of service to the people of Bangor would be the only person capable of defeating the sitting member, John Pritchard (C). Roberts' nomination was contested by the Conservatives on the ground that he was a sitting alderman, but the mayor, Thomas Lewis, ruled that the issue should be decided by the ratepayers, a decision to which both parties subscribed. Meshach Roberts defeated John Pritchard and the result of the poll was publicly declared. There was no change in the party representation in the other wards so Roberts' intervention did effectively foil the Conservatives' intentions. Two days after the election, Col. Platt, who was the Returning Officer for South Ward, publicly and without prior consultation with the mayor, declared John Pritchard elected on the grounds that Roberts was ineligible for election as a councillor since he had not cast aside his aldermanic gown at the time of the election.

The scene was set for a dramatic inaugural meeting of the new council; the proceedings had all the ingredients of action, abuse and farce to make it an unforgettable evening in the history of local government democracy. John Pritchard arrived at the meeting to claim his seat. The mayor requested him to leave; he refused to do so, whereupon the mayor informed him that he would not accept his vote on any matter. Thomas Lewis was proposed and seconded for a second term as mayor; Cllr. Douglas (C) then proposed John Pritchard and in a provocative propositional speech insinuated that Thomas Lewis had made the city the gift of a clock as a bribe to ensure his election for a second term.[8] Twelve voted for Pritchard but the mayor refused to accept Pritchard's vote; twelve voted for Lewis and Thomas Lewis declared himself the mayor for the coming year. Pritchard objected that his vote had not been counted; Lewis countered that even if there had been an equality of votes he would have used his casting vote in favour of himself. Whether or not the mayor had a casting vote as well as an original vote was contested and there was confusion as to whether Meshach Roberts voted as an alderman or as a councillor.

Amid the bitter exchanges, John Pritchard called upon his

supporters to join him at his end of the table where he would preside. A somewhat harassed but still dignified Thomas Lewis then rose to acknowledge the honour which the council had conferred upon him, whereupon John Pritchard responded by thanking his supporters for the trust they had placed in him. Thus the city of Bangor now had two mayors sitting at opposite ends of the table. In an attempt to end this farcical situation a member asked the council's legal adviser, the town clerk, to clarify the position. Richard Pritchard, a staunch Conservative, was of the opinion that John Pritchard had been legally returned to the council, that he was entitled to vote and that he had been duly elected mayor. Clearly his partisanship and the confused atmosphere of the meeting had clouded his legal judgement. John Pritchard then challenged the town clerk to stand up and proclaim him, Pritchard, to be mayor and to come over to his end of the table. The town clerk declined to do so and asked members not to force him. Thomas Lewis dismissed the town clerk's opinion as he, the mayor, had not solicited it and announced that he would proceed with the election of aldermen. Cllr. Douglas said his party would proceed with the same matter at their end of the table and called upon the town clerk once more to join them. The town clerk again refused but his suggestion that his deputy should do so was approved.

At this stage the council divided, Pritchard and his supporters proceeding at the lower end of the table with the election of aldermen, and Lewis doing likewise at the top end of the table. John Pritchard eventually declared three Conservative nominees elected and Lewis declared three Liberals elected. Both sets of aldermen were then introduced into the room and took their seats at different ends of the table. In a situation of utter chaos and farce the town clerk finally intervened to recommend an adjournment for a fortnight pending a decision by counsel on the legal points raised by the election. This suggestion was accepted and although the bizarre meeting came to an end, it became the subject of the scorn and ridicule of public opinion both locally and nation-wide.

When the council reconvened in a fortnight's time, Thomas Lewis took his usual place at the head of the table wearing the chain of office; the mayor's robe, however, had been taken by Col. Platt and placed in safe custody at the Old Bank. At the outset of the meeting it was made known that the Municipal Corporations Act clearly stated that a mayor should remain in office until his successor had accepted office and signed the required declaration. Since Thomas Lewis had signed the declaration sometime between the two meetings whereas John

Pritchard had not, Lewis claimed to be the rightfully elected mayor. After further wrangling, Ald. Pierce proposed

'that in order to carry on the business of the council pending a decision of a court of law as to who had been duly elected mayor and aldermen, Ald. Thomas Lewis, the mayor of last year, shall continue to preside over the deliberations of the council and discharge the functions of mayor without prejudice to the position of either party interested in the dispute and that the aldermen and councillors whose elections are questioned should attend and speak . . . but not vote'.[9]

The motion was carried.

Within days, John Pritchard brought an action against Meshach Roberts which was heard at the Divisional Court of the Queen's Bench sitting in Chester. The court's decision went against Roberts but the judge recognized that the law in this matter was equivocal and gave Roberts leave to appeal. The Master of the Rolls, giving judgement in the Appeal Court, said that there was nothing in the Municipal Corporations Acts which stated that an alderman could not stand for election as a councillor though he pointed out that if elected he would of course have to renounce his aldermanship. As to the duties and powers of the Returning Officer, these were prescribed in the Ballot Act: a Returning Officer's duties ceased immediately he had counted the votes and had publicly declared the result of the poll. The court declared Roberts elected and Pritchard was directed to pay the costs of the action in both courts.

John Pritchard refused to accept this humiliation; he initiated proceedings to appeal to the Judicial Committee of the House of Lords against the decision. The main point at issue this time hinged on the duties and powers of a returning officer in municipal elections. He cited the Mayor and Corporation of Bangor as defendants, thereby making the ratepayers of Bangor liable for the costs of the action should their lordships decision go against them.

Delays in the judicial process postponed until March 1888 the judgement of the Lord Chancellor. In the meantime the affairs of municipal government were in a state of confusion. The mayor was the target of the Conservatives' spite and venom; he was referred to as acting-mayor, he was deprived of the mayoral robe and he was harassed and insulted at meetings. His health succumbed under the strain and he was absent from council meetings for long periods during the year. The effect of the whole affair on Meshach Roberts was traumatic; the notorious meeting of 9 November was the last he attended. He died two months later at the age of sixty-eight.

Political passions flared up again at the election of 1887. The focus of attention this time was the candidature of Col. Sackville West for the East Ward seat which was held by a Liberal. Hirael and Garth were predominantly working class areas whose inhabitants were largely dependent upon the Penrhyn estate and Port Penrhyn for their livelihood and were mostly tenants of Penrhyn houses. These deferential workmen supported the Conservative Working Men's Club, whose Chairman was Sackville West. Of the eighteen councillors elected for this ward between 1883 and 1913, twelve were Conservative.

Sackville West's intervention, which was designed to bolster the Conservatives' waning strength on the council, infuriated the radical elements in town. They feared that his powerful presence on the council would lead to a return of power to the Castle, where, until so very recently it had firmly resided. Ominously for the Liberal cause the sitting member declined to oppose the Colonel and another, untried, politician was nominated. According to custom, Sackville West's carriage was available to convey voters to the polling stations and the albeit short journey in the Colonel's carriage must have been a source of undisguised delight for, in Liberal eyes, the scores of weak-kneed workers who voted Conservative. The *North Wales Observer and Express* caustically commented that from the appearance of the voters the carriage carried that day it would need to be thoroughly cleaned and fumigated on its return to Lime Grove! Sackville West predictably won the seat with a comfortable majority and W. Arthur Dew (C), auctioneer, won the South Ward seat from the Liberals. Both parties were equally represented on the council once more. When Thomas Lewis was elected mayor in 1885, the council agreed that it would be politic to select a mayor from each party alternately. This year it was the turn of the Conservatives to nominate a candidate. In an action which was calculated to compensate John Pritchard for his disappointment the previous year as much as it was to humiliate the Liberal faction, they nominated John Pritchard. Even though Pritchard had cited the Mayor and Corporation as defendants in his law suit he was narrowly elected. The mayoral robe came out of its hiding place and Conservatives were appointed chairmen of the principal committees.

John Pritchard (1843-1921), a native of Bangor, was the son of Robert Pritchard, Postmaster of Bangor 1836-56. In 1863 Robert Pritchard and his son established themselves as auctioneers and built up a very successful business which John extended after his father's death. He was elected onto the Local Board of Health in 1882 and topped the poll in South Ward at the first municipal election.

Four months into Pritchard's mayoralty came the long awaited decision of the Law Lords. Their Lordships rejected Pritchard's case; they argued that a returning officer had no right to question the candidature of a person whom the mayor had ruled eligible. They established the principle that the duties of a returning officer were purely ministerial and not judicial and that Platt had acted *ultra vires* in the matter. Pritchard was ordered to pay the legal costs of the case. The decision came as a great blow to the mayor personally and to the Conservatives generally. His authority and esteem were shattered and his term of office drifted uneventfully to an undistinguished close. He did not seek civic honours again.

Compared with the excitement of preceding years the election of 1888 was a quiet affair, although the Liberals gained two seats giving them a clear majority on the council once more. Their nomination of Charles Pierce for mayor won almost universal approval. Charles Pierce (1823-1901) was a classic example of the self made man who rose from rags to riches in a life-time which spanned the Victorian era. Born near Carregceinwen in the heart of the Anglesey countryside, his only schooling was a spell of a few weeks at Capel Mawr, Carregceinwen, where his teacher was the Rev. Robert Parry (Robin Ddu). At thirteen years of age he was apprenticed to his first cousin, John Davies, who had opened up a wholesale grocery and general merchandise business in Menai Bridge. The business was an outstanding success and soon Davies owned his own ships to carry a wide variety of merchandise to the Strait port. Under this clear-headed speculative genius, Pierce not only learned to read and write but also acquired the art of sound business and financial management. When John Davies died in 1847, Pierce became manager of the family's provisions establishment in Llangefni and made such a great success of it that he was eventually appointed managing director of the Davies's by now world-wide shipping enterprise at Menai Bridge. He moved to Upper Bangor to live, first at Bryn Dinas, which was built for him, and then at Bryn-y-môr. Pierce worshipped first at Twrgwyn and then at Princes Road Presbyterian chapel and made generous donations to a wide range of nonconformist causes. He was a radical in politics and a firm supporter of Lloyd George. As a J.P. and Chairman of the Bangor Bench of Magistrates he was considered to be very fair and conscientious in the discharge of his judicial duties.

On becoming mayor, Charles Pierce pledged himself to lay aside his own political and religious feelings and to dedicate himself to the welfare and interests of the people of Bangor. He invited the other members of the council to do likewise and work together as a team to carry on the business of the borough as economically as possible, consistent with efficiency. He allowed himself to be invested with the chain of office but spurned the scarlet robe when it was offered to him, despite being entreated by Platt to wear it. Some weeks later Platt officially presented the robe to the city; he then condescended to wear it.

Pierce quickly stamped his authority on the council, the *North Wales Observer and Express* commenting in March 1889 that

'men and manners are decidedly improving under the mayoralty of Charles Pierce. There is now none of that offensive squabbling and display of political partisanship which, while furnishing attractive reading for the newspapers brought the council into public disrepute and made the city and its corporation the laughing stock of the country . . . (its work) is now carried on in a businesslike, decorous fashion, and no scenes are recorded'.[10]

Pierce's mayoralty was clearly a turning point in the early history of the council for it saw the end of the deep-seated political rivalry which had characterized its early years.

In accord with the new mood of the council was the meeting of representatives of the two political parties before the election of 1889 to reach an agreement on the nomination of candidates so that a contest might be avoided. Agreement was not reached, however, and in the election the Conservatives lost a seat to Richard Davies, an architect, who was the first Liberal to stand as an Independent candidate and succeed. Of greater long term importance were the aldermanic elections of that year. Thomas Lewis, who had not attended a meeting all year because of his contined ill-health, resigned and Col. Platt was ousted. Two Liberals, T. C. Lewis, flour merchant, and Richard Grey, solicitor, were elected and Dr. Richards (C) was re-elected. This election gave the Liberals five aldermanic seats with which they were able to command a majority on the council until 1914. Charles Pierce accepted a second term of office and at the end of it he promised to donate £500 towards the cost of an infectious diseases hospital should the council decide to build one.

At the end of the year both parties again negotiated a truce and this time it prevailed. The Liberals fielded for the first time a working man, Thomas Edwards, painter, as their candidate in West Ward in place of Donald Cameron who had retired because of ill health.

However, Samuel Evans, who had been a Liberal member for the ward from 1883 to 1889 decided to enter the contest as an Independent, thereby precipitating an election. Samuel Evans was successful and the *North Wales Observer and Express*, commentating on the defeat of the Liberal candidate, said that the election

'demonstrated the danger of running a working man's candidate (for he) receives the least support from that section of the community about whose sufferings he specifically speaks'.[11]

According to the now established practice it was the turn of the Conservatives to nominate the next mayor and their nominee, Dr John Richards (1819-91), secured the unanimous support of the council. Born in Caernarfon, he began practising in Bangor in 1840, soon becoming Medical Officer to the Bangor and Beaumaris Board of Guardians. He devoted his life to the improvement of the health of the people of Bangor and made a particularly valuable contribution in this field as Chairman of the Sanitary Committee. It was during his mayoralty that the decision to proceed with the erection of the infectious diseases hospital was taken, and he donated £100 to the hospital fund. Towards the end of his term of office his health deteriorated and he died within a month of relinquishing office.

In the weeks preceding the election of 1891 the *North Wales Observer and Express* noted that there was

'not the slightest sign of activity, or the least particle of interest manifested in the constitution of the council, from which political differences, once so apparent, have now fortunately been obliterated'.[12]

The only contest was in West Ward and here the Conservatives won a seat in the person of Robert Owen, late governor of the workhouse, who stood as 'the friend of the working man'.[13] Conservatives now had nine councillors, Liberals eight and there was one Independent. Early in 1892 when Donald Cameron defeated Col. Platt in the election for a successor to Ald. Dr Richards, all six aldermen were Liberals.

Col. Hugh Savage, V.D. (1850-1912), was elected mayor for 1891-92. Born in Mold he was the son of William Savage, the north Wales agent of Messrs. Allsops, Brewers, of Burton-on-Trent. His father moved to Bangor in 1853 and Hugh was educated in Bangor and Chester. He entered the National Provincial Bank and became manager of the Beaumaris Branch. On his father's death he relinquished his post in the bank and took over the brewery agency. His principal interest was the Volunteer movement and he rose through the ranks of the 3rd Anglesey Artillery Volunteers, based at Beaumaris, to be commanding officer of the 2nd Caernarvonshire

Artillery Volunteers which he had formed in Bangor in 1868. He later became Colonel of the 1st Cheshire and Caernarvonshire Volunteer Artillery Corps, which had companies based at Bangor, Caernarfon and Llandudno. He was a member of the incorporation committee and of the first council; although nominally a Liberal he had no party attachments and often took an independent line. It was during his mayoralty that a decision was taken in principle to construct the pier.

For the first time since incorporation the election of 1892 was uncontested. The Conservatives offered the mayoralty to Lord Penrhyn but he declined it. It was then offered to William Arthur Dew (1851-1907) who, although not then a member of the council, had been a member of the incorporation committee and of the council between 1887 and 1890. William Arthur Dew was the son of William Dew of the British Hotel who had established a successful auctioneering business in 1860. William Arthur became a partner in the business in 1873 and took it over in 1881. He was highly thought of in his profession and was elected President of the Auctioneers Institute of England and Wales in 1900. A genial, kind hearted personality, he initiated a 'Mayor's Fund' to provide the necessities of life for the deserving poor of the borough. To this fund he donated £20 for the purpose of supplying coal during Christmas week and for providing soup daily during the last fortnight of the year. At the end of his term of office he presented £100 to the city to be spent, among other good causes, on an ambulance to convey patients to the infectious diseases hospital.

At the aldermanic elections that year the Liberals placed the seat vacated by Charles Pierce at the disposal of the Conservatives and Dr Langford-Jones was elected. The *North Wales Observer and Express* was quick to point out that the 'tacit abrogation of political partisanship has taken place during the Liberal regime'.[14]

Dew's term of office was dominated by discussions relating to the pier and ferry project and the matter was far from being resolved when Donald Cameron (1837-1915) was invested with the chain and scarlet robe in 1893. His was a difficult year but this shrewd and likeable Scot patiently steered the measure through its various stages to the point at which the Bangor Pier Bill received the royal assent. He also welcomed to the city the Prince of Wales and Princess Alexandra who were in the district in connection with the National Eisteddfod in Caernarfon. Cameron was a native of Inverness and at an early age had started business as a draper in Denbigh; he later moved to Bangor and, in partnership with Robert Ross, built up a high class men's outfitting and tailoring business. When the partnership was dissolved in 1880 Cameron moved to Cathedral Buildings, 205/7 High Street, where he remained until his retirement in 1912.

Despite all the controversy surrounding the pier and ferry project and the charges of extravagance that were levelled at the council, the election of 1894 was uncontested and Ald. Dr R. Langford-Jones (1856-1902) was unanimously elected mayor. A native of Bangor, he was the son of Robert Jones, plumber and gas fitter, 289 High Street, and received his education at Friars School and Dublin University. In 1878 he was appointed house surgeon at the C. & A. Infirmary and four years later started his own practice; he was medical officer to a number of institutions and surgeon major to the Bangor Company of the Artillery Volunteers. He worked energetically to establish the borough hospital, which was opened during his mayoralty, and he was chairman of the sanitary committee for many years. The council was only one of his interests in the realm of public affairs for he was also a member of the Board of Guardians, the School Board and Caernarvonshire County Council. He was a J.P. for the county of Caernarvon and Director of the Market Hall Co. He was a staunch Conservative, a zealous churchman (he was churchwarden at St. Mary's Church) and held high office in Masonic circles.

There was no contest again in the elections of 1895 and although the political rivalries which marked the early years had diminished a new alignment seemed to be emerging based on the differing philosophies of members with regard to the future development of the city. Some were of the opinion that in order to make the city a healthy, clean, attractive and prosperous trading community large sums of money would have to be spent on capital improvements. Others subscribed to the view that the council had already spent tens of thousands of pounds with little to show for it, and the high rates were imposing a crippling burden on tradesmen in particular and discouraging them from investing in their businesses. There was some substance in this argument in the mid-1890s and in the early years of the twentieth century when there were strikes at the Penrhyn quarry; the cessation of production at the quarry had an immediate effect on the employment situation in Bangor and an indirect one on the tradesmen. Those who supported capital improvements were termed 'progressives' and those who favoured a tighter control on expenditure were termed 'economizers'. These were loose affiliations and some members vacillated between both camps according to the issue of the moment.

The new alignment was not really apparent at the time of the pier and ferry issue; it was most pronounced during the gas/electricity controversies and was obvious again when such matters as the building of workingmen's houses, the construction of new seawater baths and the procuring of a permanent site for the University College were discussed. Although the council strongly supported the pier and ferry project there was, nevertheless, some persistent and logically argued opposition to it. This was articulated by Charles Pierce, T. C. Lewis and David Owen, all Liberals. Even the judicious and progressive Henry Lewis doubted its viability.

It was the electric light question however, which really polarized the council along progressive and economizer lines. At the first full scale debate on the issue in November 1895, a resolution to proceed with the installation of an electric station was carried by thirteen votes to eight. All but one of the Conservatives and four Liberals, including Henry Lewis, voted for the motion; those against were predominantly Liberals. So controversial did this matter become during the mayoralty of John Evan Roberts (L) that the municipal election of 1896 was fought on the issue. The electorate mostly gave its support to electricity candidates; Dr Grey Edwards, the proponent of electricity, scored a remarkable personal victory in South Ward where he defeated his Liberal/gas opponent by 235 votes to 73, an unprecedented margin. The result had an important outcome. So successful was the mayoralty of J. Evan Roberts (the pier was opened during his term of office) that the Liberals intended to nominate him for a second term. As a gas supporter, however, he could not possibly accept the nomination, so the progressives nominated Dr Grey Edwards in their resolve to proceed quickly with the scheme.

Those at the centre of the mayoral elections of 1896 epitomized the progressive/economizer dichotomy. John Evan Roberts (1842-1918) was the son of a small tenant farmer of Tyn y Cae, Llangwnadl, Lleyn. He had left the local school at thirteen to join his elder brother who had started up a drapery business in Bangor. After some years he set up his own business, first in Portdinorwic and then in Bangor. So successful was he that he was able to retire in 1893 at the age of fifty-one. A staunch Liberal, he was Chairman of Caernarvon Boroughs Liberal Association when David Lloyd George won his first parliamentary election; he was also a stalwart Calvinistic Methodist and held many posts in this connection such as deacon and Sunday School teacher at Twrgwyn and Treasurer of the Arfon C.M. Monthly Meeting. He was a member of the council for thirty-four years from its inception in 1883, serving two terms as mayor and twenty years as an alderman. His most valuable contribution to the council was as Chairman of the finance committee; in this office he kept a close scrutiny over council expenditure and by sound financial management steered the council through a very difficult period during the first decade of the century. Besides being a member of the city council he was a member of the Board of Guardians, member and alderman of Caernarvon County Council, a Justice of the Peace and High Sheriff of Caernarvonshire (1912-13).

By contrast, Henry Grey Edwards (1857-1913) inherited all the advantages which birth into a clergyman's family could bestow upon a child. He was the eldest son of the Rev. Henry Grey Edwards, vicar of Llanfachreth, Anglesey, and was educated privately before entering the University of Dublin to study medicine. On graduating he gained first place in his year for medicine and surgery and on the strength of this achievement was awarded a travelling scholarship which he used to continue his studies in Vienna. A keen sportsman, he represented Ireland in international rugby matches. In 1881 he came to Bangor to assist his uncle, Dr John Richards, in his medical practice and took it over on Richards' death; he held several other medical appointments in the district and he was a very popular practitioner. A Conservative in politics, he was elected parliamentary candidate for the Arfon Division but he withdrew his nomination before an election was held. He was a member of Caernarvonshire County Council and Master of St David's Lodge of Freemasons. An outgoing, genial personality, progressive in outlook, he is especially remembered for the vigour with which he campaigned for the establishment of the electricity works.

The electric light question had not been resolved when the elections of 1897 were held; the result showed a swing away from electricity candidates although they retained their majority in the council. Convention dictated that the new mayor should be a Liberal and in view of the success of the 'gas' candidates, he should be a supporter of gas. Evan Roberts was proposed for a second term by the Liberals, but the progressives nominated Hugh Hughes, one of the longest serving members on the council, a Liberal and electricity supporter. His election by a majority of one vote was a victory for the progressives who then voted a majority of their members onto the gas committee. To rub salt into the wounds of the economizers they ousted John Evan Roberts from the chairmanship of the finance committee, replacing him with David Williams a councillor of only four years' standing.

Hugh Hughes (1831-1913) owned a drapery business at Britannia House, 342 High Street. Under his ineffective chairmanship there were more scenes and incidents than there had been since the days of keen political rivalry between the two parties. Reports of meetings in the *North Wales Chronicle* referred to personal abuse being bandied about, bad language used and the alleged systematic gagging of members. The January 1898 meeting lasted five hours and the *Chronicle* reported that

'members rose simultaneously, practically no regard was made to the chair and the proceedings were altogether most disorderly'.[15]

At the March meeting the same paper informs us that

'the city fathers have been pitching into one another again in a most lively but unedifying fashion'.[16]

Hugh Hughes's term did, however, witness the compromise between the gas and electricity factions which opened the way for the settlement of the issue. At the municipal elections that year only one ward was contested and Richard Davies, a progressive, was defeated by David Owen, a Liberal, and an opponent of all progressive ventures undertaken by the council.

With the events of the previous mayoral election still rankling in their minds the Liberals determined that they should have a mayor of their own choice in 1898. Their prime objective, to rehabilitate John Evan Roberts, was successful. Robert's return to the mayoral chair seemed to catch the mood of retrenchment which was abroad towards the turn of the century. The council had committed itself to vast sums of capital expenditure and the rates stood at such a high figure that it was now necessary to exercise stringent economies. No one articulated this desire more consistently and forcefully than David Owen, who, it will be remembered, led the opposition in town to both the pier and ferry project and the electricity works. He was joined in 1900 by two kindred spirits, Owen Owen, draper, and R. Jones-Roberts, solicitor, who decisively defeated two progressive candidates in West Ward. These men, ably supported on most issues by Thomas John Williams, the aggressive headmaster of St Paul's Elementary School, carried the banner of economy into all meetings.

It was against this background of financial stringency that the council was forced to pick up the gauntlet thrown down by the University College authorities – either you find us a free site or we quit. Although the college meant so much to the economy and status of the city it took the council three years to find a suitable site. When the final vote on the resolution to buy both the Bishop's Park estate and Penrallt and to hand over a site to the college was taken in March 1902 the following voted against the resolution: Thomas Lewis (elected an alderman again in 1894), John Evan Roberts, David Owen, Owen Owen, R. Jones-Roberts and William Eames. All were Liberals and nonconformists, yet in fairness it should be stressed that the person who did more than anyone else to ensure that the University College remained in Bangor, Henry Lewis, was also a staunch Liberal nonconformist.

Henry Lewis [1847-1923, Plate 4(ii)] was the elder son of Thomas 'P' Lewis, a general provisions and flour merchant of 217 High Street, who had played a prominent part in the religious and political life of the community. Henry Lewis attended Garth and Friars School and then spent a year at the Presbyterian Church's college in Bala, but decided to work in his father's business rather than enter the ministry. He took an early interest in local affairs and became a member of the Local Board of Health in 1879. His disillusion with the Board led him to retire from it at the end of his term in order to campaign more actively for a change in city government, first as a member of the Bangor Parliamentary Debating Society and then as a member of the Incorporation Committee. He entered the city council in 1888, became an alderman in 1898, served a two year term as mayor, 1900-02, and was a member for thirty-three years.

An active worker in political and religious circles (he was a deacon in Princes Road Presbyterian Church), Henry Lewis made his outstanding contribution in the field of education. As secretary of the committee which was set up in 1882 to present Bangor's case for selection as the site for the new University College, he worked unremittingly to forward Bangor's claim. He became a member of the first Court of Governors and Council of the College and, when mayor, was the architect and champion of the plan to present a free site to the college authorities in order to keep the college in Bangor. Lewis was also a member of the governing body of the Normal College for thirty years and it was he who proposed that the college should be supported by the six north Wales counties. He was a member of the governing body of Friars School and the Girls Grammar School. In recognition of his public service, particularly in the field of higher education, he was knighted in 1911, an honour which coincided with the opening of the new college building at Penrallt which he, possibly more than anyone else, had helped to make a reality.

Henry Lewis was the epitome of the well educated, cultured, Victorian gentleman. He had a flair for writing (his books on the history of Tabernacl Chapel and Friars School make interesting reading) and a passion for justice (he was a magistrate for thirty years and chairman of the Bangor Bench of Magistrates). In recognition of his long, distinguished public career and his eminent service to the city in many capacities he was presented with the honorary freedom of the borough in 1922.

The last illustration of the manner in which developmental issues polarized opinion on the council on progressive and economizer lines relates to the building of workingmen's houses. When the council first discussed in 1897 the Houses of Working Classes Act 1890, the motion to implement the Act was carried by the casting vote of the mayor, Dr Grey Edwards. John Evan Roberts and William Bayne, among others, consistently voted against each stage in the development of the programme.

The final decision in the long drawn out controversy over the matter was taken during the mayoralty of Alderman William Peter Mathews J.P. (1860-1939) and William Bayne (1848-1931). Born in Liverpool, W. P. Mathews came to Bangor at the age of nineteen as the north Wales representative of a firm of Liverpool flour millers. He learned to speak Welsh fluently and became a member of Penuel Welsh Baptist Chapel. Joining the council in 1892 as a Conservative he was elevated to the aldermanic bench in 1904 and served the council in that capacity until his death. He has the distinction of having been the longest serving member of the council; for forty-seven years he gave active, wise and distinguished service and he was undoubtedly one of its most able members. He was chairman of the Library, Baths and General Purposes Committee for twenty-five years and played a prominent part in establishing the new library and museum. A number of institutions received his loyal support: he was the first president of the YMCA in Bangor; chairman of the Charity Organization Society; member of the C. & A. Infirmary committee, the council of the University College and the governing body of the Normal College; treasurer of the North Wales Baptist College and he supported the local cricket and golf clubs. He was a much respected chairman of the Bangor Bench of Magistrates and a prominent Freemason. In appreciation of his outstanding service to the community the council honoured him in 1935 by granting him the freedom of the borough.

William Bayne was a native of Fife but he spent most of his childhood in Ulster. He came to Bangor in 1870 and set up a drapery business in Upper Bangor (later joined by T. F. Dargie), which was a great success. He served on the council for thirty-six years, his main contribution being to the Gas and Electricity Committee whose chairman he was for twenty-six years. Bayne was an able, straightforward, and reliable man who also gave sterling service to the city's educational institutions and to his chapel, Princes Road Presbyterian, where he was treasurer for forty-five years. Ironically Bayne, who had resisted the building of the workingmen's houses, performed the opening ceremony in 1905.

With the decline of interest in party politics and in the progressive/economizer conflict, there was little to excite the electorate. In 1903 the *North Wales Chronicle* reported 'There is little excitement in our local parliament',[17] in 1904 'Scant interest because there is no burning question';[18] and in 1907 'The election is devoid of any interesting feature and public interest in it is not by any means keen'.[19] In 1910 and 1912 there was no contest and in 1913 'there was no outward and visible sign of a municipal election at Bangor'.[20]

No more visible proof of the decline in party animosity could be illustrated than by the unanimous election of Col. Platt to the mayoralty in 1906. It was the Conservatives' turn to nominate a candidate but they had no sitting member who could have commanded majority support. Colonel Platt's lack of judgement and arrogant behaviour in the sequel to the 1886 election had lost him the respect of the Liberals in particular and he had been voted off the aldermanic bench in 1889. He redeemed himself, however, by his public spirited action in acquiring the Bishop's Park and selling it to the council. As if to seal his re-instatement in public esteem, the person who proposed his election was Thomas Lewis, whom he had so grievously maligned. In his propositional speech, Lewis told Platt that

'things have changed since you were first in the chair but I can promise you a year of peace and quietness'.[21]

He reminded Platt of the difficult task he had during his first period as mayor but assured him that 'the council had now settled down to work' and he would be controlling members 'whose solitary desire was to serve the town to the best advantage, leaving party feeling aside'. Members were glad to have a man of Platt's dignity and standing at the helm that year since the King and Queen were due to visit Bangor in the July of the mayoral term for the ceremony of laying the foundation stone of the University College building.

If the Conservatives had run out of able men to hold the highest office it would seem that the Liberals shared the same fate. Their nominee in 1907 was David Owen (1851-1912) who had, before joining the council, consistently opposed the improvement measures it had initiated, and in council itself had behaved in an offensive, obstructive and petty manner. In symbolizing the drive for economy in all its activities, he was evidently acceptable to the council in its current mood of retrenchment. He presided over a very uneventful year, the only decision of note was to build the museum.

What a contrast in personality was afforded by his fellow solicitor and successor as mayor in 1908! Hugh Corbett Vincent (1862-1931) was an extremely courteous, suave and cultured man of the highest integrity. He was one of eight children of the Rev. James Vincent, Dean of Bangor 1862-76. At seven years of age he was sent to the Cathedral School at Worcester and was trained as a chorister. Later he went to Friars School and then to Sherborne School. After graduating at Trinity College, Dublin, he sought a career in law and served his articles with a Caernarfon firm of solicitors. He started in practice in 1886 with H. Lloyd Carter, a Caernarfon solicitor; when the firm acquired the well established firm of Barber and Hughes in Bangor, Vincent took charge of the Bangor office. Messrs. Carter Vincent, under his direction, became one of the largest and most highly respected firms in north Wales. Vincent entered the council in 1905 as member for East Ward and immediately made his mark; he was elected mayor within three years and an alderman in 1912. He was the first mayor to hold the office for three consecutive years. In his last term he welcomed King George V to the city when he came to open the new University College building. He also represented East Ward on Caernarvonshire County Council.

In a life crowded with interests, social, legal, political and charitable, it was the church which held first place in his affections. No churchmen of his day could forget his brilliant and unceasing campaign against the disestablishment and disendowment of the Welsh church; when the cause was lost he worked untiringly to place the finances of the church on a firm footing. He held practically every office in the church open to a layman. He met the attack on the church by the Liberal dissenters with a deeper dedication to the cause of Conservatism. He was President of the Party in the Caernarvon Boroughs constituency and as candidate in the hard fought parliamentary contest of 1910, which was called the 'battle of the giants', he reduced Lloyd George's majority to 300. Another sphere of life in which he excelled was sport; he played rugby and cricket at Friars and Sherborne Schools and while at Trinity College he was a member of the University Rugby XV and played for Wales against England. He played football for Caernarvon Wanderers and was captain for a period. He also captained Bangor Cricket Club and was one of the founders of St Deiniol's Golf Club. Vincent gave unswerving devotion to the causes in which he believed and his gifts of leadership were based on and supported by his high standards of probity, strength of character, courage and wisdom. There are probably few people who more richly deserved the knighthood which was conferred upon him in 1924 for public service.

The relative calm which had descended upon the local political scene in the Edwardian era was ruffled by the spread of new ideas and movements whose inspiration lay across the border. The impact of the growth of the labour and the suffragette movements, however, was not of great significance until after the end of the First World War, when workers and women added new dimensions to community politics and the composition of the council. It was neither from among the big unions nor from the Fabian intellectuals but rather from the small Amalgamated Society of Tailors that the first candidates of the labour movement for municipal honours were elected in 1901. Stephen Jones, who was on the radical wing of the Liberal Party, challenged the Liberals in their stronghold, North Ward; Robert Griffiths made his challenge in the working class East Ward. Both were defeated but it was an encouraging result for the labour movement. The following year, William Harvey, Postmaster at Hirael, a person with socialist leanings, contested East Ward as a Liberal and was defeated by only eight votes. He contested the ward again in 1905 and lost by twenty-eight votes to Cllr. Hugh Vincent. His colleague, Hugh Griffiths, Chairman of the recently formed Bangor Labour Organization, succeeded in capturing one of the West Ward seats. Although he stood as an Independent, he might legitimately be considered the first representative of the labour movement to sit on the council.

The year 1906 was the year of the landslide victory of the Liberals in the parliamentary elections. For the first time the Labour party stood as a discrete party and won twenty-nine seats. In October of that year a big labour demonstration was held in Bangor under the auspices of the Bangor Labour Organization. Philip Snowden, the newly elected M.P. for Blackburn, one of the leading pioneers of the Labour Party and Chancellor of the Exchequer in the Labour government of 1929-31, was invited to address a meeting at the Penrhyn Hall. The chair was taken by the Rev. T. Gasquoine and among those on the platform were four city councillors: Hugh Griffiths (I), T. J. Williams (L), Joseph Davies (L) and Dr Rowland Jones (L). After Snowden had delivered his stirring speech Mrs Snowden rose to point out that the ILP was in favour of votes for women and urged the Labour Organization to support the campaign for women's rights.

Dr Rowland Jones, President of the Bangor Liberal Association, in proposing the vote of thanks to Mr and Mrs Snowden, and possibly justifying his own presence at the meeting, emphasized that it was not only working men who supported the labour movement. 'After all', he said, 'socialism was not the creed of workmen alone'.[22] Cllr. T. J. Williams was quite overcome by the euphoria of the meeting and declared that he was prepared to withdraw his candidature at the coming municipal election in order to enable the Labour Organization to secure a bona fide working man as their representative. He promised that he would 'throw himself heart and soul into the movement to secure the return of labour representatives' and he could think of 'dozens of working men . . . who would be far more capable than many past candidates'. Stephen Jones agreed that working men could do as good a job on the council as drapers, lawyers and grocers. 'At any rate', he added, 'they could not make more blunders'. When the dust of the meeting had settled T. J. Williams remained true to his word. He withdrew his candidature in North Ward and supported David Rowlands, a railwayman of 41 Hill Street, Upper Bangor. Rowlands was the first person to win a seat as a Labour candidate.

Soon after the municipal elections of 1906, another pioneer of the labour movement who later attained cabinet rank, J. H. (Jimmy) Thomas, Secretary of the Amalgamated Society of Railway Servants, addressed a meeting of railwaymen, urging them to form a local branch of the Society. Cllr. Jones-Roberts (L) occupied the chair at the meeting. The municipal election of 1907 afforded the more confident labour movement another opportunity to launch an assault on the city council. This time two railwaymen, Martin Duggan and W. Tegarty, stood as Independent candidates but they were heavily defeated. The following year, Hugh Griffiths declined to seek re-election in West Ward and Caesar Cooil, a permanent way inspector on the railway was defeated in North Ward. However Cooil was returned unopposed for North Ward in the 1909 municipal elections when David Rowlands retired. Cooil, who lived in Euston Road, remained an active and valuable member of the council until he retired in 1919; his daughter, Mrs Elsie Chamberlain, was to become the first woman mayor of Bangor.

Thomas J. Williams returned to the council as an Independent member for West Ward in 1910. Within eighteen months he was pitched into the mayoral chair on the sudden resignation of J. Pentir Williams who, after serving only five months of his term, was appointed town clerk. In a little over ten years after first contesting a municipal election the labour movement had its most articulate and forceful proponent installed as first citizen.

A number of events in the years immediately preceding the First World War kindled support for the labour movement. In 1909 a branch of the ILP was established in Bangor; in 1913, Keir Hardie, M.P., addressed a crowded meeting at Horeb chapel (T. J. Williams presided); Fred Hudson, organizer of the National Union of Dock Labourers, succeeded in enrolling seventy-six members into his union at Port Penrhyn and representatives of seven trade unions in Bangor set up a Trades Council, whose object was to select and support Labour candidates at municipal elections. However, at the November elections 1913, both the candidates sponsored by the Trades Council were defeated and at the outbreak of war, only two representatives of the labour movement, T. J. Williams and Caesar Cooil, sat on the council.

The other movement which took root in Bangor during the first decade of the twentieth century was the women's suffrage movement. Its aim was to secure the enfranchisement of women in both parliamentary and local elections. A branch of the National Union of Women's Suffrage Societies was established in 1909; this movement was less dramatic and militant than its sister organization, the Women's Social and Political Union, a reflection of the gentler tone of politics in the more peripheral districts of Wales. The driving force behind the movement in Bangor was Charlotte White (*née* Bell) who had been an outstanding student in the Day Training College for teachers at the University College (1896-98) and who had married the city's electrical engineer Price White. Meetings were held, full use of the local press was made to articulate the objectives of the Society and pressure was brought to bear on the parliamentary member, Lloyd George, and the political parties in support of their campaign. Earlier, opposition had come from the Welsh nonconformist Liberal quarter: the Rev. T. J. Wheldon, minister of Tabernacl chapel and a prominent Liberal had taken the opportunity at the chapel Literary Society's tea in April 1907 to advise women not to become involved with the suffragette movement. The movement's objectives were finally achieved in 1919 but Charlotte White did not contest a municipal election; she was, however, elected the first women member of Caernarvonshire County Council in 1926 and proved to be a diligent and highly respected member. Her son, Col. David Price White, a solicitor in Bangor, contested the Caernarvon Boroughs parliamentary constituency for the Conservatives in 1945 and, against the national trend, won the seat.

It would now be profitable to analyse the membership of the council during the first thirty years of its existence bearing in mind the main divisions in the society from which members were drawn. Henry Platt in his acceptance speech on being elected mayor for a second term in 1907 sketched the type of person whom he regarded the ideal member of a council. Echoing the views of the incorporation committee nearly a quarter of a century earlier he emphasized that they should have

'given evidence in their own business and life of their power to carry out their work with due regard to economy and efficiency'.[23]

Cadwaladr Davies, who was on the radical wing of the Liberal Party and the first Registrar of the University College, giving his reasons for not nominating a working man at the election of 1883, stated that

'the working men themselves felt that their interests demanded councillors with experience and knowledge of business to bring to bear upon their work in council. These were qualifications which they could scarcely hope to find in a working man'.[24]

Moreover, had a working man been elected he would have found it impossible to attend meetings since from 1883 to 1889 they were held at 10 a.m. on Wednesdays and from 1900 at 5 p.m. In fact, only those persons who were well established in their practices or businesses could afford to take the time to participate in council affairs and judging by the attendance in the early years even these persons found it difficult enough.

By analysing the occupation of every member on the council of 1883 and of each council at ten yearly intervals from that date it is possible to determine the social class composition of the council during the period under review (Appendix, Table 15).

Not surprisingly the data reveal that apart from the one railwayman who sat on the council in 1913 the membership was unquestionably middle class. All were prominent persons in the community on account of their business or professional interests and their leadership in such spheres as the church, chapel and the militia. They divided into two groups, businessmen and professionals. Rather more than half the businessmen were shopkeepers and merchants, particularly drapers, and the rest were agents of various kinds and master craftsmen who ran their own businesses. The professional group may be divided into the higher, fee-earning professions, e.g. doctors, solicitors, dentists and architects and the lower salariat, e.g. postmasters, workhouse governors and headmasters. A wide range of interests was represented and there was little change in the groupings over the period. Notable for their absence from the council chamber were members of the new higher education élite. Only one member of the staff of the University, Professor E. V. Arnold (L), contested a seat; he stood as a gas candidate at the time when the establishment of electricity works was the main election issue and was defeated. John Price, Vice-Principal of the Normal College, a Liberal, made a valuable contribution to the council between 1886 and 1892. An analysis of the occupations of the mayors elected during this period shows that doctors and solicitors were as numerous as shopkeepers and merchants and one can therefore conclude that the council was not ruled by a shopocracy (Appendix, Table 16).

Colonel Platt may have been generalizing when he divided the affluent middle class into those who had inherited money and those who had made good because of their exceptional ability.[25] However, it is not difficult to apportion members to these groups. To the first belong Hugh Vincent and Grey Edwards, sons of wealthy clergymen, and a group of men whose fathers came from obscure enough backgrounds but had been successful in business and had provided their sons with grammar school and possibly university education, e.g. Henry Platt, John Pritchard, Hugh Savage, Arthur Dew, Langford-Jones, Henry Lewis and H. R. Pritchard (Town Clerk). The second group comprised those who had risen from humble families and had had little formal education: Charles Pierce, Don Cameron, J. Evan Roberts and William Bayne. The careers of these mayors have been sketched earlier in the chapter. A notable representative of the latter group is Francis Williams, Alderman from 1883-6. Born in 1825 at Felin Rhydhir near Pwllheli, he spent his early working life as a traveller for a Sheffield cutlery firm, doing his rounds in Lleyn on horseback. In 1851 he set up an ironmongery business in Bangor (opposite the market place) and built up a very successful business. His success enabled him to indulge his passionate interest in antique furniture, oil paintings, china and curios and at his home, Vron, in Upper Bangor, he built up one of the finest collections in North Wales, including among his paintings an original Reubens.

Although some members of this middle class élite continued to live above their shops or their practices in High Street, the majority had by

1883 sought the more relaxed and healthier environment of Upper Bangor, where they lived in large detached and semi-detached villas which proclaimed by their grandeur the success of their owners. Many of this group were extraordinarily wealthy: Charles Pierce (obit 1901) left £142,567 (£4,890,000); Francis Williams (obit 1905), £45,493 (£1,820,000); John Evan Roberts (obit 1918), £37,268 (£465,000); Hugh Vincent (obit 1931), £41,885 (£803,000). More modest sums were left by Hugh Savage £5,544 (£156,000) and David Owen £5,632 (£158,000) both of whom died in 1912. Colonel Platt left an estate valued at £407,539 (£7,866,000). Several would be considered multimillionaires today. This élite in its turn used its wealth to enhance the life chances of their sons by buying for them the best education that was available, frequently in the most reputable public schools in the land. Dr Grey Edwards's son went to Winchester, Hugh Vincent's to Rugby, Dr J. E. Thomas's to Charterhouse and Henry Lewis's to Epsom, Arthur Dew's sons went to Cheltenham and Rugby and T. C. Lewis's and William Bayne's to Rydal.

Clearly there were very considerable financial rewards for entrepreneurship in Victorian and Edwardian times, but at the same time there were hazards. During the early years of the present century Liverpool millers swamped the north Wales flour market and drove scores of local millers out of business. Among them were Thomas Lewis and Henry Lewis who had built up very profitable businesses in this product in the last decades of the previous century. Cllr. D. E. Thomas, who took over Meshach Roberts' well established chemist's shop in 1886, was declared a bankrupt in 1911. Financial difficulties led others to resort to illegal practices. Robert Hughes (L), Plas Llwyd, a marine insurance agent and secretary of the Bangor and Arfon Building Society and deputy mayor (1895-96), disappeared from the city in July 1897. Six weeks later he was arrested in Antwerp and charged with forgery and embezzlement of sums of money amounting to £360 (£13,750). He was sentenced to five years penal servitude. Albert Colin Downs, an accountant, collector of income tax for the Bangor District, and member of the council 1904-6, was found guilty in 1906 of forgery and embezzlement while being responsible for the accounts of Bangor Temperance Tavern Co. He served a prison term of six months. While service on the council enhanced the status and esteem of most members, for the few who were unsuccessful or just unlucky exposure to the public limelight compounded their misfortune.

The unity which membership of one social class gave to the council was deeply fractured by the political and religious affiliations of members. Moreover, the cleavage was remarkably clear cut since all but one or two of the Conservatives were Anglicans and all the Liberals were nonconformists. Although the Conservatives won the first election they formed the majority party for only two years. By manipulating the election of alderman the Liberals were able to secure a majority on the council from 1888 to the end of the period (see Appendix, Table 18). For the majority of members, affiliation to a religious denomination was no mere badge of respectability. Most were committed and hard working members of their church or chapel. The nonconformists in particular had learned the art of public speaking and discussion in chapel services and the Sunday school. As deacons, Sunday school teachers, precentors, secretaries and treasurers they had shown leadership and had attained prestige in their chapel milieu before seeking new challenges in the broader horizons of the council and other Boards. Nine of the eleven nonconformist mayors were deacons and/or Sunday school teachers. Among the Conservative mayors were generous benefactors of the church (Henry Platt), tireless laymen (Hugh Vincent) and diligent churchwardens (John Pritchard and Robert Langford-Jones).

The strength on the council of Welsh speaking, Liberal nonconformists had a constraining effect on its progress and enterprise. Opposition to the great issues of the period, the building of the pier, the establishment of an electric light plant, the choice of a site for the University College and the building of working class houses all came from this group of members. Their puritanical sabbatarian views and attitudes were expressed in a host of other matters affecting the community. They stubbornly opposed the sale of alcoholic drinks at the Gazelle Inn and insisted upon the sale there of tea and coffee; their chagrin was undisguised when, in 1911, the council learnt that £400 worth of beer, wines and spirits had been sold there but no tea at all! Cllr. T. J. Williams urged the council to 'wash its hands of the unclean thing'.[26] Entertainment, apart from sacred concerts, was banned on the pier on Sundays and David Owen summed up the disapproval of his group to the standards of entertainment which the council contracted to provide on the pier by insisting that 'entertainment on the pier in a university town should elevate young people and not teach comic ditties'. He prophesied that the council was 'sowing seeds which the town would have to reap'.[27] This group of councillors also wanted to segregate men and women bathers at the baths, and to prohibit bathing, the running of the ferries and the sale of newspapers on Sundays.[28] Concern for moral standards was expressed by Joseph Davies in opposing the spending of £5 on fiction books for the library. Figures from the library revealed that in July 1913, 550 volumes of fiction were issued but only two on religion and philosophy and Davies contended that 'the library was erected for better purposes than to provide frivolous books'.[29] Furthermore Henry Lewis in 1906 demanded that the seats which the council had placed in Menai Woods should be removed since

> 'what takes place (there) is a disgrace to civilization . . . and we ought not to do anything to encourage it'.[30]

It is difficult to determine the extent to which members were Welsh speaking but one can assume that all but five members of the first council were able to speak Welsh. This number showed little variation over the period. Most of the principal officers were Welsh speaking. Meetings were conducted entirely in English and all minutes and communications were written in English. Yet there was always strong support for the Welsh language and culture. Owen Owen, who adopted the bardic name Castellfryn, was an ardent promoter of these; he was prominent in persuading the council to support the holding of the National Eisteddfod in Bangor in 1902 and in 1914 (it was actually held in 1915). Addresses to T.R.H. the Prince and Princess of Wales on the occasion of their silver wedding in 1888 and to the Duke of York and Princess Mary on their wedding in 1893 were presented bilingually. A Welsh title was given to the library and a precedent was established in 1905 of fixing bilingual name-plates to streets; from 1907 practically every new street was given a Welsh name.

Membership of the Masonic Lodges was yet another factor which divided the council. Bangor has a long history of freemasonry extending back to 1827 when the St David's Lodge (No. 384) was established – one of the first in North Wales. In 1880, Col. Platt founded the Royal Leek Lodge (No. 1849). Most of the Conservative councillors and all the Conservative mayors during this period were Masons, some of them holding high office in the movement provincially. The only Liberals who were masons, Savage and Cameron, were not brought up in the Welsh nonconformist tradition and neither of them was a member of the local party. Two of the three Town Clerks and several of the principal officials were Masons. The radical mouthpiece, the *North Wales Observer and Express*, often referred to the 'masonic hall clique', which was a term it used to denigrate the Conservatives in the early days of intense political rivalry.[31]

Colonel Platt set the tone of the council by giving it a measure of dignity and prestige. Being a military man he had a keen sense of duty, ceremonial and dress. He presented the council with the trappings of authority – the mace, the mayor's chain of office and a splendid scarlet mayoral robe; he insisted on members wearing gowns at council meetings and formal occasions and on their adherence to the rules of debate. He also instituted the tradition of the mayor and corporation processing to the cathedral to attend divine service on the Sunday following the installation of the mayor. This custom did not easily take root. When Thomas Lewis, a deacon at Horeb Welsh Wesleyan Chapel, became mayor he graciously attended the cathedral service but asked the council to accompany him to his own chapel the following Sunday. Most members did so but Platt was a notable absentee. Liberal members showed their disdain for John Pritchard by boycotting his ceremony and Charles Pierce repudiated the whole idea of holding one. After Grey Edward's service the custom lapsed for twelve years under a succession of nonconformist mayors but it was revived again in 1908 by Hugh Vincent.

The council operated with very few paid officials in its early days. Its first town clerk, Richard Hughes Pritchard (1850-1901), was a native of Bangor being the son of William Pritchard, a partner in the firm of Thomas Bros., slate and stone manufacturers of Penlon works. Educated at Friars and Beaumaris Grammar Schools and the Liverpool Institute he won a scholarship to Jesus College, Oxford, to study Classics. In 1876 he joined J. W. Hughes's firm of solicitors, became a partner in 1880 and principal two years later. He was a staunch Conservative and Anglican and held the offices of Diocesan Registrar, Chapter Clerk and Bishop's Secretary. He was Clerk to the Magistrates for twenty years and to Friars School Governors for many years. In masonic circles he held high local and provincial office. Pritchard was a cultured and warm hearted man who died in the prime of life.

Pritchard was succeeded by W. Huw Rowland (1864-1912), the son of a Welsh émigré to Liverpool. From St George's School he won a scholarship to Liverpool College and in 1886 he established his own solicitor's practice in Bangor. Unswervingly Liberal in politics he entered the council in 1899 and was appointed town clerk in 1901. His first major assignment was to steer through its various stages the Bill enabling the council to present the land on which to build the new

University College. Rowland was a faithful member of Tabernacl C.M. chapel and a popular Sunday school teacher. He died at the age of forty-eight and was succeeded by John Pentir Williams, another prominent Liberal and nonconformist who held office for twenty-seven years.[32]

The post of town clerk was a part-time appointment. Of the full time officials, three persons deserve special mention. John Gill (1853-1929) came to Bangor from Ramsbottom, Lancs., in 1876 on his appointment as Surveyor and Clerk to the Local Board of Health. Although he was Surveyor at the time of the typhoid epidemic and must therefore share some of the responsibility for the defective state of the water supply, he was appointed surveyor and water engineer to the city council at its inauguration. He was responsible for the laying out of the Bishop's Park Estate and Deiniol Road, Garth Gardens and Menai Woods, and he designed and constructed the Twrgwyn reservoir, the Siliwen baths, the borough hospital and the Caerdeon housing estate (1924). Gill was a modest and conscientious official of the council which he served for forty-one years.

One of the most outstanding servants of the council over the hundred years under review was E. Smith Owen (1857-1951), who was first borough accountant and then treasurer from 1884 and 1935, a period of fifty-one years. Owen was a shrewd financier and managed the council's accounts with distinction. At the outset he set up a department for the issue of bonds for short period loans and a sinking fund for their redemption which proved highly advantageous. Despite the large capital expenditure in which the city was involved he succeeded in obtaining loans at low rates of interest and under his wise financial direction the city was able to keep its rates at a comparatively low level. Owen was a native of Bangor.

Price Foulkes White (1874-1952) was appointed to install the electricity generating plant in 1900 and to manage the electricity department. He was the son of David White, who managed the gas undertaking for the Local Board of Health from 1878 to 1883. Price served his apprenticeship in the electrical section of the Post Office telegraph department in London and shared for a time the same workbench as Guglielmo Marconi, the eminent Italian radio inventor and engineer. A keen sportsman he played association football for Tottenham Hotspur, Sheffield United and Leicester City and was selected to play for Wales against England. He steered the electricity undertaking through a difficult period initially and on John Smith's retirement as gas manager in 1906 Price White was appointed to manage both utilities, a task he undertook with devotion until his retirement in 1940.

In the somewhat closed society of Victorian times in particular the 'local parliament' made a considerable impact on the life of the community. Although the council gave the city a focus and a sense of unity and identity, elections to it were often keenly contested and improvement measures involving large capital expenditure were hotly debated both inside and outside the council chamber. Predominantly middle class in composition, divisions among council members reflected their political and religious denominational norms and values. Yet, whatever the differences between members, it is plainly evident that during this period the council attracted men of high calibre who were respected leaders within the small community. Such men sought office because they wished to serve their community and at the same time enhance their status and prestige. Membership gave them the opportunity of becoming the city's first citizen, of obtaining thereby a seat on the magisterial bench, of welcoming royalty and gaining a seat on public bodies. These were just rewards for hundreds of hours spent in often tedious committee and council meetings. The involvement in the council of highly respected and acknowledged leaders of the community secured for it the social acceptance and authority it needed to complement the legal authority granted to it by the Charter of Incorporation. In all its activities it was supported by able servants who laid down the foundations for an efficient administration.

*Notes*

1. Taken from a letter written by 'Old Bangorian' and printed in NWC, 25 March 1899.
2. UCNW, Belmont MS 310.
3. UCNW, Belmont MS 294.
4. W. Ogwen Williams, pp. 75-88.
5. NWOE, 23 October 1885.
6. For biographies of T. 'P.' Lewis see Biographical Magazine, September 1888, and GAS, XM/2765. See also Belmont MSS in UCNW Library.
7. For biography of Meshach Roberts see GAS, XM/2765.
8. The clock was made in Leeds from designs of Lord Grunthorpe, then the greatest authority on clocks in the world. The clock tower is forty-seven feet high and built of red brick in the Queen Anne style. It was built by T. J. Humphreys, a local builder, and was presented to the public in April 1887.
9. NWOE, 26 November 1886.
10. NWOE, 8 March 1889.
11. NWOE, 7 November 1890.
12. NWOE, 16 October 1891.

13. NWOE, 6 November 1891.
14. NWOE, 18 November 1892.
15. NWOE, 7 January 1898.
16. NWOE, 11 March 1898.
17. NWC, 24 October 1903.
18. NWC, 5 November 1904.
19. NWC, 8 November 1907.
20. NWC, 7 November 1913.
21. NWC, 9 November 1906.
22. See NWC, 5 October 1906 for a report of the meeting.
23. NWC, 15 November 1907.
24. NWOE, 3 November 1883.
25. NWC, 15 November 1907.
26. NWC, 5 May 1911.
27. NWC, 10 January 1903.
28. NWC, 9 August 1912.
29. NWC, 1 August 1913.
30. NWC, 5 October 1906.
31. NWOE, 10 December 1886.
32. See Chapter 6 p. 195.

# CHAPTER 5

## 1914 — 1945

'. . . the most humane bit of work Bangor has ever accomplished'.[1]

WHATEVER divisions there were in the community 'were instantly forgotten' and 'all parties were one' at the outbreak of war in August 1914.[2] In a wave of patriotic fervour practically everyone wholeheartedly supported the war against Germany and worked together to achieve a victorious outcome. The catalyst for the war itself, the German invasion of small, defenceless Belgium, offended the liberal values which Welshmen had fought so hard to attain on their own soil. At a public meeting the Dean of Bangor, several nonconformist ministers and others prominent in various walks of city life pledged their support for the war. Academics, particularly Principal Reichel of the University College and Professor Henry Jones, addressed meetings urging young Welshmen to volunteer for service in the armed forces. Professor Hudson Williams, Vice Principal, and Principal Harries of the Normal College urged the creation of a battalion in the name of the University of Wales, whose members would be confined to past and present students of the University and Normal Colleges and past pupils of the intermediate schools 'on the principle that those who had worked together shall fight together'.[3] Cllr. Owen Owen floated the idea of holding a big meeting in the National Eisteddfod pavilion to which Lloyd George or Winston Churchill should be invited; he thought that either would 'inspire the people of Eryri with the great spirit that was in Owen Glyndwr and Llywelyn, the last Prince of Wales' and predicted that 'hundreds of young men would join the army at once'.[4]

Immediately mobilized for war were the officers and men of the Royal Garrison Artillery and the 6th Battalion, R.W.F.(T.A.). The gunners left for Pembroke Dock and embarkation for France on 5 August and the Territorials were posted to Northampton. Women were quick to respond to the war effort. Within days of the outbreak a Women's Patriotic Guild was formed under the presidency of the mayoress to collect items of clothing, blankets and other comforts for the troops and it continued with this task throughout the war. As nurses, they helped to staff the new Poor Law Hospital in Glanadda, which was requisitioned as a Red Cross Hospital for wounded soldiers, the convalescent hospital set up in Bodlondeb and the V.A.D. Hospital at Llwyn Eithin, Upper Bangor.

The war on the continent soon became a reality when in September 1914 a group of sixty-two Belgian refugees, which the council had undertaken to billet, arrived. Lord Penrhyn leased Wellfield House near the town centre for the purpose and a house in Melinda Terrace was similarly used. Before their return to Belgium in 1919 the refugees presented a brass plaque, surmounted by the motto 'Union fait la Force' (union makes for strength) on which their gratitude to the people of Bangor is recorded and which was erected in the foyer of the Town Hall. Encouragement was given by the council to all young men in its employment to volunteer for service: 'any workmen in the employ of the council who enlist . . . be assured that during their absence this council will pay to their direct dependants one half of their present wages and will re-instate them when they return'.[5] A room in the Town Hall was set aside to act as a recruiting centre and two committees of the council were set up to co-ordinate relief, namely, the War Emergency Committee and the Distress Committee.

The mayor and leading members of the council personally identified themselves with the war effort and a number of members' sons enlisted in the early stages. Richard Williams, the Mayor, Hugh Vincent, William Bayne and Smith Owen, the Accountant, each had one son in the army, Caesar Cooil had two and Henry Lewis and Rowland Jones had three. John Roberts went to France with the Royal Garrison Artillery, Thomas Vallance and T. J. Williams joined the Special Constabulary and Hugh Vincent and J. L. Vaughan enlisted in the Bangor Volunteer Battalion, the forerunner of the Home Guard.

Responding to a general desire in the city to make a worthwhile contribution to the war effort, the council petitioned the War Office to designate Bangor a Soldier Training Centre, pointing out that there was ample accommodation in the city and that Lord Penrhyn had made his park available for military training. February 1915 witnessed the arrival of the 11th Service Battalion of the South Lancashire Regiment, the 'St Helens Pals', who received a rousing reception when they marched through the streets of the city on their way from the railway station. Their officers were billeted in the Castle and British Hotels and the men in lodgings throughout the city. The Penrhyn Hall was made available to them for use as a recreation centre. Although they were in Bangor for less than two months, lasting friendships were forged and the council arranged for survivors of 'the Pals' to return to Bangor after the war. A year later men of the West Lancashire Engineers were billeted in the city for a short time.

When conscription was introduced in May 1916, military tribunals were set up to examine the cases of those persons who for one reason or another claimed exemption from military service. The mayor presided over the Bangor tribunal and among its members were Henry Lewis, Hugh Vincent, T. J. Williams and T. E. Taylor. Bangor was justly proud of its recruiting record: 1,014 men served in the forces compared with 966 from Caernarfon and 943 from Llandudno. Inevitably there was a price to pay. Over a fifth of those who served, 220 men, laid down their lives and council members were not spared the trauma of losing sons in battle. The first of their war casualties was the nineteen year old son of Hugh Vincent who was killed while leading his platoon against the German trenches at Richebourg, St. Vaast, on 9 May 1915. Henry Lewis lost his youngest son and Caesar Cooil and Charles Pozzi each lost two sons. Sons of two former councillors were awarded the M.C. for gallantry: Lieut. Henry Grey Edwards, a member of the R.F.C. received his award in 1915 and Lieut. Ioan Y. Glynne, the son of J. Glynne Jones, won his medal for displaying the highest qualities of leadership and gallantry on the Italo-Austrian frontier in 1918. He became mayor in 1950.

Throughout the war the council exercised the strictest economy in all its activities. In September 1915 the Local Government Board urged it not to undertake any work involving capital expenditure and later that year a Retrenchment Committee was set up to scrutinize the expenditure of every committee. Little more could be done than to maintain services in the face of escalating costs. In recognition and appreciation of their outstanding services to the nation during the war the council honoured the Prime Minister, D. Lloyd George, and the Commander of the British Expeditionary Force in France, Field Marshal Haig, with the freedom of the city. Each leader attended a discretely arranged ceremony in 1920.[6] A memorial was erected in honour of those who sacrificed their lives in the war. Designed by Frank Bellis, a local architect, who also designed the layout of the surrounding grounds, it was unveiled on the occasion of the Armistice Day service held in 1923. Ever since then it has become the focus of the city's yearly tribute to the fallen of the Great War and succeeding wars.

Bangor's response to war savings appeals (the last three war loans raised £450,000), prompted the War Office to present the city with a tank which was positioned in the grounds of the Town Hall opposite the library. The Rev. J. D. Jones, Vicar of Bangor and Secretary of the War Savings Committee, proudly accepting the tank, viewed it as an 'expression of the courage, sacrifice and cleverness of the British race'.[7] In the more sober days of the mid-1930s the presence of a rusty old object of carnage offended scores of citizens and the council responded in October 1937 to calls for its removal.

The depressed state of the local economy for the greater part of the interwar period has been referred to in Chapter One. One effect of economic depression and unemployment on landlords, small businessmen and craftsmen and householders generally was to arouse intense interest in the level of the rates, the major source of the council's income. Items of the council's expenditure were closely scrutinized and every attempt was made to keep the rates down to acceptable levels. Circumstances of financial stringency made it difficult for the council to initiate any spectacular development projects and for the most part its activities were necessarily confined to the maintenance and gradual improvement of its basic services to the community. The principal initiatives that were taken were in the field of housing and these were taken in response to pressure, suitably accompanied by financial incentives, from central government. Indeed, a notable characteristic of the interwar period was the greater involvement of central government in affairs of local government authorities. The effect was to carry through to a successful conclusion an unprecedented house building and slum clearance programme which transformed not only the appearance of the city but also the lives of a sizeable proportion of its inhabitants. So vast was the scale of the housing programme in terms of monies involved, the time required to be given to it by council members and officials, and the controversies it generated that it dominates the work of the council in the interwar period. However, let us first examine the more traditional activities of the council during the period.

A commitment to ensure and enhance the health and general well-being of the community continued to be one of the council's priorities. Three notable improvements were made in the water supply. Firstly, in the early 1920s the whole length of pipe from the intake on the Llafar down to Bangor was renewed and in 1933 a duplicate main was laid down. Secondly, to overcome the erratic nature of supplies in the Upper Bangor area an elevated storage tank was erected on the top of Bangor Mountain in 1927. Thirdly, in June 1932, a new screening house was built near the water intake; after passing through new filter beds the water was then chlorinated and small quantities of lime were added. Regular checks were made on the purity of the water so that high standards were maintained. These improvements helped to meet the increased demand for water brought about by an increase in the number of new houses that had been built each equipped with a hot and cold water system, bath and flush toilet. As new housing estates were developed so the water mains and distribution system were extended. That these improvements were successful is borne out by the fact that supplies were quite adequate during the exceptional drought of the summer of 1933.

Improvements in the existing system and its extension to areas of new housing estates also dominated work in connection with the sewerage system. The main improvement was the laying of a new 2.5 feet diameter trunk sewer in 1936 from the railway bridge to the coast and the construction of a new outflow further out to sea.

The River Adda continued to cause problems. People living near its banks dumped household waste and rubbish into it and flooding occurred periodically. The flood of 18-19 September 1922 was particularly severe; in a period of fourteen hours over 1.75 inches of rain fell and caused the river to overflow, flooding Orme Road and Beach Road to a depth of 14 inches in places. Boats were brought into service to evacuate people from their flooded homes. Water Street, Fountain Street and Foundry Street were also flooded in consequence of a sewer at high tide being surcharged with water coming down from the higher parts of the city. Another severe flood in February 1929 followed a fall of 2 inches of rain in less than an hour and streets in Hirael, the Dean Street area and in West End were flooded. Determined to eradicate the problems once and for all, the council approved a scheme involving the conduiting of further stretches of the river and the construction of a new outflow at the coast. The scheme proved a complete success.

In 1932 the rubbish destructor was shut down. A new boiler was needed but since the city was now obtaining most of its electricity in bulk from the grid system its replacement was not justified. This was not an unwelcome decision since there were continual complaints about the noxious smoke the destructor emitted from time to time. The preferred method of rubbish disposal pioneered in the 1920s was controlled tipping whereby depressions in the land's surface were filled in by stages to a predetermined height and then covered over with either soil or hardcore, depending on their ultimate planned use. Controlled tipping was first introduced in Bangor in 1932 when an area bordering the River Adda near the Crosville Bus Depot was earmarked for the process. Later, an area adjacent to Heol Dewi in Glanadda and then a fifteen acre site called Wern Fields on the Caernarfon Road were similarly developed. All three sites were eventually laid out for recreational purposes.

As soon as the war ended the council took up once again the contentious issue of a public abattoir. Finally, it decided to convert for the purpose one of the buildings at Deanfield, Glanadda, which had functioned as a brewery and then as a slate works. Bitter opposition from the residents of Glanadda was overcome and the abattoir opened in 1922. In furtherance of its campaign to improve the quality of milk retailed in the city, the council supported the Milk and Dairies Order issued by the county's Medical Officer of Health which came into operation in October 1926. Milk retailers had to register with a local authority; they had to undertake precautions designed to minimize contamination and their cows had to be examined periodically by a veterinary officer. In April 1932, the Chairman of the Health Committee reported to the council that all the milk sold in the city was tuberculin tested. Bangor was one of the first towns in north Wales to claim this important advance. Samples of food sold in the shops and on the streets were regularly taken for analytic examination.

Throughout the interwar period there was a general improvement in the health of the community in line with national trends. A reduction in the incidence of infectious diseases in particular had an effect on the number of cases admitted to the Infectious Diseases Hospital. Between 1924 and 1929 inclusive an average of only twenty-seven patients each year were admitted. Faced with a reduction in numbers the council agreed in 1934 to admit patients from the neighbouring local government areas of Bethesda, Ogwen and Llan-fairfechan. To comply with the provisions of the Public Health Act 1936, an extension had to be built to accommodate five individual wards and this was opened in July 1937. Soon after the end of the war the council had to turn its attention to the need for another cemetery. Among the options discussed in 1923 was the building of a crematorium but it did not gain much support. After the consideration of a number of sites within the borough, to each of which there were strong objections, it was decided to go beyond the borough boundary. A ten acre site adjacent to Allt-y-Marchogion on the A5 road south of the city was bought from the Penrhyn Estate in 1924 for £2,722 (£43,550). Another £5,222 was spent in laying it out and erecting a lodge, railings and gates. The first body to be interred there, in November 1931, was that of Dr John Edward Thomas who had been mayor 1920-21.

Significant developments took place in the provision of open space and recreational facilities during the period. Two sites in Upper Bangor overlooking the Strait were presented to the council. Pen-y-Bonc, at the junction of Princes Road and Temple Road, was presented by T. F. Dargie in memory of his son who was killed in the war. A local solicitor, W. Ashley Jones, purchased from the Penrhyn Estate in 1928 thirteen acres of land below Siliwen Road and presented them with the stipulation that they should remain public open space in perpetuity. In 1934 the council obtained a lease until 1990 of Camp Field, commonly known as 'Roman Camp' on the summit of the Upper Bangor ridge. Land adjoining the Town Hall was laid out in 1929 as a crown bowling green and a putting green. In that year too the old rubbish tip along the coast south of the Adda outflow became a playing field as did subsequently the tips on Garth Fields and Heol Dewi. Price Davies, the Surveyor, conceived the idea of a pleasure park on Garth Fields which included an open air swimming pool, a yachting and paddling pool, a bowling green and putting green, tennis courts and a rose garden.[8] Only six tennis courts and the putting green were actually laid, however. Other open spaces emerged as a result of the comprehensive redevelopment scheme at Pen-y-Bryn at the eastern approach to the city and of the housing scheme at Maes Tryfan. An offer made by the Dean and Chapter of the cathedral to dispose of the disused cemetery, Tan-y-Fynwent, was accepted by the council in 1939. The latter did not respond, however, to the suggestion articulated by the mayor in 1934 that it should construct a boating marina between Hirael and Port Penrhyn and a promenade along the Strait from the pier to the George Hostel, thereby missing an opportunity of enhancing public access to this stretch of the coast.

Swimming in the Siliwen Baths remained a popular recreational activity; an average of over 15,000 persons a year used the baths between 1925 and 1932. Yet, by 1937 there was a general feeling that the baths had outlived their usefulness and in the following year the council considered applying for a grant under a scheme sponsored by the National Fitness Council for the building of indoor swimming baths. However, since the council's financial commitment would represent a rate of 4.5 pence in the pound the proposal gained little support. Throughout the period the baths returned an annual deficit.

Far greater deficits were incurred by the pier and ferry undertakings. Silt, which had accumulated at the pier head during the war years, had rendered the water there too shallow for the Liverpool steamers to land passengers. A major renovation programme was undertaken in 1922; the channel was dredged, the pontoons were rebuilt, large areas were redecked and the iron understructure was chipped, tarred and painted. Damage caused by the steamer *Christiana*, which ran into the pier in a storm in December 1914 and severed it, had also to be made good.[9] Improvements at the pier head were of little avail, however, since the Liverpool and North Wales Steamship Company had replaced their shallow draught paddle steamers with boats which drew more water and only an occasional one called at the pier head thereafter. An attempt in 1935 by the Llandudno based Cambrian Shipping Company to revive the link between Llandudno and Bangor pier, using the steamer *Lady Orme*, generated little public support.[10] The expectation of thousands of visitors landing off the pleasure boats had been a major factor in inducing the council to build the pier in the 1890s; the drying up of this source of revenue made the pier a financial embarrassment.

The principal cause of the decline of the ferries to Llandegfan and Beaumaris was the growing use of the bus service to Beaumaris which was more regular, safer, cheaper and more comfortable than the ferry. In 1926, the ferry service was described as 'a thing of the past'.[11] Declining numbers of passengers had a ruinous effect on trade at the Gazelle Inn and in the face of mounting losses the council sold the inn in March 1930 for £1,000. The purchaser took a five year lease on the ferry and bought the *Cynfal*, one of the ferry boats. When the deal was revealed at a council meeting a councillor expressed the wish 'that like the inn they could sell the pier'.[12]

It proved difficult after the war to revive interest in pier entertainments. Occasional band and variety concerts were held and dancing to the sound of amplified gramophone records was a regular feature. Some sacred concerts attracted up to a thousand people and in 1925 a profit of £600 was made on pier entertainments. The pier, however, practically ceased to be a rendezvous for entertainment by the early 1930s.

References to the 'poor old pier' were made in 1919; in 1929 it was termed a 'bug bear' and in 1927 a 'white elephant'. And so it was. In the early 1930s an annual loss of at least £2,000 was being incurred, equivalent to a rate of 7.5 pence in the pound, a greater sum than that raised for all the housing schemes that had been completed by 1935. The chairman of the Finance Committee, presenting his budget for 1937-38, asked the council 'to consider whether it can afford to continue running an undertaking which imposes such a serious burden on the rates' and added: 'If I felt we could get anything like a reasonable figure for the pier as old iron, I would gladly see it disappear'.[13]

In the face of mounting pressure to rid itself of the ferry and pier the council in 1937 sponsored a Bill in Parliament to amend the Bangor Corporation (Pier, etc.) Act of 1894 so that it could discontinue wholly or in part the ferry to Llandegfan and sell the pier. A public meeting in December gave the council the authority to proceed with the Bill but the County Councils of Anglesey and Caernarfon objected. Their reason was that since a major reconstruction of the Menai Suspension Bridge was imminent, and might have resulted in the bridge being out of service for some time, the retention of an alternative means of communication across the Strait was essential. There were also fears that the bridge might be a target for enemy aircraft should war break out. The council amended the Bill to meet the objections of the County Councils and it became law in May 1938, but first the Munich crisis and then the outbreak of the Second World War frustrated the council's intentions.

Another municipal service, the library and museum, also faced hard times since the council was able to levy only a penny rate for its upkeep and it was £800 in debt by 1925. A new librarian in 1930 succeeded in raising the number of books issued from around 8,000 a year in the late 1920s to 40,000 in the late 1930s, but the museum was a more intractable problem. A suggestion made in 1929 that its contents should be housed in the University College was accepted by the university authorities and when it took over the old Girls' Grammar School building in 1940 part of the building was set aside to exhibit the council's collection. Ald. W. R. Jones saw this as 'another gesture in cementing the cordial relations between town and gown'.[14]

In 1915, at the time the 'St Helens Pals' were billeted in the city, the council had installed hot and cold water baths in the basement of the library. This facility was well patronized in the 1920s but, as the number of council houses equipped with a bath steadily increased, the number of people using it declined; for 1937 and 1938 the average was only 1,325 persons and the enterprise was losing money.

Undoubtedly the most bizarre of all the council's services was the fire service. The only significant modernization of the brigade to take place was the substitution of a lorry for the horse to draw the fire engine. On the occasion of a fire at the margarine works in Aber in 1922, the lorry was not available so a charabanc was quickly pressed into service. One can visualize the old engine drawn by the charabanc trundling along the road to Aber and arriving at the scene of the fire some fifty minutes after it had been called out! Discussion at the subsequent council meeting revealed that the appointed lorry was in any event normally out all day delivering coal and was not immediately available should a fire break out. After much discussion the council decided in 1926 to buy a motor engine. The one they bought was found to be heavier than the maximum weight allowed for vehicles crossing the Menai Bridge. To overcome the limitation the trailer carrying part of the tackle was detached from the engine at one side of the bridge, manhandled across it and reconnected at the other side. Eventually the engine was sold and a smaller one purchased.

When consideration was given to a quicker method of calling the firemen out to deal with a fire the council decided to fix a siren on the roof of the Central Garage, rather than install telephones in firemen's houses, since that was the cheaper alternative. Citizens protested on the grounds that it was absurd to wake up the whole city in order to inform a handful of men. There was another disadvantage: the siren was an invitation to all and sundry to flock to the scene of a fire to watch the spectacle, thereby restricting the firemen's freedom of action. There was much consternation among the firemen while they were attending to a fire in 1929 when the supply of water was suddenly reduced to a trickle: an inquisitive motorist had parked his car on the pipe! Two years later the main hose burst while being used to extinguish a fire and, in explanation, a confession was made that the pipe had deteriorated through having been constantly used for pumping sewage. A fire in the market hall in May 1935 drew a large crowd into High Street; to disperse it the firemen turned their hoses on it 'drenching many, including several ladies, to the skin'.[15]

An impressive amount of work had been carried out on the city's streets and footpaths in the first thirty years of the council's existence. This work continued throughout the period under review with several improvements and extensions into the new housing estates. Among the major improvements were the realignment of the main road at the Penrhyn Arms Hotel and the widening of Beach Road (1933-35); this stretch of road in conjunction with Garth, Deiniol and Holyhead

Roads, was designated part of the A5 trunk road and created an inner by-pass. Other improvements included the levelling and re-surfacing of High Street (1926), the extensions of Glynne Road to Garth Road (1930), the widening of Holyhead Road between the station and Upper Bangor and at the Look Out (1935), of Garth Road between the town clock and the police station (1936) and of the Caernarfon Road between Brynllwyd and the new borough boundary (1938). Responsibility for the main roads was transferred to the county authority in 1927 although the council acted as the county's agents in improving and cleaning them. In 1938 all trunk roads, and there were seven miles of them in the borough, became the responsibility of the Ministry of Transport.

Throughout the 1920s and 1930s there was an exponential increase in the number of motor vehicles using the roads. For example, the number registered in Anglesey and Caernarvonshire alone rose from 4,200 in 1926 to 9,200 in 1938.[16] Traffic congestion in High Street, already considered a problem in 1914, became progressively worse. Although responsibility for the control of traffic rested with the Chief Constable, the council was able to make recommendations to him with a view to finding a solution to the problem. Cllr. Wartski, who owned the largest shop along the High Street, considered that 'congestion on the High Street was the worst possible thing for business in the street',[17] and pressed for the adoption of a one-way system for buses in particular which were the main cause of the congestion. Much argument centred on the preferred system; in 1930 it was decided that buses entering from the direction of Caernarfon and Holyhead should proceed along High Street to the town clock and the bus station, now established adjacent to Tan-y-Fynwent, and leave via Deiniol Road; buses entering from the east were to proceed up lower High Street to the town clock and leave via Garth Road, Beach Road and Strand Street. In June 1932 the council suggested that congestion on High Street might be relieved if parking were allowed on one side of the street only but the suggestion was not implemented. Five years later it succeeded in getting buses banned altogether from High Street.[18] Even so it was evident that congestion would continue as long as a two way system was in operation.

Significant developments took place in connection with the council's gas and electricity enterprise. In 1925-1926 practically all the gas lit street lights were replaced by electric lights. Thereafter the use of gas was restricted almost entirely to dometic appliances. A growing demand for electricity exceeded the output of the works but rather than increase the generating capacity the council decided that it would be cheaper to buy bulk supplies of electricity from the North Wales Power Company which had established a hydro-electric station at Dolgarrog in the Conwy Valley. A 20,000 volt transmission line was erected from Bethesda to Bangor in 1923 and the local electricity station soon became a subordinate source of supply. The Electricity Supply Act 1926 provided for the establishment of the Central Electricity Board with responsibility for a national grid; consumers connected to it were guaranteed a regular supply of electricity which came to be increasingly used as a source of power in homes to operate cookers, vacuum cleaners and heaters. A hire purchase system was introduced to assist people with the purchase of electrical appliances. Between 1919 and 1939 the annual consumption of electricity increased from 265,000 units to 3,300,000 units. Among other initiatives taken by the council at this time was the purchase of the market hall in 1935 and Bron Castell in 1936. Bron Castell, which had housed St Winifred's Girls' School, was sold to the B.B.C. in 1940 and remained in its possession until 1976.

Concern for the well-being of its citizens had always motivated the council to act in support of the more unfortunate members of society. When he was mayor in 1892, W. A. Dew had initiated a Mayor's Fund to relieve those in distress and to add a little cheer at Christmas. At the time of the Penrhyn Quarry strike of 1901-03 unemployment in Bangor was high and the council directed the surveyor to engage unemployed persons on various minor improvement projects. Contractors who built the library were asked to take on the local unemployed. After the war unemployment became an even more pressing problem; the number out of work rose to 300 by the end of 1922 and during the General Strike of 1926 the mayor opened a distress fund. When the number of unemployed had reached 300 again in December 1927 the council established a committee to find work on council projects for as many as possible. Up to seventy men at a time were employed in laying new sewers and water pipes and in the improvement of roads, grants for which were available from the government if unemployed labour was used. In spite of this, 456 people were unemployed by Christmas 1932, representing about 17 per cent of the working population.

Outstanding among all the activities of the council during the inter-war period was its housebuilding and slum clearance programme. Its record in this field is impressive by any standards and is a magnificent testimony to the initiative, farsightedness and perseverance of council members and to the skill and dedication of its staff. Housebuilding had been at a minimum nationwide in the years preceding the war and during the war was virtually at a standstill. The war time government perceived an urgent and unprecedented need for houses when hostilities ceased and pledged itself to the most ambitious housing programme ever considered by a British government. Housing policy lay at the heart of its plans to reconstruct British society after the trauma of war, and, under the slogan of 'homes fit for heroes to live in' the government sought a better world for those whose sacrifices had been so great. Within three years it aimed to build half a million houses of much higher quality than had hitherto been available to the working class. The Tudor Walters Report recommended that each house should have at least two downstairs rooms, three bedrooms, a lavatory, bathroom and larder; it should receive adequate light and ventilation; it should be sited in attractive and varied layouts at a density not exceeding twelve houses to the acre. Much of the inspiration of the committee was drawn from the 'garden city' movement which had achieved such a notable success at Letchworth, Welwyn, Bournville and Port Sunlight in the decade or two before the war. A Local Government Board circular to local authorities incorporated the recommendations of the Tudor Walters Report and contained appropriate model house plans and designs for the guidance of local architects.

The government's post-war housing policy was embodied in the Housing and Town Planning Act 1919 (Addison's Act). There was an assumption in the policy that houses in the number and of the quality envisaged and at rents which working class tenants could afford could not be provided by private enterprise and so the onus was placed firmly and unequivocally on local authorities. The Act required local authorities to assess and provide for the housing needs of their areas; their powers in connection with the compulsory purchase of land were defined; compensation to owners of this land was set out and generous housing subsidies were introduced. Losses incurred in excess of the product of a penny rate were to be borne by the Treasury. The Act also required local authorities to set up housing committees. This scheme of state subsidized housing represents a marked shift from the permissive housing acts of 1875, 1890 and 1895 and a clear acceptance by the state of its responsibility in this field. It also marks a significant intrusion by the state into the affairs of local authorities.

Even before the end of the war the Local Government Board had refused to countenance a scheme the council had presented to it in

November 1915 for the building of houses on a site on Sackville Road.[19] The council therefore approached the Penrhyn Estate with a view to purchasing land on Caernarfon Road and on either side of Penchwintan Road for the building of its first post-war houses. Sir Henry Lewis's suggestion that four local architects should be invited to submit plans so that a variety of designs might be obtained was accepted and three ladies were co-opted onto the relevant committee to advise on the selection of designs. In March 1919 Lord Penrhyn gave a plot of land on Caernarfon Road to the council as a gift and plans were drawn up for the construction of eighteen houses. Sir Richard Williams, who had been appointed chairman of the newly created Housing Committee in July 1919, laid the foundation stone in October 1920. The layout, comprising two blocks of four houses each fronting onto Caernarfon Road and five pairs of semi-detached houses in a cul-de-sac, was called Pennant Crescent. Built of brick with cement rendering under a slate roof, the houses measure 1,000 feet super. and are the largest two storey houses which the council has built (Appendix, Table 19 and Map 2).

Building costs in the immediate post-war years were almost twice the very considerable increase in general prices so the building of Addison houses became a very expensive activity. Repeated calls for economy during the winter of 1920-21 led the government to slash public expenditure with what has been termed the 'Geddes Axe'. One of the government's prime targets was the housing programme and in 1922 it terminated all projects under the Addison Act. The Conservatives, who won the General Election of 1922, passed a new Housing Act in April 1923, the Chamberlain Act. Houses built by local authorities according to higher density and reduced space standards could now qualify for an annual flat rate subsidy of £6 on each house for a period of twenty years. A narrow strip of land on the north side of Penchwintan Road was bought by the council from the Penrhyn Estate and eight pairs of semi-detached houses were built on the site under the 1923 Act. These were followed in 1924 by four pairs of semi-detached houses on a portion of the Deanfield site which the council had bought in 1920 for the purpose of locating its abattoir. Built in a short cul-de-sac off Ainon Road these houses, called Caerdeon, were designed by John Gill, the Borough Surveyor.

Since all the houses up to this point had been located on the western side of the city, the next instalment was built on the eastern side at Maes-y-Dref, which had been the city's football field, and at Pen-lôn, which was an open space. Both plots had been bought from the

Penrhyn Estate and the layout in both cases took the form of a cul-de-sac. In 1924 the Penrhyn Estate provided another 7.5 acres of land, lying between Caernarfon Road and Penchwintan Road for the council's next housing scheme, the Heol Dewi Scheme. The new surveyor, T. P. Francis, planned an attractive layout here comprising a cul-de-sac, winding roads and semi-circular patches of greensward and thirty-two Ministry of Health Type A (non-parlour) houses. All the houses are semi-detached, built of brick with cement rendering and have a variety of roof designs. Councillors expressed approval of the plan; Ald. John Roberts thought it was 'the nicest layout he had ever seen – a veritable garden city'.[20] The council decided to let these houses at lower rents than they had fixed for the earlier houses. This policy decision was motivated by the realization that even the subsidized rents charged for the houses were well beyond the reach of families living in the most miserable housing conditions. Cllr. Thomas Williams (Lab.) asked in November 1924, 'What is the use of building houses at rents no-one can pay?'.[21] The Housing Acts were intended to help 'those in need' yet the new council tenant was, in the main, the better paid skilled working man and white collar worker (Table 5).

TABLE 5

*Social class of Household Heads on two Council Housing Estates, 1935*

|  | No. of houses | No. of Houses for which information obtained | Social Class 2 3 4 5 |
|---|---|---|---|
| Pennant Crescent | 18 | 14 | 5  9 |
| Pen-lôn Gardens | 18 | 17 | 3 12  1  1 |

*Source: P. E. Jones (1973) Table 6.11, p.412*

Twenty-five per cent of household heads were in Social Class 2 and included a primary school headmaster and a school teacher, the station master and the undermanager of the gas works. Sixty-eight per cent were in Social Class 3 and included railway engine drivers, Post Office engineers and clerical workers.

Overcrowding in the city's houses had not been alleviated in any way by the council's early housing programme. Indeed, housing data

for the censuses of 1921 and 1931 show that the situation had
deteriorated in the 1920s in those houses in which overcrowding was
most acute.

TABLE 6

*Housing Density Data, 1921 and 1931 Census*
(Density of more than 2 persons per room)

| No. of persons | | Percentage of population | | No. of private families | Percentage of total private families |
| --- | --- | --- | --- | --- | --- |
| 1921 | 1931 | 1921 | 1931 | 1931 | 1931 |
| 407 | 458 | 4.14 | 4.69 | 64 | 2.34 |

*Source: Censuses 1921 and 1931*

Although it was evident that the houses built by the council were
not fulfilling their intended role the attitude of the council was
incredibly complacent. Sir Richard Williams was of the opinion in
July 1926 that once the Heol Dewi Estate was complete the council
'should rest a little'.[22] Many felt, even taking government subsidies
into account, that the housing programme was placing a heavy burden
on the rates. Ald. Bayne, who since 1899 had opposed municipal
housing, expressed the view that the council should 'hesitate before it
went in for another housing scheme because the general body of
ratepayers did not benefit'.[23]

While the council was apparently burying its head in the sand an
organization formed in Bangor early in 1925 sought to draw to the
notice of the public the chronic state of the housing stock and the
intolerable conditions under which a high proportion of the citizens
were living. At a conference in Birmingham in April 1924 members of
an organization under the title of 'Christian Order in Politics,
Economics and Citizenship' (COPEC), considered the report of the
Archbishop of Canterbury's committee of enquiry into housing in
Britain. The report stated that 'insufficient and insanitary housing is
the source of moral weakness and spiritual degradation' and issued a
challenge by declaring that 'there are few more urgent duties for
Christian men and women than to play their part in removing this
great, inveterate evil from the life of the community'.[24] Pious Welsh
nonconformists earlier in the century, as we have seen in Chapter

Three, were fully aware of the relationship between poor housing conditions and moral decline.[25] This same concern was evidently still felt in Bangor in the 1920s for a group of enthusiasts invited a regional COPEC conference to Bangor in November 1924. One result of the conference was the formation of a COPEC Housing Group in Bangor. Recognizing that an exact knowledge of the facts concerning the state of housing could only be secured by means of a survey it urged the health committee of the council to make such a survey, pledging itself to provide volunteer workers to conduct it. The council, in December 1925, agreed to undertake the survey and welcomed the offer of assistance from the COPEC committee. It contributed a sum of £30 towards the cost and appointed a temporary sanitary inspector to assist in the work. The COPEC group contributed £50 and enlisted the help of eighty women.

Between April and August 1926, 2,621 houses were surveyed and the findings, published in September, exposed the insalubrious state of the houses occupied by the poorer members of society and the degree of overcrowding in them. Some of the facts which came to light are tabulated below (Table 7) and relate only to areas which experienced the highest degree of overcrowding and the poorest physical condition of the property. These areas comprised 35 per cent of the city's housing stock.

TABLE 7

*Selected Data from the Housing Survey Report, 1926*

| | |
|---|---|
| Number of houses isolated for special study | 908 |
| Number of persons | 3,450 |
| Number of houses that are back to back | 18 |
| Number of houses with one bedroom | 190 |
| Number of such houses occupied by four or more persons | 74 |
| Number of houses with two bedrooms | 459 |
| Number of such houses occupied by six or more persons | 87 |
| Number of cases of two or more families residing in one house | 71 |
| Number of houses that are overcrowded | 199 |
| Number of houses considered totally unfit for habitation | 87 |
| Number of rooms under seven feet in height | 187 |
| Houses affected by damp | 266 |
| Single bedroom houses without window in rear wall | 125 |
| Houses with kitchen window not opening | 232 |
| Houses without food stores | 116 |

TABLE 7 [continued]

| | |
|---|---|
| Houses without cooking facilities | 151 |
| Houses without copper boilers | 853 |
| Houses without wash houses | 826 |
| Houses without slop sinks | 815 |
| Houses without baths | 884 |
| Number of houses provided with sanitary bins | 100 |
| Cases where one tap serves two or more houses | 8 |

In their introduction to the report the sanitary inspectors hoped that it would 'meet the requirements of those earnest men and women who want to know . . . what can be done to promote better housing for the working classes of Bangor'. Coinciding with the publication of this report came the report of the District Medical Officer of Health for Caernarvonshire for 1925-26. Referring to Bangor, he stated 'while the council deserves credit for the effort it has made to build more houses we must face the fact that no relief is reaching those on whom the pressure is greatest . . . The resources of the poor are not equal to the minimum demands for the new houses and they are therefore compelled to remain in houses that warrant demolition and which are becoming more delapidated each year'.[26] When these two reports were discussed by the council in November 1926, Cllr. Vallance summed up the mood of the council by saying that the reports 'make us uncomfortable', and noting that the council 'was not building houses to relieve the bona fide working man neither was it relieving the congested areas'.[27]

Having initiated the enquiry the local COPEC branch took a bold step in helping to relieve some of the appalling housing conditions in which about a third of the city's population lived. A plot of land belonging to the Friars School Estate was conveyed in March 1927 to Miss Rathbone, secretary of the group. A short road, Seiriol Road, was laid down and two terraces of ten houses each were built on either side of the road. Perceiving the need for smaller, less expensive houses, which might be let for rents which low income families could afford, the group constructed houses not exceeding 680 feet super. Built of brick cavity walls under a slate roof, each house contains two downstairs rooms and three bedrooms and has a bath, lavatory and hot water boiler on the ground floor.

Contrary to stimulating the council to follow its example, the COPEC initiative seemed to discharge it from any further action. Cllr. Wartski, on the completion of the Heol Dewi scheme in July 1927, called for the disbanding of the housing committee since he did not believe the council would be building any more houses. The mayor, John Roberts, thought instead that the committee should be allowed to die a natural death.[28] In a further discussion on housing in December 1928, the chairman of the housing committee expressed the belief that the council would not have to build houses again in his lifetime. These attitudes strengthen the notion that the council, despite progress to date in this field, was not fully committed to the concept of municipal housing and that its concern for the level of the rates was greater than for the living conditions of a high percentage of the citizens; they are the more reprehensible since at that time legislation was already on the statute book for the building of smaller houses at higher densities which could be let at much lower rents. The Housing Act 1924, Wheatley's Act, passed by the first Labour government, granted local authorities a subsidy of £9 for every house built, payable over a period of forty years. Rents for these houses were to be fixed at the general level of pre-war rents for working class houses and to achieve this, local authorities were obliged to make a contribution of up to £4.50 a year on each house from the rates. Such a contribution may have been a factor in deterring the council from implementing the Act; another factor was certainly its aversion to building small houses or 'rabbit hutches' as they were contemptuously referred to by councillors.

Pressure was, however, mounting for the council to take a new initiative and in October 1929, the chairman of the housing committee advised the council that it should now consider building 'a smaller and cheaper type of house at a lesser rent than the houses previously erected' and to 'advertise in order to ascertain whether there was a demand for them'.[29] The council authorized the committee to proceed and accordingly it bought two plots of land, Gardd Denman off Penchwintan on the west of the city and a portion of the Friars School Estate on the east. When plans for the houses were presented to the council in December there was a heated debate, with accusations that 'instead of doing away with slums we are going to create slumdom'.[30] A Leader in the *North Wales Chronicle* admonished councillors for this defeatist attitude and, referring to the houses built by the COPEC group, stated that there were 'no complaints . . . no change of tenants, no arrears of rent and the group was considering reducing the rents by fourpence a week. If Bangor COPEC can provide dwellings which can be let at rents moderate enough to suit the purse of working men, surely the council can do likewise'.[31]

Sixty-three houses were built at Gardd Denman, known as the Ty'n-y-Caeau scheme, and seventy on the Friars School Estate and named Maes-y-Llan. Despite their smaller size, 830 feet super, they met the Ministry of Health 'A' class specifications. Outwardly they present a contrast to houses built under previous schemes. Apart from five semi-detached pairs in Maes-y-Llan they are built in variable length terraces of from four to eleven houses. Frontages of the longer terraces are relieved by bringing out the fronts of some houses and by incorporating bay windows in others, each projection being crowned with a gable. Variety is also achieved by facing the ground floor elevations with red brickwork and rendering the wall above the ground floor string line with rough cast cement. By building in terrace formation more houses could be constructed on the available land and a density of 14.6 houses to the acre was attained. Each house cost an average of £350 and the rents worked out at nine shillings a week for houses with bay windows and eight shillings and sixpence a week for the others. These rents compared with nineteen shillings and £1 a week for the earlier houses. Demand for them was overwhelming; there were 400 applicants for the first twenty-four houses at Ty'n-y-Caeau. Overall there were 560 applicants for the 133 houses and some method had to be devised to allocate the houses to the most needy. In response the council had to consider building more houses. Shortage conditions only exacerbated the plight of low income families and Sir Richard Williams flayed landlords who were charging fifteen shillings a week for hovels and twelve and thirteen shillings for cellars without any light. There were instances of from twelve to sixteen shillings a week being charged for two rooms in large subdivided houses.

For its next instalment of houses the new surveyor, Price Davies, presented the council with an imaginative plan for the comprehensive redevelopment of the old, run down sector near the eastern entrance to the city. The plan embraced the re-alignment of the main London-Holyhead road down Beach Road, the demolition of the now derelict Penrhyn Arms Hotel and outbuildings and several abandoned industrial premises along the coast at Hirael. The grounds of the former hotel and some adjacent land were scheduled for development as a public park and a triangular plot was set aside for building houses. The housing component of the plan generated passionate debates in council. Opponents claimed that the site was unique in that it presented charming views across the Strait towards Beaumaris and should be preserved as an open space for everyone to enjoy; some councillors enlisted the support of the Council for the Protection of

Rural Wales for this opinion. There was apprehension too that should council houses be built here visitors' first impression of the city would be an unfavourable one. The layout itself had its critics; since it was surrounded on all sides by busy roads concern was felt for the safety of the 200 or so children who would eventually live there. A more fundamental objection was the small size of the project; it was thought that the council should consider building 600 houses in two large estates at either end of the city in an elevated and healthier environment rather than nibble at the housing problem piecemeal on the floor of the valley. Those who supported the plan dismissed the environmental argument by stating that the surveyor had prepared a very attrctive plan, that the entrance to the city at this point had never been a salubrious one and, as Cllr. Chamberlain put it: 'It was no use telling people that there was a beautiful view at the bottom of town when they were herded together like cattle in other parts'.[32] Supporters also emphasized the dire need for houses and of a site which was near the the employment spots of the working men.

The opponents, having lost the environmental argument, raised the twin bogies of 'rabbit hutches' and 'creation of new slums' once again. This was probably the more powerful argument since, following the collapse on Wall Street in 1929 and the economic blizzard which swept the world in its wake, the Ministry of Health refused to sanction, under the 1924 Housing Act, the building of houses of more than 760 feet super. and reduced the subsidy payable on each house to £4.50 a year. Several appeals to the Ministry to be allowed to build larger houses and to site the lavatories outside rather than inside the houses, for which the council seemed to have a preference, were to no avail. As pressures on the government steadily mounted to withdraw all subsidies under the 1924 Act following the publication of the May Report on National Expenditure, the council in July 1932 accepted a *fait accompli* and hurriedly activated the plan for building thirty-five houses. The final plan for Maes Isalaw attempted to mitigate some of the environmental objections that had been raised. Houses built at a density of 14.5 per acre and in varying block sizes and styles face out towards the encompassing roads so that no back yards are visible from them and archways connect adjacent blocks to further exclude back yards from view. The estate screens the older properties of Hirael from the view of travellers descending onto Beach Road and a broad area of greensward separates the development from the main road. Each house cost an average of £335 to build and a rent of eight shillings and ninepence was fixed. When the houses were ready for occupation in November 1933 there were 800 people on the council's waiting list.

The completion of Maes Isalaw marks the end of the third phase of the council's post-war housing programme and also the resignation of Sir Richard Williams as Chairman of the Housing Committee and his replacement by Cllr. Richard Jones. In spite of the fact that 318 houses had now been built, the problem of overcrowding in insanitary dwellings remained; indeed because of the lack of alternative accommodation, few such houses had been demolished, although closing orders had been issued. This was a nationwide problem and slum clearance became an issue in the parliamentary election campaign of 1929. A Labour administration was returned at that election and a new Housing Act, Greenwood's Act was passed in 1930. In essence the Act gave financial support to local authorities for demolishing slum property and for rehousing those who were rendered homeless on that account. Local authorities were also urged by the government to take advantage of the falling building and labour costs of the early 1930s and to build houses at substantially lower rentals. Responsibilities of local authorities under the Act were threefold: to identify unfit houses and to submit a five year programme of demolition to the Ministry; to acquire land on which to build houses for those families displaced and redevelop the cleared sites where appropriate.

The council's survey of unfit houses was completed in July 1932 and its five year plan to demolish 580 houses and replace them by a similar number of new houses was approved by the Ministry of Health in February 1934. This was a most ambitious plan for a small authority, the number of houses ranking eleventh in the list submitted by non-county boroughs and urban districts throughout England and Wales. It was, moreover, a measure of the acute problem of unfit houses in Bangor, a legacy of the early nineteenth century, and of the commitment of the council at that time to tackle the problem. The main area scheduled for demolition was the Dean Street area, or the Central Area as it was referred to; smaller number of houses in Hirael, Garth, Britannia Square, Kyffin Square, Mountain Street, Lon-y-Popty, Glanadda and Hendrewen were also earmarked for demolition. Rehousing displaced families on the scale envisaged and at the low densities required by the 1930 Act made it necessary to purchase large tracts of land near the periphery of the city and, to ensure that land would be available for the city's future development, the boundaries of the borough were extended in 1934. The first site to be selected was one of thirty acres on Ffriddoedd Farm on the Upper

Bangor ridge, which was purchased from the Penrhyn Estate. Land fronting two of its boundary roads. Ffriddoedd Road and Belmont Road, was reserved for development by private builders so that the better class houses would be visible from the main roads and in March 1934 five and a half acres were sold to the Local Education Authority for building a new Girls' Grammar School. A further ten acres of steeply sloping ground were scheduled an open space and recreation ground.

This was an excellent site for house building since fine views of the Snowdonia Range are obtained from it. There was much opposition to the council's choice of site on the grounds that such a prime position should have been reserved entirely for private building. Furthermore, residents of Upper Bangor objected to the prospect of hundreds of slum dwellers in their midst.

Price Davies planned another attractive estate of 162 houses and two shops at an average density of twelve houses to the acre. Known as Maes Tryfan, the estate comprises 130 three bedroom houses and, on account of some of the large families which were to be displaced, thirty-two four bedroom houses. Blocks varying from two to six houses in number and of two and three storey construction are built in juxta-position and each block displays a variety of front elevations, roof patterns, facing materials and constructional details. All the houses are of the more expensive parlour type; Mrs Chamberlain, a former school teacher, made a strong case for this type of house on the grounds that children should have a separate room in which to do their homework. Each house cost either £319 or £370, according to the number of bedrooms, yet the council charged a fixed rent (including rates) of five shillings and sixpence (27.5p) a week irrespective of the size of the house. The whole project added another eight pence (3.33p) to the rates.

The first tenants, from Brook Row, moved into Lôn Glyder on 1 April 1935. By the end of 1936 all the houses were occupied and 633 persons had been rehoused. Cllr. Brooks reckoned that it 'was the most humane bit of work Bangor has ever accomplished'. A tenant on the estate told Ald. Matthews that living in Maes Tryfan 'was like heaven', and Matthews was pleased that people had been given an opportunity to raise themselves 'physically, morally and spiritually'.[33]

Two smaller housing projects followed. Both the Tan-y-Maes –Gernant scheme (eighteen non-parlour type houses) and the Brynllwyd scheme (fifty-four parlour type houses) were planned to rehouse people from the Hendrewen Road and Glanadda districts.

Houses had now been built to accommodate 234 families but another large scale development of 300 houses was needed to meet the council's objective. Four sites on the periphery of the city were examined, namely, Coed Mawr and Eithinog in the west and Tanybryn and the Penrhyn Home Farm in the south-east. Not one of the landowners was prepared to sell any of this land but Lord Penrhyn, who owned the latter two, offered the council seventy acres of another farm, Maesgeirchen, on the southern slopes of Bangor Mountain and overlooking the Cegin Valley. Compulsory purchase orders could have been issued for any one of the four sites but the council was totally opposed to these measures because of the unpleasantness they would have engendered; it did not wish to offend Lord Penrhyn, in particular, since he had willingly sold practically all the land on which the council had built houses up to that time. Most councillors were opposed to a development on Eithinog Farm since they had it in mind to develop that farm for private houses at some future date. The Housing Committee finally decided that the building would have to take place either at Coed Mawr or at Maesgeirchen. An inspector from the Ministry of Health who was asked to examine the two sites reported that the Coed Mawr site would be a very expensive one to develop and recommended Maesgeirchen.

The Housing Committee's commendation of the Maesgeirchen site at the council meeting in January 1936 was greeted with a storm of protest which reverberated throughout the city, becoming the main topic of conversation for months. The committee's case was based on the inspector's report and on the fact that the site could be bought without resort to compulsory puchase procedures. Had this been necessary, long delays would have ensued and it might not have been possible to build all the houses before 31 March 1938, the deadline fixed by the Ministry for granting a subsidy.

Principal among the arguments against the site were psychological and geographical ones; Maesgeirchen lay the other side of Bangor Mountain and to rehouse people there would be tantamount to turning them out of the city. Up to this time all developments had occurred between the two embracing ridges with the main thrust up the Adda Valley. The argument that Maesgeirchen was nearer than Coed Mawr to the town centre – it was only a quarter of a mile from the town clock as the crow flies – did not impress Ald. John Roberts who asked 'what was the good of telling that tale to a harassed mother who wanted to send her children to the Central School as though her family consisted of crows'.[34] Actually, by road the journey was 1.4 miles. A

*Plate 4.*  (i) Col. Henry Platt, C.B., J.P.; Mayor 1883-85 and 1906-07.
(ii) Sir Henry Lewis, J.P.; Mayor 1900-02.
(iii) Sir Richard J. Williams, J.P.; Mayor 1913-20.
(iv) Ald. W. R. Jones, J.P.; Mayor 1928-31.

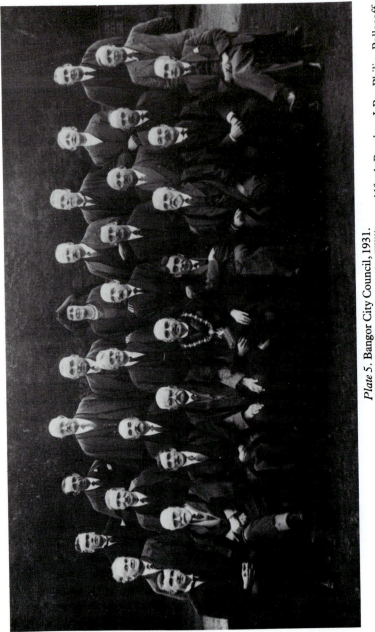

*Plate 5.* Bangor City Council, 1931.

*Back row, left to right:* T. Rogers Jones (Sanitary Inspector), W. S. Williams, Alfred Brooks, J.P., Philip Pollecoff, Mrs Chamberlain, W. O. Williams, O. T. Owen, Rev. O. Madoc Roberts, Ithel Williams.

*Middle row:* J. W. Burns, Thomas Davies, J.P., R. Stephen Jones, E. H. Jones, M.A., John Williams, Evan Edwards, Isidore Wartski, Richard Jones, Price F. White (Electrical and Gas Engineer).

*Front row:* B. Price Davies (Surveyor), Thomas Vallance, Major John Roberts, T.D., W. P. Mathews, J. P., W. R. Jones, J.P. (Mayor), J. Pentir Williams (Town Clerk), Sir Richard J. Williams, O.B.E., J.P., Richard Thomas, E. Smith Owen (Treasurer).

suggestion was mooted that a tunnel might be driven through the mountain as had been done by the railway company ninety years previously. The contention that people would be taken some distance away from their familiar shops, schools, chapels, churches and public houses was a potent one, particularly in view of the fact that four shops were the only concession to community facilities planned for the whole estate. Cllr. Wartski, a Jew, explained how the Jews had built their communities all over the world around their Bethels and village forges and he was concerned about the social and moral disorientation people would experience in their isolated locale. His opposition to the site was not entirely altruistic, however. As a High Street businessman he shared with other shopkeepers and the Chamber of Commerce the fear that the transfer of people to peripheral housing estates would inevitably have a detrimental effect on trade in the High Street. Tradesmen urged the council instead to redevelop the Central Area but in no way would the Ministry of Health sanction the building of more than eighteen houses to the acre there and at that density nowhere near enough houses could be built. Yet another argument against Maesgeirchen was the high cost of developing the isolated site; roads and sewerage, water, electricity and gas mains would have to be laid over considerable distances and this factor would outweigh the higher cost of building the houses themselves at Coed Mawr for example.

The matter came to a head at a crucial meeting of the council held on 15 June 1936 when the resolution to build houses on the Maesgeirchen site was carried by one vote. Surprisingly, only eighteen councillors attended this important meeting and the mayor abstained from voting. A Leader in the *North Wales Chronicle* later that week under the heading 'Maesgeirchen by one vote!' regretted that 'such a momentous decision, which must have weighty and serious implications financially and otherwise and which may or may not . . . hang like a millstone around the neck of the city's progress, had been taken by a solitary vote'.[35] The decision was a personal triumph for Cllr. Richard Jones and his committee who had laboured incessantly against determined opposition in order to ensure that the three hundred houses, which were so desperately needed, would be built before the ending of the Exchequer subsidy.

Price Davies prepared a geometrical plan for the estate comprising concentric circles of streets and houses connected to the A5 by a main development road and a parallel cycle track; the centre was reserved for shops and community facilities. The tender of Messrs. M. A.

Bosworth, Builders, of Wolverhampton for £120,840 was accepted in February 1937.[36] Houses of different block lengths, sizes and elevations were skilfully juxtaposed to give a sense of harmony and unity. Privet hedges were planted along house boundaries and trees along the roads which, when matured, would help to make it a 'real garden suburb of the city'.[37] The council departed from its custom of giving Welsh names to all the streets: the road joining the estate to the A5 was called Penrhyn Avenue in honour of Lord Penrhyn who had provided the site; Greenwood Avenue commemorates Arthur Greenwood who, as Minister of Health in the 1929-31 Labour Government was the architect of the Act under which the estate was built, and Kingsley Avenue honours Kingsley Wood, who was Minister of Health at the time the houses were built. The estate was officially opened by Lord Penrhyn in November 1937 and the first tenants moved in the following week. At the opening ceremony Cllr. Richard Jones referred to Maesgeirchen as 'the most important single development in the history of Bangor'.[38] Few would agree with Richard Jones's assessment although the estate certainly added a new dimension to the physical shape of the city and created a discrete working class suburb detached from the rest of the city. The last families were rehoused in Maesgeirchen in April 1939.

Condemned houses, when vacated, were demolished. Much of the rubble from the Dean Street area was used as hard core for the new roads and houses at Maesgeirchen. A comprehensive redevelopment scheme was planned for the Dean Street area. A new street plan was laid down and forty-two houses were built at the prescribed density of eighteen houses to the acre. Built in the Georgian style, they comprise two-storey three bedroom houses and three-storey four bedroom houses which were ready for occupation before the end of 1939. The outbreak of war held up the demolition of much of the area east of Dean Street and in the changed circumstances of the post-war period the council failed to implement in its entirety its original redevelopment plan for that area.

When war broke out in 1939 the greater part of the massive slum clearance, house building and rehousing programme initiated in 1934 had been consummated. Five hundred and seventy-six houses had been built and 1,871 people, almost a fifth of the city's population, had been rehoused. This was a tremendous achievement for such a small local authority. It was a task which required much planning and resourcefulness: clearance orders had to be posted street by street and defended at Ministry of Health Inquiries; landlords and agents had to be negotiated with and sometimes litigated against; occupiers had to be persuaded to leave homes and surroundings in which they had lived a lifetime for new, distant housing estates, and many shopkeepers, publicans, craftsmen and businessmen with commercial premises in the condemned areas had to be compensated. Each individual's circumstances had to be taken into consideration and treated with patience, tact and sympathy. For instance, there were thirty-two couples drawing a pension, twenty widows and spinsters and nine widowers who lived on their own and five elderly and infirm persons who, in some cases, were bedridden. It would have been unreasonable and impracticable to remove such people and arrangements had to be made for them to interchange with occupants of nearby houses which were not on the lists for immediate demolition. The council also moved to the new estates the belongings and furniture of the displaced persons after first disinfecting the latter with hydrocyanic acid gas to ensure that no vermin were carried into the new houses. Once the new tenants had settled in, the council sponsored an annual competition for the best kept garden in an attempt to encourage them to cultivate their gardens and keep them tidy. The winner was presented with the City of Bangor Challenge Cup.

Despite the constraints placed upon the council by the adverse economic and financial situation which prevailed in the inter-war years the period is notable in a number of respects. In the first place, the council greatly enhanced and extended its functions in the sphere of health and environmental improvement. More competent surveyors, together with technical advances, helped to ensure a pure and more plentiful water supply, a greatly improved sewerage and rubbish disposal system and a successful flood prevention scheme for the River Adda. Hand in hand with advances in medical science went stricter inspection of the slaughter of animals and of milk and food retailed in the city and the provision of more open space and recreational facilities. By building more than 900 well designed houses at low residential densities in healthy surroundings and by demolishing over 500 houses, unfit for human habitation, in crowded localities, the council greatly improved living conditions for a high percentage of the people of Bangor.

Secondly, by its involvement in the sphere of housing, it extended still further the process of municipal socialism which had begun in the mid-nineteenth century. By 1939 the council owned about 30 per cent of the city's housing stock and had become the city's largest landlord, the posture once of the Penrhyn Estate.[39] Power had been gradually transferred from the castle to the town hall, albeit with the active acquiescence of the lord of the manor.

Finally, the period witnessed the insidious intrusion of central government into the affairs of local authorities. This process was particularly marked in the sphere of housing. Conflict arose when central government refused to sanction any local deviation from its directives, for example, when the council wished to build larger houses with outdoor lavatories at Maes Isalaw. Councillors complained of dictation from Whitehall and Cllr. E. H. Jones said 'It is about time local authorities started taking notice of what Whitehall is doing in the way of interfering with the powers of local authorities'. He prophetically added, 'It is going to undermine local government in this country. Who knows the needs of Bangor, the council or some official sitting in an armchair in London?'[40] The chairman of the Finance Committee, in presenting his estimates for 1938, complained about the 'spate of legislation' enacted by Parliament which imposed new duties on local authorities'[41] and Elwyn Jones, shortly after his appointment as town clerk in 1939, in a prospective view of local government, observed that 'Whitehall was taking a growing share in the regulation and control of the work of local authorities'. Referring to the fact that an increasing percentage of local government expenditure was being borne by the Treasury, he perceptively remarked that 'he who pays the piper calls the tune'.[42]

The outbreak of war in 1939 diverted the council's attention to more pressing activities in the field of civil defence such as the issue of gas masks, the building of air raid shelters, the reception of over 3,000 evacuees from the Liverpool area, the release of land for allotments and the collection of salvage. Railings were removed from around the town hall, town clock and many other buildings, which led one citizen to remark 'Our streets are almost naked now'.[43] In view of the fact that the council immediately before the war was anxious to sell the pier, for scrap iron if necessary, it is strange that it did not snatch the opportunity provided by the shortage of metal during the war to dispose of it. In any event, the pier was closed throughout the war since the War Office had ordered the council to remove the decking as a precaution against the pier's use as a potential enemy landing point! The only enemy object which did land was a mine dropped by a German aeroplane over Maesgeirchen and which did some damage to property there. Searchlight batteries were located along the Strait and an army camp was set up on the Beach Road playing field. Some of the

council's property was made available to the B.B.C.'s Variety
Department which was evacuated to Bangor in 1940. Famous radio
programmes like *ITMA, The Old Town Hall* and *Music Hall* were
broadcast from the Penrhyn Hall, and the B.B.C.'s music library was
housed in the public library.

Throughout the War the council struggled to maintain services
with a smaller labour force and to administer the new obligations
which were placed upon it in the sphere of civil defence and
evacuation. Among the events which marked the end of the War in
Europe were the ringing of church bells, community singing, a
bonfire on the Ja Ja ground, a service of thanksgiving and a sports
meeting.

*Notes*

1. Cllr. Alfred Brookes's view relating to the transfer of the first families from slum
   dwellings in Brook Row to the Maes Tryfan estate, NWC, 5 April 1935.
2. NWC, 21 August 1914.
3. NWC, 4 September 1914.
4. Ibid.
5. Ibid.
6. The enmity which existed between the two leaders is well known. The 'freedoms'
   were conferred at the County Theatre within a fortnight of each other in July 1920.
7. NWC, 9 January 1920.
8. See NWC, 2 June 1933 for a plan of the development.
9. For report of accident see NWC, 11 December 1914.
10. See NWC, 7 June 1935 for the opening of the service.
11. NWC, 12 November 1926.
12. NWC, 7 November 1930.
13. NWC, 9 April 1937.
14. NWC, 27 October 1939.
15. NWC, 24 May 1935.
16. From data supplied by Motor Taxation Offices, Caernarfon and Llangefni, in
    1972.
17. NWC, 30 May 1930.
18. NWC, 10 December 1937.
19. See p. 63.
20. NWC, 30 July 1926.
21. NWC, 14 November 1924.
22. NWC, 30 July 1926.
23. NWC, 6 May 1927.
24. UCNW Bangor MSS 19232-19234.
25. See pp. 60 and 62.
26. NWC, 10 September 1926.
27. NWC, 12 November 1926.
28. NWC, 29 July 1927.
29. NWC, 4 October 1929.
30. NWC, 6 December 1929.

31. Ibid.
32. NWC, 4 March 1932.
33. NWC, 3 May 1935.
34. NWC, 19 June 1936.
35. Ibid.
36. The tender was for 300 houses and comprised 230 large 3-bedroom, 50 small 3-bedroom and 20 4-bedroom houses. Rent charged was seven shillings and sixpence a week irrespective of size.
37. NWC, 3 December 1937.
38. Ibid.
39. It owned 950 houses which were occupied by 3,752 people. NWC, 6 December 1940.
40. NWC, 3 February 1933.
41. NWC, 8 April 1938.
42. NWC, 21 July 1939.
43. NWC, 19 November 1943.

# CHAPTER 6

## 1914 — 1945

**'They worked with only one aim, the advancement of the city.'**[1]

THE COMMUNITY described by Henry Lewis in the early 1880s had undergone substantial change even before the outbreak of the First World War. Technical advances had helped to break down its comparative isolation. After the turn of the century English language newspapers were being read by an increasingly more literate society and national events gradually diverted attention from local issues. Through the medium of the silent film the public was regaled with scenes from all over the world. More holiday makers arrived by train and, after the opening of the pier, by boat; the motor car, bus, charabanc, motorcycle and bicycle all helped to extend people's horizons.

The War itself accelerated the process. News from the battlefields of Europe and the Near East and the seas around our shores riveted people's thoughts onto the wider scene. The presence in Bangor of war-torn refugees, Lancastrian troops in training and wounded soldiers brought home to the community the reality of war as much as did the departure of over a thousand young men to serve on distant battlefields and the shock of the casualty lists. Servicemen returned after the war with wider experience of life.

After the War, national and international events came to play a more important role in the daily lives of the community. The national railway strike of 1919 and the General Strike of 1926 affected workmen in Bangor no less than in other parts of the country; the economic depression triggered off on Wall Street in 1929 left its mark on the people of Well Street. Contact with the wider world was extended by the coming of radio into homes and 'talkies' to the cinema (after 1929). Famous filmstars, comedians, singers, footballers, cricketers and jockeys became household names as entertainment and sport took a grip on people's minds and betting and the football pools took a share of their incomes. The gathering clouds of war in the 1930s produced a peculiar reaction in Bangor; the Maes Tryfan housing estate, opened in 1935, was facetiously called Abyssinia and the Maesgeirchen estate, over which controversy raged in 1936, was called Madrid.[2] People became aware of preparations for war nearer home when an R.A.F. station was established in Penrhos, near Pwllheli, in 1936 and when the submarine H.M.S. *Thetis* failed to surface during an exercise off the coast of south-east Anglesey in 1939. Within a few months of the tragedy men were being conscripted for military service, air raid precautions were being taken and plans for the reception of children who were to be evacuated from Liverpool were being drawn up. On 1 September 1939 the Germans unleashed their blitzkrieg on Poland and Britain was once again at war, this time on a global scale.

The community underwent great social change as it emerged from its comparative isolation. The First World War had cruelly treated the aristocracy, particularly the Penrhyn family, as both the heir to the estate and his brother were killed in action in France in July 1915. Soon after the war almost half the estate, albeit the more outlying portion, was sold and the slate industry was in sharp decline. Although the influence of the estate and the family waned to some extent during the period, the estate was still a major employer of labour and owner of land and houses in the city and the third Lord Penrhyn (1864-1927) and his son, the fourth Lord (1894-1949), maintained an active interest in local and county affairs. They gave nominal leadership in a number of fields, especially those relating to politics, the church and agriculture. As owners of practically all the land the council needed for its house building programme they always negotiated sympathetically with it. The council sustained a happy relationship with the family and in recognition 'of the long and honourable connection which had existed between the city of Bangor and the house of Penrhyn, and in particular the great public service and generosity' rendered by the third baron, it granted him the freedom of the borough in 1926.[3]

Of Henry Lewis's two middle orders (see p. 96), the professional one increased in number and influence during the period. Opportunities in professional and clerical occupations multiplied with growth in educational and medical services, banking and office employment. These fields began to be manned by the upwardly mobile products of the county grammar schools and redbrick universities and colleges rather than by the privileged sons of the wealthy, as hitherto. Openings for businessmen or for those working on their own account, on the other hand, were not so favourable. Small businesses in slate working, flour milling, coach making, etc. either faced competition from larger regional manufacturers or else their products were no longer in demand. The invasion of High Street by multiple stores and national agencies created a new breed of shop and office manager who was invariably a newcomer, seeking further promotion and without any great attachment to the city. Few local entrepreneurs in the retail, craft and service trades now hired more than ten employees.

Numerically still the largest class, the working class had come increasingly to work for large firms and institutions rather than for small scale entrepreneurs. The big employers of labour were the railway and bus companies, the post office and the county council, all of whom were corporate and remote bodies. Even the larger building contractors who were engaged to build houses for the council were not local firms. Labour in all these branches of activity became heavily unionized and terms and conditions of work and rates of pay were negotiated, approved and applied nationally.

Each residential area within the city reflected the social standing of its inhabitants. Pre-eminent in social prestige and status was the Siliwen Road–Victoria Park district in Upper Bangor. Here, in large villas built in the late Victorian period, resided the academic élite of the University College and successful professional and business men, most of whom were still able to retain the services of a domestic servant up to the outbreak of the Second World War. Increasingly, professional and business men began to occupy the smaller three and four bedroom houses built along Meirion Lane, Menai Road, lower Ffriddoedd Road and Penrhos Road in the 1930s by speculative builders for owner occupation. The smaller size of family, the high cost of keeping servants and the labour saving amenities with which these well designed houses with garages were equipped, made these houses an attractive investment for the middle classes.

In terms of size, ground density and rateable values there was little difference between the speculatively built houses at the lower end of the owner occupation market and those built in the early phases of the council's post war building programme. There was a convergence too in the social class of their early occupants: salaried clerks and school teachers shared common frontages with the aristocracy of the working class, engine drivers, signalmen, and railway and post office engineers. Seventy-seven per cent of the owner occupiers in the estate built adjacent to Ffriddoedd Road and Belmont Road were in Social Class III (35 per cent of them were railwaymen) as were 67 per cent of the council's tenants in Pennant Crescent and Penlon.[4] The features which distinguished the privately built houses from the others were the greater variety in outward design and superior fittings.

Each successive phase of building by the council was marked by the erection of smaller houses let to people further down the occupational and social scale. The rehousing of slum dwellers at Maes Tryfan and Maesgeirchen painted these estates with an image which all council estates eventually came to acquire.

Despite the buoyancy of house building in the inter-war period, the majority of citizens still lived as tenants of private landlords in houses built before the Great War. These houses varied from the large three and four storey terraced houses to the four roomed terraced cottages, many of which were already earmarked for demolition when war broke out in 1939.

During the Great War the Conservative and Liberal Parties buried their political differences for the united purpose of pursuing the war effort. Immediately after the war, Lloyd George, the Prime Minister, went to the country as leader of a coalition government and won a convincing victory at the polls. Unprecedented economic problems in the immediate post war period gave rise to high inflation, industrial turbulence and tensions in the coalition itself. When Lloyd George went to the country again in 1922 the coalition had been dissolved and the Conservatives won a small majority, this time over a much stronger and more confident Labour Party. The Liberal Party was decimated although its support held up in the rural constituencies of Wales and Lloyd George did not lose his magic touch in his Boroughs constituency. The election was a watershed in the fortunes of the Liberal Party which ceased thenceforth to be a significant force in national politics. As the heir to the traditional radical vote the Labour Party made great strides, particularly in industrial south Wales. Constituted as a political party in 1918, it had gained considerable support by 1922 and in the election the following year it formed a government, albeit a minority one. From that time the main contest nationally has been between the Conservative and Labour Parties.

At the local level in 1919 the Labour Party fielded a candidate, the General Secretary of the North Wales Quarrymen's Union, in the Caernarfon constituency which was an amalgamation of the former Arfon and Eifion constituencies. He was narrowly defeated by the coalition candidate but his colleague in Anglesey, the war veteran

Brigadier-General Sir Owen Thomas, won the seat for Labour. This seat, however, was recaptured by the Liberals in 1922 and all four constituencies in north-west Wales remained loyal to the Liberal cause until 1945.

Another element of the Welsh political scene in the inter-war years was the re-emergence of Welsh national feeling, reminiscent of the Cymru Fydd movement in the closing decades of the previous century. Plaid Genedlaethol Cymru (later Plaid Cymru) was formed in August 1925 and its basic message was as much cultural as it was political. In the forefront of its programme was the promotion of the Welsh language by giving it official recognition and status in administrative and public life and throughout the educational system. Not surprisingly its earliest members were drawn from among Welsh intellectuals and the movement found fertile ground in which to germinate in the centres of higher education in Bangor. Prominent among the party's early leaders were Ambrose Bebb and Professor J. E. Daniel.

William Ambrose Bebb (1894-1955), a native of Cardiganshire, was active in Welsh cultural and protest movements as a student in the University College at Aberystwyth. Between 1920 and 1925 he held lecturing appointments at the Universities of Rennes and the Sorbonne and came under the influence of right wing French nationalist writers and Roman Catholicism. In 1925 he joined the staff of the Normal College and remained there until his death. John Edward Daniel (1903-62) was a native of Hirael. His father was a Congregational minister who held several pastorates including one in Patagonia. Educated in Hirael, Garth and Friars Schools, John won a scholarship to Oxford in 1919 and shortly after graduating was appointed Professor of Theology at the Bala-Bangor Independent College. Another prominent member of Plaid Cymru and editor of the Party's newspaper, *Y Ddraig Goch*, in the 1930s was a lecturer in the Extra Mural Department of the University College, A. O. H. Jarman.

Nurtured and inspired by intellectuals such as Bebb, Daniel and Jarman, student activists at the University College took a more militant path. One of their first acts of protest was to enter Caernarfon Castle on St. David's Day in 1932 and pull down and tear up the Union Jack which was flying there. Professor Daniel said that 'it was a necessary protest' and 'he rejoiced at it'.[5] Both Bebb and Daniel contested parliamentary seats in Caernarvonshire in the 1930s but were decisively beaten. The Party made little impact on the political stage; its main support came from Welsh speaking intellectuals and rather conservative, nonconformist elements. Indeed, it entirely misjudged the patriotic mood of the majority of Welshmen by its implied support of the Facist régimes on the Continent, by burning installations at the R.A.F. station at Penrhos in 1936, by organizing a boycott of celebrations to mark the coronation of King George VI in 1937 and by totally opposing war and conscription in 1939.

Sharp divisions between Anglicans and nonconformists which rent the community in pre-war days and which were continually stirred up by the disestablishment campaign became less apparent after the Church was disestablished in 1918. As an independent Welsh church within the Anglican communion it identified itself more closely with Wales and the needs of Welsh people. Ordination of priests came to be held in Welsh as well as in English and a new hymn book (1934) and prayer book were printed in Welsh.

The First World War marks a watershed too for the nonconformist denominations. After a century of continuous growth membership of the Presbyterian Church of Wales, the strongest denomination in Bangor, reached a peak during the war years but during the inter-war period declined by about 5 per cent. Although the data indicate only a small reduction in membership, they do not reveal the decrease in regularity with which members attended chapel services. A more ominous trend between the wars was the halving of the number of children and Sunday School members in the Welsh Presbyterian chapels in Bangor. Cultural activities which centred on places of worship continued to attract considerable support, however. Slum clearance and the redistribution of the population made a number of mission halls redundant but no places of worship were built on the new housing estates. Churches and chapels maintained their Sunday services and their clergy and ministers. There was no significant erosion of the Welsh Sunday as it had evolved during the Victorian and Edwardian eras and the spirit of Sabbatarianism remained strong. In wartime there was much support for designated days of prayer. A united bilingual service of thanksgiving at the cathedral at the end of the war in Europe in May 1945, 'in token of deliverance from a great peril and of victory over a powerful and cruel enemy', attracted a congregation which overflowed into the street.[6]

The mayor of Bangor throughout the Great War was Ald. Richard John Williams [1853-1941, Plate 4 (iii)]; he was elected in 1913 and re-elected each year until 1920. Born in Blaenau Ffestiniog, he entered the service of Evan Morris, a wholesale grocer in Liverpool, in 1872. Williams was soon appointed his representative in north Wales, charged with extending the firm's influence there. He was an energetic, shrewd and successful businessman and he established the firm as one of the principal wholesale grocers in north Wales. He was taken into partnership by Morris and when the firm became a company, trading under the name of Morris and Jones, he was appointed to the board of directors. Richard Williams was elected onto the council in 1907 and his exceptional qualities were soon recognized. Within six years he was elected mayor and although it was a very difficult period he devoted himself not only to the office itself but to innumerable committees of which he was invariably chairman. For his outstanding services he was awarded the O.B.E. in 1920 and for their services to the city he and his wife, who had supported him with equal dedication in a wide range of community activities, were granted the freedom of the borough in 1921. While still mayor he was elected the first chairman of the council's housing committee and laid the foundations of the council's inter-war housing programme. His talents were not confined to the city council: he became a member and alderman (in 1926) of Caernarvonshire County Council and its chairman, 1932-33, a Justice of the Peace and Deputy Lieutenant of the county. He gave loyal and devoted service to his chapel, Princes Road Presbyterian, where he was an elder for thirty years. For his long and distinguished public service he was awarded a knighthood in 1922.

During the war there was a moratorium on municipal elections; vacancies were filled by nominees elected by the council and among them were two members of the Labour Party, T. E. Taylor and J. H. Willington, both railwaymen. In September 1918 the local Trades Council was reconstructed and among its aims was assistance to Labour Party candidates at municipal elections. Its secretary, R. A. Carter, another railwayman, won a seat in a by-election in 1919.

A few weeks before the first post war municipal election, Ald. Henry Lewis, by now the council's *eminence grise*, in a long letter to the *North Wales Chronicle*, appealed to businessmen, the better educated and ministers of religion not to lose the opportunity of serving the city. 'We want men accustomed to study as well as men accustomed to act', he said. Using a familiar war time expression he asked 'Was there no one on the staff of the colleges who would attempt to go over the top?' He praised the high qualities and usefulness of the four Labour Party members on the council – 'they were a power on the council, they had something sensible to say on most questions and they were thoroughly in earnest'. However, he spurned them for having 'no experience of public affairs', and he struck a note of caution and concern lest less competent candidates 'who have no idea in their heads but follow a leader' should be elected by the working man. In essence, he perceived the lack of interest the educated, middle class was showing in municipal government and warned them that if they did not supply men of the right calibre for municipal office 'then we shall soon see the council filled with Labour men'.[7]

No member of the staff of the city's colleges responded immediately to Henry Lewis's challenge and only four were to do so subsequently. His call to ministers of religion was made relevant by a clause in the Representation of the People Act 1918 which allowed them to seek election for public office. Two ministers eventually did so. The Act, which was largely the government's response to the suffragette movement, not only gave women over twenty-eight years of age the vote in parliamentary elections but also gave the wives of ratepayers the right to vote in municipal elections. It also confirmed that women could stand as candidates in municipal elections, a right accorded them by an Act of 1906. Henry Lewis made no reference to women in his letter to the *Chronicle* but they were not to be denied the rights they had fought to achieve; three women were elected during the period. His challenge was not really heeded by the middle class yet his apprehension of a working class take over was entirely unfounded.

Four trends in the constitution of the council during the inter-war years are interesting to note. Firstly, there was the dominance of the council by Independent members, secondly, the struggle of the Labour Party to gain influence in it, thirdly, the entry of women into a hitherto male preserve and finally, the attempt of Plaid Cymru to win support for its cause at local government level. Each of these trends will now be considered.

Conservatives and Liberals closed ranks during the war and during the period of the post-war coalition government. In the first three post-war municipal elections the councillors who had entered the council before the war under political labels (there were only six of them left) now stood as Independents, as did all new candidates other than Labour ones. Ald. Richard Williams in 1919 proudly asserted that the council 'was not divided into sections. They worked with only one aim, the advancement of the city and they knew no party'.[8] After 1922, with the rout of the Liberal Party nationally and the rapid growth of the Labour Party, there was no desire on the part of Conservatives and Liberals to return to the party politics of the pre-war period. At no time up to 1945 were there fewer than nineteen Independent members on the council and all but one of the aldermen and all but two of the mayors were Independents (Appendix, Table 18). Under the Independent banner, however, all shades of political opinion were represented ranging from staunch Conservatives to traditional Liberals and an active member of a professional union.

While the local Conservative and Liberal Parties were inactive in local elections the Labour Party throughout the period attempted to increase its representation. At the first post–war election it fielded candidates in each of the wards and four were successful: T. J. Taylor held his seat in East Ward, George Williams, a signalman, replaced Caesar Cooil in North Ward and Richard Thomas, a printer, and Stephen Jones, a tailor, were successful in East and South Ward respectively. The Party now had six members and seemingly was all set to become a force within the council. The *North Wales Chronicle* attributed the success of the Labour Party members to the solid vote of the wives of the working men. 'They rallied in support of the Party, while the wives of the other sections of the community showed marked apathy.'[9] However, at the 1920 election the Party lost a seat and for the next forty-five years (apart from 1947) it never had more than five members. Although the Party generally lacked people of the calibre able to command the support of the electorate, four of its number made a significant contribution.

Stephen Jones of Field Street was a member from 1919 to his death in 1940 and became the only Labour alderman in 1933. A native of Betws-y-Coed, he had emigrated when a boy to the U.S.A. with his father. On his return he gained employment as a tailor with Messrs. Aronson in Bangor and thereafter served two other high class drapers in the city, Cameron and Vallance. Alfred Brooks, a railwayman, served on the council from 1922 to 1934 and was deputy mayor in 1928 and 1929. He was the first working man to be appointed a Justice of the Peace in Bangor. William Samuel Williams (1900-57) was a native of Bangor and joined the staff of the engineering department of the railway company after leaving Garth school in 1914. He entered the council in 1929, became the second Labour mayor in 1943 and an alderman in 1945. He was chairman of the Housing Committee during the period of acute housing shortage after the Second World War and despite many difficulties and frustrations steered the Coed Mawr housing scheme to a successful completion. A faithful churchman and advocate of the temperance movement, he was a churchwarden at St Mary's Church, a member of the Governing Body of the Church in Wales, and President of the Chester and North Wales District Council of the L.M.S. Railway Temperance Union.

The most capable and certainly the most outgoing of the Labour members was Mrs Elsie Chamberlain [1886-1972, Plate 6 (i)]. Born in Liverpool, she came to Bangor in 1891 when her father, Caesar Cooil, took up an appointment with the railway company. She attended Glanadda and Cae Top Schools and Cynffig Davies's 'grammar school' in Menai Bridge. Having decided on a teaching career she did her pupil teaching at Garth School and after certification taught at Vaynol and Cae Top Schools. In 1910 she married F. T. Chamberlain, a bridge and works inspector on the railway. Experiencing the trauma of losing two brothers in the First World War, she became an active member of the British Legion from its inception, was vice-chairman for Wales of the women's section and a member of the Central Committee in London. She entered the council in 1930 for West Ward and represented it with a break of one year only until 1950. She showed a deep concern for the health and living conditions of the low income groups and actively supported the council's housing programme in the 1930s and in the post-war years. She helped organize the reception of evacuees in Bangor at the outset of the War and was involved in the Citizens Advice Bureau and the Sailors, Soldiers and Airmen's Families Association. She was chairman of the Health Committee when she was elected mayor in 1941, the first women to hold this office. In her induction speech she conceded that there was no money for any new initiatives but at that particularly crucial time in the War she made a promise that she would always endeavour to remember that she had a neighbour and hoped that everyone else would do likewise. She planned a unique event for the day on which she was installed mayor for a second term: she arranged for the flying of the Russian flag, alongside the Union Jack, from one of the masts in front of the town hall as a mark of admiration for the valiant struggle of the Russian people, and particularly of the Red Army in the defence of Stalingrad. Her public service extended beyond the local council chamber; she was a member and chairman of Caernarvonshire County Council and took a keen interest in educational matters, particularly those relating to the Normal College of which she was a governor for many years. In 1934 she was appointed a Justice of the Peace, once again the first woman in Caernarvonshire to hold this office. At St David's Church she was a faithful worshipper and chorister. For her valuable contribution to so many aspects of public life she was awarded the M.B.E. in 1947.

Women had shown interest in the political and public life of Bangor over many years. A women's section of the County Liberal Association and the Primrose League had been established in the 1890s and there was an active branch of the suffragette movement in the early years of the twentieth century. Women actively campaigned for the establishment of a grammar school for girls in 1898 and contributed generously to the war effort. Mrs Richard Williams, by her devotion to the community during her busband's long term as mayor, was an inspiration to all. It was not surprising, therefore, that women were confident enough to stand for municipal honours when their legal right to do so was finally established in 1918. Both Mrs Chamberlain and Miss Selina Williams, the headmistress of Glanadda Infants' School, contested seats in the election the following year but neither was successful.

Soon after the war a branch of the National Council of Women was established in Bangor, pledged to foster co-operation between men and women in social, moral and religious work. At the municipal elections of 1921 the branch supported the candidature of both Mrs Chamberlain and Miss Williams. This support drew a fierce attack from Dr E. V. Arnold, Professor of Classics at the University College and President of the Borough Liberal Party, who was a candidate for the North Ward. In a letter published in the *North Wales Chronicle* he claimed that 'the attempt on the part of women to be elected on public bodies (was) nothing less than a sex conspiracy against men' and considered the activities of the National Council to be 'a conspiracy of women against the good of the community. Candidature by sex', he stated 'is even more open to objection than that by class'.[10] A spokeswoman for the National Council repudiated the Professor's views and held that since questions of housing, the care of mothers and children, health and education, and the price and quality of food were being dealt with by the city council it was essential that women should co-operate with men in these fields. 'This is really housekeeping on a large scale', she wrote.[11]

The male chauvinist Arnold won a seat in the ensuing election and Mrs Chamberlain was defeated once again. Miss Selina Williams, however, won a seat and became the first woman councillor. She was swept into the council on a wave of indignation felt by the inhabitants of Glanadda towards the council's resolution to locate an abattoir at Deanfield, opposition to which Miss Williams had fervently orchestrated. She retired from the council in 1930 and Mrs Chamberlain won her West Ward seat. In 1941, Miss Rena Hughes, headmistress of Hirael Infants' School, became the third woman schoolteacher and second headmistress of an infants' school to serve on the council.

Plaid Cymru first contested an election in Bangor in 1937; it was for the North Ward on the County Council when Ambrose Bebb challenged the sitting member, John Williams, a former mayor. The *North Wales Chronicle* considered his intervention 'an ill-timed intrusion', especially in view of the known attitudes of the Party to the Coronation and to the arson attack on a R.A.F. station.[12] Bebb was defeated but he was well satisfied with the 183 votes he gained, particularly since the election occurred 'in one of the most conservative towns in Wales'.[13]

Emboldened by this result both Ambrose Bebb and Professor Daniel contested seats at the municipal election of 1937. They were two formidable candidates and, apart from Prof. Arnold and W. J. Hughes, a lecturer at the Normal College, were the only academics who responded to Henry Lewis's call nearly twenty years earlier. Professor Daniel came out against the sitting member for East Ward, the Rev. W. J. Owen, much to his chagrin. Owen claimed that he was as keen and ardent a Welshman as any member of the Welsh Nationalist Party, as indeed he was. He wrote poetry under his bardic pseudonym 'Afallen' and was a prolific writer in Welsh. The *North Wales Chronicle* perceptively observed that local politics 'should have been the initial cockpit for the attempts of the Party to start their political activities rather than the parliamentary arena'.[14] It took the Party another thirty-five years to realize this. Both Plaid candidates were defeated though Bebb polled 25 per cent of the vote in a three cornered contest and Daniel 38 per cent in a straight fight.

These were encouraging results and both candidates were back in the field the following year. This time Bebb got to within seven votes of victory and Daniel's share of the poll increased to 42 per cent. At the declaration of the poll Bebb set a precedent by delivering in Welsh the customary thanks to his supporters.

February 1939 was a significant month for the Welsh Nationalist cause in Caernarvonshire. On the tenth of that month a young school teacher, Hywel D. Roberts, was elected onto the Caernarfon Town Council and a week later Ambrose Bebb won a seat on the Bangor council in an uncontested by-election. The Party had arrived at last, however fortuitously. Bebb took his seat at the council meeting held on St David's Day and declared that his 'debut on that day would carry with it some significance'.[15] His hope was not fulfilled, however, for within six months the country was at war again and a moratorium was placed on municipal elections. Bebb and his Party became thoroughly discredited for their opposition to the war and when his seat came up for election in 1946 Bebb resigned. His Party withdrew from municipal affairs for the next twenty years.

Neither the challenge of the Labour Party, which drew its main support from the railway community in West Ward, nor of Plaid Cymru, which drew some support from the more intellectual sector of the city, North Ward, succeeded in toppling the hegemony of the Independents. It would be interesting to speculate as to whether the absence of the cut and thrust of political argument and rivalry had become a reason for the apathy of the electorate towards municipal government. Even though 75 per cent of a much enlarged electorate voted in the 1919 election the *North Wales Chronicle* was not reticent in admonishing the electorate for its apathy. 'This lack of interest in municipal affairs', it regretted, 'is as deplorable as it is detrimental to the welfare of the city'. The paper claimed that 'there were few candidates of outstanding merit (and) as to their calibre it is doubtful whether in fifty years hence any of them would be remembered by name'.[16] Already doubts were being raised about the merits of persons standing for election and of their effectiveness once elected.

That the attitude to municipal affairs was one of great indifference between 1919 and 1938 is evinced by the fact that in six of those years there was a contest in only two of the four wards on average. An attempt was made in 1929 to inject a modicum of interest into the election. Two wards were contested and an organization offered odds and took bets on the likely outcome. Church leaders in particular were deeply incensed; in a sermon the vicar of St David's Church condemned the practice as 'deplorable and degrading . . . It is only another incontrovertible proof of the low standards to which public morality had descended throughout the land. Even twenty years ago', he said, 'such a thing would not have been heard of or tolerated in Bangor. The curse and vice of gambling and betting has even reached the quiet villages of Caernarvon and Anglesey'.[17] Clearly Bangor and district had accepted national norms and despite the doubtful morality of the practice, the flutter succeeded since the highest turnout at the polls in the inter-war years, 85 per cent, was recorded! Large crowds turned out to hear the declaration of the results and a leader in the *North Wales Chronicle* the following week commented that interest in the election was 'eloquent proof that the accustomed apathy had for once been dispelled'.[18] Interest was not sustained, however, for three of the subsequent five elections were uncontested. Lack of interest may be accounted for by the dearth of contentious issues in the council's programme during these years. Improved water supplies, sewerage and rubbish disposal arrangements, cleaner and better surfaced roads and pavements and more recreational facilities generated public support. Municipal housing, which constituted the major sphere of the council's activity, did give rise to some controversy but it focused on the siting of estates, especially those at Maes Isalaw, Maes Tryfan and Maesgeirchen, rather than on the concept of municipal housing itself. A degree of ambivalence which marked the council's response to the Housing Acts of 1923 and 1924 gave way to a more positive and remarkably farsighted approach to the 1930 Act. Between 1934 and 1939 the council carried through the largest slum clearance and rehabilitation programme of any town of its size in the country.

Underlying this extraordinary achievement was a deep sense of Christian duty which seemed to unite people of widely differing political views and positions in the class structure. The admirable initiative of the COPEC group of Christian men and women stirred the conscience of council members who came to regard the provision of decent housing for the poor and underprivileged people of the community as a Christian responsibility. The church itself exploited the theme. In a hard hitting sermon preached in the cathedral in May 1933, at the time the council was about to consider its slum clearance programme, the Rev. Glyn Simon, Warden of the Church Hostel, dwelt upon the Christian's duty to conquer the problems of slum housing and other anti-Christian evils in their midst. Bangor 'had a city council of professing Christians for years', he declared, 'yet there were many houses . . . in which no Christian should expect his fellow man to live'.[19] To allow this situation to continue was to condone the 'sin of unfaithfulness to God', which was the theme of his text, the 101st Psalm. From 1935 to 1937, when important decisions were taken in connection with the housing programme, the mayor was the Rev. Madoc Roberts who had served on the housing committee. In a speech at his installation Ald. Mathews drew attention to the mayor's commitment 'to improve the living conditions of the people of Bangor, helping them transfer to dwellings which were the envy of everybody. That was practical Christianity'. he said, 'putting into practice what he (the mayor) preached on Sunday'.[20] Mrs Chamberlain dwelt on the same theme in a heated debate in council in March 1936 on whether or not to proceed with the Maesgeirchen scheme. Citing a family tragedy which had occurred in one of the slum houses she stridently declared 'We don't know the meaning of the word Christianity and citizenship unless we hurry with the housing scheme'.[21]

The contentious Maesgeirchen scheme was passed by a majority of one in June 1936, yet the municipal election of that year was an uncontested one. Sir Richard Williams thought that there should have been a contest. 'It does not speak well for the interest the people of Bangor take in municipal affairs that they should have allowed this occasion to pass without a contest',[22] he said. Others took the view that it was an overwhelming endorsement by the electorate of the council's decision.

An analysis of the membership of the council during this period in terms of its social class composition reveals that it was still predominantly middle class, although the appearance of Labour Party members made it slightly less so than in the period before 1914. There was a decrease in the number of businessmen working on their own account and an increase in the professional/salariat class, the reasons for which have already been given (Appendix, Table 15). This trend is hardly manifest, however, in the occupational groupings of the mayors (Appendix, Table 16). Businessmen still outnumbered the other occupational groups. With the general improvement in the health of the community, doctors were not induced to serve on the council to the same degree and, surprisingly, no solicitor became first citizen. The council certainly attracted the most prosperous and influential businessmen, especially those in the drapery trade. Isidore Wartski, Philip Pollecoff, Charles Pozzi and Thomas Vallance, for example, owned the largest departmental stores in the High Street and they were very wealthy men. All four had migrated to the city; two of them, Wartski and Pollecoff were Jews whose fathers had emigrated from Poland and the Ukraine respectively, Pozzi's family hailed from Italy and Vallance was a Scot. Most of the other businessmen operated on a more modest scale and the lower salariat and working men were persons of limited financial means. Most were content to send their sons to the local grammar school and to live, in the 1930s, in the new, smaller, detached and semi-detached houses which had been built along Ffriddoedd, Belmont and Penrhos Roads. A motion presented in 1922 that the mayor should be voted an allowance to meet his out of pocket expenses is a reflection of the lower degree of affluence of many who entered the council in this period. The motion was defeated but Mrs Chamberlain raised the matter again in 1934. She contended that a mayor should be elected on his merits not on whether or not he could afford to accept the post. Expressing sentiments which were very common fifty years earlier, she said: 'The council is our local parliament (and) our mayor is looked upon as our prime minister, and the country pays the Prime Minister thousands a year'.[23] On the casting vote of the mayor, the council decided to make the mayor an annual allowance.

The strength of Christian feeling among members of the council has already been referred to. Their sabbatarian views were as pronounced during this period as they had been before the Great War. A majority of members, particularly those who attained the rank of alderman and mayor, were regular worshippers at their churches and chapels and held office in them. Nonconformists outnumbered members of the Church in Wales in a ratio of three to one, which probably reflected the proportion of these two groups in the community. All the aldermen between 1914 and 1931 and all the mayors between 1914 and 1934 were nonconformists; eight of the eighteen aldermen were chapel deacons as were five of the mayors. A Wesleyan minister, the Rev. Madoc Roberts, has the distinction of being the only minister of religion to hold the office of alderman and mayor. When Cllr. Wartski was elected mayor in 1939 he was the first Jew to hold the mayoralty of any town in Wales. At his installation luncheon, Wartski said that he regarded his election as a 'deliberate assertion of the principle of religious toleration, or rather religious equality, which was one of the noblest features not only of public life in this country, but also of municipal and political institutions throughout the Empire'.[24] Whether churchman, nonconformist or Jew each mayor led the council in procession to the traditional service held in the cathedral at the outset of the civic year.

A majority of the members were Welsh speaking, including sixteen of the aldermen and twelve of the mayors. The council continued its policy of giving Welsh names to most new streets and the mayor set a precedent in the boroughs of north Wales when he read the proclamation of the accession of King George VI to the throne in December 1936 in Welsh as well as English. Three councillors were members of the 'Gorsedd' of bards, Owen Owen, Richard Thomas and W. J. Owen and it is significant that the National Eisteddfod was thrice held in Bangor during the period: in 1915, 1931 and 1940. Compared with the earlier period the social composition had not changed to any significant degree. Despite the foothold gained by working class men, and the toe hold won by women, the majority of members were middle aged, middle class business and professional men who were Welsh speaking and nonconformist. Mayors elected between 1914 and 1945 illustrate these characteristics (Appendix, Table 17).

Three members of the pre-war council were elected mayor in the years after Richard Williams's retirement. The first, in 1920, was Cllr. Dr John Edward Thomas (1868-1931) who had been deputy mayor throughout Williams's mayoralty. A native of Holywell, Clwyd, he graduated first from the University College, Aberystwyth and then from the University of Edinburgh where he obtained his M.D. degree. An appointment in 1890 as a surgeon at the C. and A. Infirmary brought him to Bangor where he eventually set up in general practice. His medical background made him a fitting chairman of the Health Committee which he served with distinction. He was a Justice of the Peace and devoted much of his time to his chapel, Twrgwyn, and to Welsh cultural activities.

Ald. Owen Owen (1849-1929), who followed Thomas in 1921 was, at seventy-two years of age, the oldest person to hold the mayoralty. He was born in Newborough, Anglesey, but moved with his family first to Bangor then to Blaenau Ffestiniog where his father established drapery businesses. At sixteen years of age Owen was apprenticed to a drapery firm in Birkenhead and three years later he was appointed its representative, first in the north of England then successively in Ireland, south Wales and north Wales. In 1881 he opened up his own drapery business in Birkenhead but a few years later moved to 163/5 High Street, Bangor. Owen, an ardent 'eisteddfodwr', helped to promote the National Eisteddfod in Birkenhead (1878), Liverpool (1884) and Bangor (1890, 1902 and 1915). He was no mean bard and took for his pseudonym the title 'Castellfryn' from the stretch of High Street commonly called 'Castle Hill', where his shop was situated. He promoted also the naming of buildings and streets in Welsh. Owen was an ardent Baptist and a staunch Liberal. On the council, to which he was elected in 1900, he identified himself with the drive for municipal economy.

Owen was followed in 1922 by William Thomas (1867-1935), a native of Holyhead, who came to Bangor in 1887 to manage Dicks Boots and Shoes, the first multiple shop to open in the city. Six years later he opened his own business at 298 High Street and for the next thirty-five years ran a thriving business which was noted for its reliability, courtesy and cheerfulness. He took a deep interest in the religious, moral and cultural affairs of the community. At his chapel,

Tabernacl, he was an elder, secretary (for twenty-five years) and a Sunday School teacher. He was elected onto the council in 1911 as a Liberal and served on it for sixteen years.

The third successive High Street shopkeeper to become mayor was Cllr. Thomas Vallance (1863-1933), a native of Dumfries. He came to Bangor in 1880 to work with another Scot, William Bayne, and then he set up his own business at 246/50 High Street, which he built up into a large and successful one. He was one of the founders of the Bangor Trades Association, the forerunner of the Chamber of Commerce, in the early years of the century and he was a promoter and subsequently chairman of the Bangor Blue Motor Company. He was an elder at Princes Road Presbyterian Church and joined the council in 1918.

Major John Roberts T.D. (1872-1939), a native of Bangor, was elected mayor in 1924. He was the son of Griffith Roberts, a coachbuilder; when the business declined John and his brother set up as house painters. John's particular passion was for the Volunteer Movement. He rose through the ranks of the Caernarvonshire Artillery Volunteers to gain a commission in the Royal Garrison Artillery in 1916. He saw service with the regiment at the Battle of the Somme and at Vimy Ridge and in 1920 he was promoted to command the local battery. He was elected to the council in 1908 as Conservative member for West Ward and served as chairman of the Health Committee and of the Finance Committee. As chairman of the former he was deeply involved in the slum clearance programme of the 1930s. Roberts had a wide range of community interests: the Hot-Pot fund, which rendered excellent service to the indigent, the athletic sports committee, Bangor City Football Club (he was a football referee), the North Wales Society for the Blind which elected him general secretary, the C. and A. Infirmary contribution scheme and Penuel Welsh Baptist chapel. He conducted a choir which he had formed from members of the mission church in Kyffin Square and which won Eisteddfodic successes.

The first person in this period to hold the mayoralty for three consecutive years was Ald. W. R. Jones, J.P. [1874-1949, Plate 4 (iv)]. A native of the Nantlle Valley, he trained to be a teacher at the Normal College and obtained a teaching post at Garth School in 1897. He remained there for forty-two years, thirty-five of them as headmaster. He worked diligently for the improvement of teachers' conditions of employment; he was secretary for thirty-four years of the Caernarvon County Teachers Association and was a teachers' representative on the County Education Committee. At national level he was a member of the N.U.T. Executive Committee and the Burnham Salary Committee. He served on numerous educational bodies: the Court of Governors of the University of Wales and the National Museum of Wales, the Council of University College, Bangor, the Central Welsh Board and the governing bodies of Friars and the Girls' Grammar School. At his chapel, Twrgwyn, he was an elder and chapel secretary and he became Moderator of the Arfon Presbytery in 1932. He was appointed a J.P. in 1919 and was chairman of the Juvenile and Matrimonial Courts. Co-opted onto the council in 1917, he was active on the Pier and Ferry Committee, though his greatest contribution lay in his efforts to secure playing fields and recreation facilities for children. In recognition of his public services he was awarded the O.B.E. in 1936.

John Williams, a native of Bangor, was the other person to serve a three year term as mayor. In 1911 he joined a well known Liverpool firm of colliery agents and in 1925 was appointed their representative in North Wales. He played an active part on a number of charitable committees in the city and was a deacon and treasurer at Pendref Congregational Chapel. He joined the council in 1919 and was mayor at the time when important decisions were made concerning slum clearance and the building of the Maes Tryfan housing estate. Williams represented North Ward on Caernarvonshire County Council for many years.

Another native of Bangor followed John Williams as mayor in 1934. Ald. Richard Thomas (1878-1952) was born in Hirael, the son of Richard Thomas, a sea captain. He became a printer, working for the *North Wales Chronicle*, and entered the council as Labour member for East Ward in 1919. The following year, he took over the Sackville Printing Works and, having become an employer, loosened his ties with the Labour Party and sat as an Independent. He gave valuable service as vice-chairman of the executive committee of the 1931 National Eisteddfod at Bangor and in recognition of his work in this connection was appointed an honorary member of the 'Gorsedd' of bards, taking the bardic name 'Risiart o Hirael'. For many years he represented East Ward on Caernarvonshire County Council; he was a member of St Mary's Church and a lay reader.

In 1935 a well known figure in the religious, social and literary life of north Wales was elected mayor. The Rev. O. Madoc Roberts (1867-1948) was a native of Portmadoc and after holding several pastorates came to Bangor in 1917 to take charge of the Wesleyan bookshop. He was President of the Welsh Wesleyan Assembly, Secretary of the Wesleyan Home Missions Society in north Wales and a popular preacher at 'cyrddau mawr'. As a writer he had a popular and attractive style and among the books he had published is a commentary on the Book of Amos and the novel *Pobl Nant y Gro*. In aiding the poor in Bangor he worked unostentatiously and he ardently supported the council's slum clearance and house building programme. He was mayor at the time of the Maesgeirchen controversy and worked hard to get the measure through council. Loyal and thorough in all his duties, he was a popular mayor.

William Owen (1882-1953), who became mayor in 1937, was brought up in humble circumstances in Hirael. After a period on the staff of the *North Wales Chronicle* he set himself up as an auctioneer and estate agent. Possessed of a shrewd mind and sound business acumen, he built up a successful business in Bangor and later in Llandudno also. He was highly regarded in his profession, becoming President of the Liverpool and North Wales Branch of the Chartered Auctioneers and Estate Agents. An efficient organizer, he first showed his skill in this area as Secretary of four Royal Welsh Shows held in Caernarvonshire in the 1920s and 1930s. He was elected onto the council in 1921, became Chairman of the Gas Committee and the Parks and Open Spaces Committee and was mayor at the outbreak of war in 1939. During the war he was chairman of the local National Savings Committee and organized several successful War Savings Weeks; he was also Chairman of the local Food Control Committee, the Welcome Home Committee and, after the war, the local Festival of Britain Committee. He also served on Caernarvonshire County Council.

Isidore Wartski (1878-1965), mayor from 1939-41, was a devout Jew and a member of the Board of Deputies of British Jews. His father set up a drapery business at 204 High Street in the 1880s and later opened premises in Llandudno. Isidore took over the Bangor business, greatly expanded it and moved into new premises, 196-200 High Street. He was active in promoting Bangor as a shopping centre and gave valuable service to the Chamber of Commerce, as chairman for many years, and the North Wales Holiday Resorts Association. He was elected to the council in 1924, served on most of its committees and was formidable in putting forward his point of view.

At most periods in the history of the council there were exceptionally gifted members who made an invaluable contribution to its work but who, for one reason or another, did not attain the rank of first citizen. Two such persons deserve recognition. Richard Jones (1878-1938) or 'Dickie town', as he was affectionately known, was a native of Hirael and a painter by trade. In his youth he played football for Bangor City and represented Wales in international matches. He was a Bangorian through and through and a tireless champion of the poor and underprivileged. Elected to the council in 1926 he gave unfailing support to its housing programme at every stage and became chairman of the Housing Committee in November 1933, just at the time when the council was about to embark on its slum clearance and house building programme under the Act of 1930. He steered through almost to completion the council's ambitious programme and will be particularly remembered for the determination with which he persevered with the Maesgeirchen scheme. He resolutely defended the decision to build houses there against fierce opposition and had the satisfaction of seeing tenants move in before he died.

Elias Henry Jones, M.A. (1883-1943), had a very different upbringing and career. Born the eldest son of Dr Henry Jones, Professor of Philosophy at the University College, he had a brilliant career in the Universities of Glasgow, Grenoble and Oxford, and at one of the Inns of Court. In 1906 he joined the élitist Indian Civil Service and held appointments in Burma before enlisting for active service when war broke out in 1914. Captured by the Turks in Mesopotamia in 1915, he escaped from a prisoner of war camp in Anatolia and subsequently wrote a book, *The Road to Endor*, in which he recounts how he and fellow prisoners enlisted the aid of the occult to win their way to freedom.[25] After the war he returned to Burma and became a member of the Burmese Legislative Council. His draft scheme for the constitution of the projected University of Rangoon was not accepted and in his disappointment he resigned from the civil service and returned to Wales. He became editor of *Welsh Outlook*, a commentary on Welsh public affairs and lectured at Coleg Harlech for a short time before being appointed Registrar of the University College of North Wales in 1933. Entering the council in 1928, he quickly made his mark, and was soon elected Chairman of the Gas Committee and then of the Finance Committee. He showed a masterly grasp of corporation finance and skilfully brought the council through the very difficult period of the 1930s. Poor health, largely a result of privations under captivity during the war, induced him to resign from the council in 1937 and from his post at the University in 1942.

The council was fortunate in this period in having the services of well qualified, diligent and trustworthy officials. From 1912-39 the town clerk was John Pentir Williams (1867-1939). Born at Tan-y-Foel Farm, Pentir, he was educated at Friars School and became one of the first students to enrol at the new University College in Bangor. After graduating he decided on a career in law and having served his articles with a Bangor solicitor, he set up his own practice in the early 1890s. He entered the council in 1902 as Liberal member for West Ward and was elected mayor in 1911 but he resigned in order to apply for the post of Town Clerk to which he was appointed. During his twenty-seven years in the office he gave wise counsel, particularly in the field of municipal housing which was new and unfamiliar ground for local councils. Pentir Williams was an ardent Liberal in his early days and was an elder at Berea Chapel in Glanadda. His special interest was choral and church music and he was a keen 'eisteddfodwr', giving valuable support to the national eisteddfod held in Bangor in 1915 and 1931. He was an esteemed member of Caernarvonshire County Council, the Council of the University College and the Rotary and Masonic organizations.

On John Gill's retirement in 1924 the council appointed T. P. Francis, a gifted municipal engineer, to the post of Surveyor. He had won a gold medal of the Institute of Municipal and County Engineers and was a Fellow of the Institute of Civil Engineers and of the Surveyors' Institute. To him was given the task of designing the Heol Dewi, Maes-y-Dre and Pen-lôn housing estates. He finally solved the problem of the water supply to Upper Bangor and directed the re-surfacing of High Street, a much needed improvement. He left Bangor in 1929 to become surveyor at Dagenham which was then developing rapidly under the shadow of the new Ford plant. By 1933, however, he had been appointed city engineer of Cape Town, South Africa, but his meteoric career ended suddenly in 1935 with a heart attack.

Possibly the most outstanding servant of the council during the period was B. Price Davies (1889-1954). He came to Bangor with impressive qualifications and an excellent record of service. Trained as a municipal engineer, he served with the Royal Engineers in France in the First World War. After the War he became Surveyor of Works to Cardiff City Council and was involved in that council's early municipal housing schemes. He wrote a book in 1922 entitled *Estimating for Buildings and Public Works* which ran into several editions and his papers on 'The Economics of Road Surfacing' and 'The Arrangement and Economics of a Town Plan' were published in the *Journal of the Institution of Municipal and County Engineers*. For each of three papers on town planning and house design he won a prize awarded by professional organizations. In Bangor he was responsible for improving the reliability and purity of the water supply; he finally solved the problem of the flooding of the Adda and he masterminded the main phases of the council's slum clearance, house building and redevelopment programmes. The sensitive arrangements of houses of differing sizes, height and block lengths on attractively laid out estates and in a variety of design patterns are a living testimony to the expertise and vision of Price Davies.

Even a small city such as Bangor could attract the services of men of high calibre and their genius is indelibly inscribed on the face of the city. With such gifted officers, who were able to comprehend, interpret and give advice on 'the spate of legislation' emanating from Whitehall, the council was able to propel the city forward at what might seem to have been a most unpropitious period in its history. A good representation of the principal men in local business and the professions sought seats on the council during the period and maintained its high standing in the community. An analysis of the membership of the council reveals that it was little changed from the earlier period (Table 15), despite the fact that it now included a few representatives of the Labour Party and a token representation of women. Two forces which divided the council in the pre-1914 period had moderated in their effect: the rivalry between Conservatives and Liberals was replaced by co-operation under the Independent appellation, and the antagonism between members of the Anglican communion and nonconformists gave way to a realization that in rehousing hundreds of families from the nineteenth century slum houses they were jointly discharging a Christian duty. With a greater meeting of minds and fewer controversial subjects to deal with, particularly during the war years, the council appeared to be a more united body. Council elections failed to excite the populace and a degree of contentment if not apathy crept into civic affairs.

*Notes*
1. Words spoken by Ald. R. J. Williams at his installation as mayor for the seventh term in 1919. NWC, 14 November 1919.
2. Although the council decided on 15 June to proceed with the Maesgeirchen scheme, the battle over the site was still raging when the Spanish Civil War broke out on 18 July 1936.
3. NWC, 8 August 1926.
4. See P. E. Jones (1973) Table 6.11, p. 412a.

5.  NWC, 4 March 1932.
6.  NWC, 11 May 1945.
7.  NWC, 19 September 1919.
8.  NWC, 14 November 1919.
9.  NWC, 7 November 1919.
10. NWC, 28 October 1921.
11. Ibid.
12. NWC, 26 February 1937.
13. NWC, 12 March 1937.
14. NWC, 29 October 1937.
15. NWC, 3 March 1939
16. NWC, 7 November 1919.
17. NWC, 29 November 1929.
18. Ibid.
19. NWC, 2 June 1933. The Rev. Glyn Simon later became Archbishop of Wales.
20. NWC, 15 November 1935.
21. NWC, 6 March 1936.
22. NWC, 13 November 1936.
23. NWC, 9 November 1934.
24. NWC, 10 November 1939.
25. *The Road to Endor* (London 1930).

# CHAPTER 7

## 1945 — 1974

'. . . a voracious Whitehall busily monopolizing civic work'.[1]

IN THE period which followed the end of the Second World War the range of services administered by local authorities greatly expanded and there were growing demands from a public whose standards of living and expectations were constantly rising that these services should be efficiently managed. Many of the initiatives for improved and developing services came from central government which, out of Treasury funds, helped to finance the escalating expenditures involved. Indeed, soon after the War, government grants had outstripped rates as a source of local government revenue. The range and importance of local government activities forced national government to take a close interest in the way local councils exercised their powers and they were subject to a spate of regulations, circulars and reports of inspectors which emanated from various government departments.

Soon after the War it had become apparent that some of the services which small municipal authorities provided, such as the gas and fire service, might be better administered by larger bodies or taken out of the control of local authorities altogether. As the years went by the ability of small authorities to command the physical and human resources necessary to cope adequately with the business of government was increasingly questioned. By the mid 1960s it was obvious that the administrative structures created in the nineteenth century were no longer appropriate for the needs of the second half of the twentieth century. In 1966, therefore, the government set up a Royal Commission on Local Government in England under the chairmanship of Lord Redcliffe-Maud to consider the future structure of local government. Evidence which the Commission collated convinced members that major surgery to the system was necessary and that existing structures needed to be replaced and not simply amended.

Although the main recommendations of the Maud Commission's Report,[2] published in 1969, were not accepted by the Conservative government in 1971, they did form the basis for reform. The Local Government Act 1972 swept away the existing system and instituted fundamental changes in structure of local authorities and the assignment of functions to them. The new system came into operation on 1 April 1974.

A review of the Council's activities between 1945 and 1974 must, therefore, be considered against the background of these developments. Although working within the constraints of small size and external control, the council nevertheless had a wide range of discretionary powers, especially in the field of housing and the provision of recreational facilities. The council was, therefore, to retain some degree of initiative in areas which enhanced the quality of life of its citizens. A threefold approach to a study of the council's activities during the period is considered appropriate. Reference will be made in the first place to those services which were removed from the council's jurisdiction; secondly to those services which it continued to administer and finally to the response of the council to the government's plans for the reorganization of local government.

The first of the services over which the council lost control was the fire service. Under the Fire Services Act 1947 all local units were amalgamated to form county services and responsibility for them was vested in county authorities. When proposals for the new Caernarvonshire service were revealed the council considered them to be much too grandiose. In 1939 the Bangor fire service had twelve part-time firemen; under the new scheme the establishment at the Bangor station was fixed at ten full-time and twenty part-time firemen. This was regarded as excessive, particularly in view of the fact that the number of fires dealt with averaged only ten each year in the borough and two in adjoining districts. A rate of 8s. 8d. in the pound was required to support the new service whereas the rate to maintain the Bangor service had been 8d. So began the process of centralization, loss of local control, overmanning and increased costs which came to characterize so many sectors of the public service after 1945. 'This happens', said Huw T. Edwards, a prominent Trade Union leader in North Wales, 'when local government is taken out of the hands of local people and administered from a distance . . . I think this is planning gone mad'.[3] In 1964 the county authority built a new fire station near the junction of Beach Road and Garth Road.

In July 1948 the council handed over its isolation hospital to the

Regional Hospital Board which was created under the National Health Service Act of that year. In the fifty-three years since its establishment the hospital had dealt with 2,860 cases from the borough itself and 1,026 from adjacent local government districts. However, since the early 1940s infectious diseases had almost become a thing of the past so its *raison d'être* no longer existed. In its reorganization and rationalization plans the Regional Hospital Board designated one of the Caernarfon hospitals, Bryn Seiont, an isolation unit, and the Bangor hospital a convalescent unit.

Under the Town and Country Planning Act 1947, planning authority was removed from borough and urban councils and vested in county councils. The lower tier councils were permitted, however, to inspect all plans relating to their areas and to make recommendations to the county authority. County planning authorities henceforth came to exercise a dominant influence over the development of the city in its broader environmental setting. The 1947 Act required the county planning authority to draw up a development plan for the whole area under its jurisdiction and to prepare town plans for the main urban areas. The Bangor Draft Town Plan was published in 1964; the council spent much time discussing its proposals and made a number of recommendations. Many of these were incorporated in the final plan which received Ministry approval in 1968. From that time all developments had to conform to the plan, although procedures were available for these to be amended in appropriate circumstances.

The Electricity Act 1947 created the British Electricity Authority which was given responsibility for the generation and distribution of electricity throughout the country. Assets of local authorities in this field were vested in one of the fourteen area boards set up under the Act. The transfer of Bangor's assets to the Merseyside and North Wales Electricity Board took place on 1 April 1948. Likewise, on 1 May 1949 the assets of the gas department were transferred to the Wales Gas Board, one of the twelve Area Boards set up under the Gas Act 1947.

The last of the city's utilities to be transferred to a larger authority was the water utility. During the post war years the consumption of water rose rapidly due to an increase in the population, particularly in the number of students. New housing estates and student hostels were built and baths and/or showers were installed in scores of houses. To meet the increased demand new storage reservoirs were built at Bryniau (1958) and at Twrgwyn (1959). The Bryniau reservoir was designed to improve the pressure and flow of water in the higher districts between Upper Bangor and Penrhos where the main building developments were taking place. Included in the schemes were new trunk mains to carry water to the reservoirs, new distribution mains and new metering and recording devices. Even so, the needs of the several communities in Caernarvonshire could not be met by the piecemeal developments of each local authority and there was an urgent demand for a comprehensive system which would cut across local government boundaries. The Eryri Water Board was created on 1 April 1967 to take over responsibility for planning and developing a water supply system for the greater part of the county. Later, in 1974, the Eryri Water Board was itself assimilated by the Welsh Water Authority which assumed responsibility for water and sewerage services over the greater part of Wales. Regional headquarters for the Board were built in Penrhos in 1979.

Despite the loss of these major services the council had plenty to concern itself with in the fields of public health, housing and environmental management. The sewerage system was extended and repaired as the need arose but throughout the 1960s it became increasingly apparent that the whole system, laid down and replaced piecemeal, was in need of a major overhaul to meet the increasing demands made upon it. The inadequacy of the system delayed the planned development of land scheduled for private building between Eithinog and Penrhos with a result that builders opened up housing estates for owner occupation along the north shore of the Menai Strait rather than in Bangor. Furthermore, the traditional discharge of sewage in a raw state into the sea was no longer compatible with rising standards of environmental health and the need for a sewage treatment plant became urgent. The council addressed itself to these problems but was deterred by the scale and cost of a major new system. Procrastination seemed justified in the late 1960s when reorganization of local government was imminent and although plans were submitted to the Welsh Office for approval in 1973 there was no possibility of their being implemented. At the time of reorganization the problem was transferred to the Welsh Water Authority which undertook a major sewerage and sewage treatment scheme between 1982 and 1984 costing £2.5 million.

Population growth and rising living standards resulted in an increase in rubbish which had to be collected and disposed of. Tipping at the Wern fields ceased in the early 1960s and the ground was converted into rugby and football pitches. Tipping started on the site of the old reservoir at Hendrewen in 1962 but this was filled within ten years. In the absence of further sites within the city itself the council joined with the Bethesda Urban and Ogwen Rural District Councils to develop a large disused gravel pit near Pentir for tipping purposes, a move which emphasizes the fact that it was necessary for small local authorities to combine in operating basic services even before reorganization of local government occurred.

Environmental health services, the responsibility of the Public Health Inspector, broadened in their scope and had to comply with more stringent standards set by central government. Among the matters for which the Inspector was responsible were the control of pests and air pollution, the inspection of houses as habitable dwellings, of foods retailed, of hotels, cafes and other premises where food was consumed by the public, of factories, shops and other places of employment and the council's abattoir. The state of the abattoir frequently came under close scrutiny. When, in 1949, it was proposed to advance a large sum of money for improvements to it, many councillors were of the opinion that a new one should be built. Periodically over the next twenty-five years proposals to close down the abattoir or to build a new one were discussed. A final decision to close it was taken by the Arfon District Council in 1977.

The administration and upkeep of cemeteries remained under the aegis of the council. In 1947 the idea of a crematorium was mooted by Cllr. Dr Idwal Griffith but his suggestion was premature.[4] The matter was raised again in 1963 and in April 1966 the council decided to proceed with the venture. First of all it sought the support of neighbouring local authorities so that the cost might be shared but apart from Holyhead Urban Council which promised that it would abandon its own plans for a crematorium if one were built in Bangor the response was negative. There was strong opposition in the council to a project lacking adequate outside support; the cost, estimated at £110,000 was too high; the average number of deaths a year in Bangor did not justify it and there were more pressing projects on which to spend such a large sum of money. After much controversy the motion to build a crematorium was carried by sixteen votes to seven in August 1971, by which time the cost had risen to £137,000 (£562,000). Built on a site adjacent to Mynwent Dinas Bangor it was opened by Sir Michael Duff of Vaynol in September 1973.

After the election of a Labour administration in 1945 the building of subsidized public housing was to be a major objective of the government in its effort to overcome the chronic housing shortage of the post-war years. Throughout the period 1945 to 1974 successive governments involved local authorities in the administration of a range of housing initiatives which were wider in their scope than those during the inter-war years yet fluctuated in their impact and degree according to the ideological persuasion of the political party in government at any given time. Reasons for the shortage of houses at the end of the war were several and were related to demographic and social factors. The immediate reason was the fact that no houses had been built for six years. People were living longer and therefore occupied houses for a longer period, a higher proportion of the population was getting married and people were marrying at a younger age. These trends were to become more marked as time went by.

Anticipating a demand for between 400 and 500 houses when the war ended the council submitted a plan for that number to the Welsh Board of Health for its approval. Until the plan became a reality the demand for houses was quite overwhelming as is illustrated by the fact that in November 1945 thirty-nine persons had called at a councillor's home within a few days soliciting his support for the tenancy of a house which was not yet vacant.[5] In January 1945 there were 316 applicants for one house!

Two schemes of a temporary nature were introduced to relieve the immediate problem. Thirty-nine army huts which had been erected during the war on the Beach Road playing field were taken over and converted for family use. The Welsh Board of Health reluctantly sanctioned this expedient on the grounds of the extreme pressure on accommodation at the time. The huts were restyled and were first occupied in 1948. Residents were very dissatisfied with their makeshift homes, however, and constantly drew the attention of the council to their plight. They were resettled in 1951 whereupon the Beach Road site was cleared and reverted to a playing field. The government's short term response to the post-war shortage of houses was to provide factory constructed pre-fabricated bungalows which were relatively cheap to produce and erect. Bangor was allocated fifty of these bungalows and the council sited them at Maesgeirchen. Another ten were put up at Brynllwyd to house key workers employed by British Electrical Meters which had taken over the nearby Daimler factory at the end of the war. Although scheduled to last only ten years the bungalows were not removed until 1966.

The cornerstone of the Labour Government's post-war housing policy was the Housing Act 1946 which was steered through the

House of Commons by Aneurin Bevan, the Minister of Health. Basically the housing programme was intended for 'general needs' rather than for the poor and underprivileged as was the case with the 1930s programme. Bevan strongly criticized the inter-war system which had seen speculative builders construct houses for one income group and local authorities for another with the social polarization it had caused. No clearer example of a 'castrated community', to quote Nye Bevan, could be found than Maesgeirchen. Local authorities, he proposed, should build houses to meet the varied needs of the community and to bring a wide range of social classes together, as occurred in the traditional English village. It was envisaged that house building in the post-war period should be undertaken principally by local authorities and private building was to be severely restricted by the issue of building licences. Generous subsidies of £16.50 per dwelling per annum for sixty years were given to local authorities.

Bevan was also anxious to improve the quality of council built houses and accepted the recommendations of the Dudley Committee on housing standards. These proposed a minimum of 900 feet super. for a three bedroom house, the improved arrangement of space in the house by eliminating the separate parlour for instance, the provision of better amenities, particularly in the bathroom and kitchen and the installation of gas or electric cookers rather than solid fuel ranges. Subsidies under the 1946 Act encouraged the council to embark upon its first major programme of permanent houses. A thirty-four acre site, comprising portions of Coed Mawr Farm, Cae Mab Adda Farm and Bryn Seisyllt had been purchased in stages between 1944 and 1946 and a lay out reminiscent of the formal, geometric shapes of the inter-war period was adopted. The estate was developed in a number of stages. The first contract for 140 houses was awarded in October 1946 and this phase was scheduled for completion in March 1948. However, the contractors ran into difficulties over the site which fell steeply from Penrhos Road and a shortage of building materials and skilled craftsmen compounded their difficulties. Only half the planned number had been built by May 1949 but the contract was completed in the following year.

Besides causing frustration and resentment among those on the waiting list the delay had longer term effects which added to the council's embarrassment. A chronic shortage of materials nationwide induced the government to regulate the number of houses each local authority could build; the standard of reference was the number of houses a council had built in a given period and it was allowed to build only a fixed percentage of that number. Bangor's allocation for 1951 was twenty houses, a totally unacceptable figure in view of the fact that there were 876 persons on the waiting list. Even Bethesda and Menai Bridge were allocated more. Representations to the Welsh Board of Health did result in a slightly higher allocation.

Inevitably the selection of tenants for new houses became an extremely sensitive task. Priority was given to the following groups in this order: sufferers from T.B., those living in overcrowded dwellings, war veterans, married couples in rooms, key workers, and families living in insanitary houses. Accusations were levelled at the Housing Committee from time to time for the inconsistent criteria and the 'hush hush' methods it employed in selecting tenants. Following a spate of complaints the Welsh Board of Health conducted an investigation in January 1949. The Housing Committee, to whom the council had delegated the task of selecting tenants, threatened to resign *en bloc* unless it obtained from the council a vote of confidence for the way it administered the selection procedures. This it received in February 1949.

Between 1950 and 1952 four separate contracts for 118 houses at Coed Mawr were awarded. When completed in 1953 the Coed Mawr scheme comprised 258 houses, 110, or 43 per cent, in semi-detached pairs and 148 in terraces of four houses. Being larger in size and built at lower densities than most of the council's inter-war houses and those it built after 1953 they have higher rateable values, command higher rentals and house a higher class tenant than most of the other council estates.[6]

Contemporary with the major development at Coed Mawr were other smaller housing projects. Two of them were in Hirael. In 1947 the council bought a small plot of land along Seiriol Road from the Trustees of the COPEC group and built nine pairs of semi-detached houses on it. Before the war the council had declared a portion of central Hirael ripe for redevelopment and demolition of insanitary dwellings had begun. Demolition continued in 1946 and on the cleared site twelve houses, twenty-two flats and nine garages were built between 1947 and 1951.[7]

The presence of large numbers of elderly people in the community, many of whom lived on their own, induced the council to erect flats to accommodate them. Flats were built both in slum clearance areas such as Hirael and Britannia Square in Upper Bangor and on the large inter-war council estates where there was by now an ageing population. Britannia Square, where over thirty small cottages had been built in the 1850s on not much more than half an acre of land, was the subject of a demolition order in 1936. Demolition commenced in 1939 and continued after the war. When the time came to redevelop the site in 1951 there were acute shortages of building materials and the council was obliged to comply with a government regulation to build a prescribed proportion of all new houses from pre-fabricated sections. Twelve flats in three two-storey blocks were built in non-traditional materials in 1951-52. The first flats built on an inter-war council estate were on Penrhyn Avenue, Maesgeirchen, where a block of twenty-four was built in 1950.

The Conservative Party in opposition was highly critical of the Labour administration's record on housing. In its 1951 election manifesto it pledged itself, if elected, to build 300,000 houses a year by cutting bureaucratic procedures and encouraging private enterprise and owner occupation. Houses built by local authorities were to contribute to the total and the Housing Act of 1952 raised the standard annual subsidy on such houses to £35.60. Stimulated by the subsidy the council planned a development of 238 houses on a portion of the Penrhyn Estate which lay to the west of the existing settlement at Maesgeirchen. Built between 1953 and 1958 the houses reflect the lower quality and space standards which the government had introduced in order to meet its widely acclaimed target. Houses are smaller in size (750-850 feet super.), are built on smaller plots of land and are generally in longer terraces than those at Coed Mawr.

Houses built in the late 1940s and 1950s are more uniform in their design than those built in the inter-war years. Monotonous rough cast elevations contrast with the exposed brick facings or brick and rough cast facings of the earlier period. Bay windows are entirely absent in the Maesgeirchen houses and there are no gables to add interest to the longer rows of terraces. Roof styles are more uniform with some hipped types in Coed Mawr but straight ended forms in Maes-geirchen. Once the government had met its commitment to build 300,000 houses a year it was free to pursue the principal objective of its housing policy which was to encourage the private housing sector. Whilst giving a range of incentives to owner occupiers it passed the Housing Subsidies Act 1956 which cut the subsidy payable to local authorities for 'general needs' houses. House building by the council came to an abrupt halt and national resources were diverted to the private sector.

The council gave every support to the private builder. In 1953 it bought Eithinog Farm near the western margins of the city for

£28,000 (£210,000); it laid roads and mains services and divided the land into plots for private development. It was specified that the minimum size of dwelling should be 1,050 feet super. and, due to the predetermination of plot size, a low density development was ensured. House building began in 1955 and by 1974 one hundred and twenty-one dwellings had been built. Since several builders were involved in developing the estate a variety of house designs was achieved. Government funds were also available to enable the council to advance money to potential owner occupiers on the security of their property. Powers to advance money for house purchase had first been given to local authorities under the Small Dwellings Acquisition Act 1899 and about £130,000 had been lent by the Bangor Council under this and later Acts. The Housing (Financial Provisions) Act 1958 empowered local authorities to lend up to 100 per cent of the value of a house. Between 1955 and 1970 the council under its mortgage loan scheme advanced £227,000 to prospective home owners.

Although subsidies for houses for 'general needs' were cut by the Housing Subsidies Act 1956, exchequer grants were still available for certain categories of 'special needs', such as people displaced by slum clearance and the elderly. This Act gave councils a renewed incentive to demolish slum property. Further areas of Hirael were declared clearance areas in 1955 and 1959 and on the cleared sites ten three bedroom houses, a three storey block of flats and a four storey block of sixteen maisonettes were built. This phase of redevelopment obliterated the previous street plan and brought back greensward to an area which had been covered by buildings at high density for nearly 150 years. Demolition of houses on Caernarfon Road near the junction with Ainon Road was followed by the construction of a block of eighteen flats and maisonettes on the site in 1961. Smaller demolition schemes followed in Berllan Bach (1965-67), in Lon-y-Popty (1968) and in Upper Bangor, in Albert Street, Victoria Street, Hill Street (1970) and Vron Square; in the main these more confined areas have been converted into temporary car parks. More flats for the elderly were added to inter-war council estates: Greenfield Avenue, Maesgeirchen (1961), Ffordd Cynfal (1963) and Lon-y-Glyder, Maes Tryfan (1964).

Demolition was only one solution to the problem of sub-standard housing. Another was the repair and modernization of houses, which, although old, were soundly constructed. Improvement grants had been available to both landlords and owner occupiers under the Housing Act 1949 and these were raised by the Housing Repairs and

Rent Act 1954. The Housing Act of 1959 made it mandatory for local authorities to give grants to people for home improvements and a stream of applications flowed into the Town Hall. In scores of homes a bedroom was converted into a bathroom with a W.C., an extension was added to the rear of houses to accommodate a larger kitchen and/or bathroom with a W.C. and hot and cold water systems were installed. Grants were also made towards the cost of converting large houses into flats, a process which the council encouraged in the 1950s to help alleviate the chronic housing shortage. Many large villas and terraced houses in Upper Bangor in particular were converted at this time.

The council was assiduous in upgrading its own housing stock. An extension, comprising a scullery, bathroom and W.C. was added in 1955 to the houses built under the Workmen's Dwelling Act 1890, and onto a row of six cottages at Ael-y-Bryn which it had purchased in 1926, both in the teeth of opposition from tenants. Sculleries were built onto houses in the Maes Tryfan Estate (1965) and the Tyn-y-Caeau Estate (1970). As a result of the considerable reduction in personnel employed at the station, the British Railways Board in 1966 offered for sale the whole of its estate of sixty-seven houses. The council bought the estate and undertook the installation of working kitchens, bathrooms and W.C.s: in three bedroom houses the smallest bedroom was converted into a bathroom and W.C. and onto the rear of two bedroom ones an extension was built to accommodate a larger kitchen, bathroom and W.C.

By the beginning of the 1960s there persisted a shortage of houses nationwide for members of the lower income groups. The Conservatives in their Housing Act 1961, therefore, restored subsidies for houses built by local authorities for 'general needs'. In response to the Act the council in 1961 purchased Tan-y-Bryn from the Penrhyn Estate together with twenty-four acres of land. The fields lying between Tan-y-Bryn and the A5 road were designated an open space under the terms of the purchase agreement, the house itself was sold to the Youth Hostels Association and land adjoining the original settlement at Maesgeirchen was set aside for housing. With the return of a Labour government in 1964 there was a greater commitment once again to build public sector houses. Housing had been a key issue in the election of that year, the Labour Party pledging itself, if elected, to build 500,000 houses a year by 1970. Assisted by subsidies under the Housing Act 1961 the council proceeded in 1966 with a planned development of 234 dwellings and 125 garages at Tan-y-Bryn at a contract price of £800,000 (£4,240,000).

Incorporating many aspects of advanced planning design and having more flats and maisonettes than houses, the appearance of Tan-y-Bryn is in marked contrast to other council estates. In planning the estate the natural environment, layout, design and elevation of buildings, and the arrangement of play areas, open space and street systems were considered together in one unified design. Only one through road traverses the estate and the other roads are culs-de-sac which afford a high degree of penetration to each housing group. The estate comprises 102 three bedroom houses, ninety-four two bedroom flats and maisonettes in four storey blocks and thirty-eight two bedroom flats in two storey blocks. Housing units are grouped together to form six courts each having its own identity and name evocative of the Knights of the Round Table. There is a pleasing blend of housing units and styles which is enhanced by different shades of facing brick and pre-fabricated units. Solid fuel central heating was installed in the houses and gas ducted warm air in the flats and maisonettes, thereby obviating the need for the traditional chimney. Garages were built in two batteries on each side of the estate but twenty-four houses were provided with integral garages, an innovation on a council estate. Open space, greensward and mature trees make this an aesthetically pleasing development [Plate 8 (ii)].

The estate, which was opened by George Thomas M.P., Secretary of State for Wales, in October 1968, has not been without its problems, however. Dampness and condensation, for which new building materials and constructions are probably to blame, have proved intractable; some tenants find central heating expensive; children playing on the central stairways of the blocks of flats cause annoyance; and rubbish accumulates in the stair wells. To this day the council has often had difficulty in letting parts of the estate.

The country's economic difficulties, culminating in the devaluation of the pound in 1967, forced the government in 1968 to drastically reduce its house building programme and to encourage instead the improvement of old houses. Compared with comprehensive re-development, rehabilitation was a cheaper alternative. The Housing Act 1969, which raised substantially the grants available for rehabilitation, embodied the government's new philosophy. Additional grants were available for councils to acquire old property for the purpose of improving it. The council purchased two terraces of houses in Fountain Street, Hirael in 1971 and approved plans for upgrading them. A few months before reorganization in 1974 the council approved a scheme costing £2 million for the improvement of 600 of its inter-war houses; bathrooms were to be extended, new windows inserted, central heating was to be installed and complete re-wiring to be carried out.

With the Conservatives in government between 1970 and 1974 the emphasis again shifted to the encouragement of owner occupation. Council housing, on the other hand, was reduced to the role of providing accommodation for the poor and the elderly. The Housing Finance Act 1972, which reduced government subsidies on council houses and raised council house rents to levels which might be considered 'fair', had as an objective the transfer of the better-off council tenants to the owner occupied sector. The legislation also gave to the government the power of determining council house rents, a move which further eroded the powers of local authorities. In order to protect the worse off council tenants a system of rent rebates was inaugurated and councillors and their officials spent long hours deliberating as to who among their tenants were eligible for rent rebates. The government also encouraged local authorities to sell council houses and housing associations to provide private rented accommodation. Bangor Council finally decided not to sell any of its houses[8] but it did sell land on the Eithinog Estate to a company which raised two blocks of flats for private rental. The Llys Mair development (1974) was highly contentious and hotly debated in council since it was considered an unwarranted intrusion into a private housing estate and it disfigured the Belmont skyline as seen from Anglesey.

When the census was taken in 1971 nearly half the households and half the population of Bangor lived in council property. These are higher percentages than those obtained in any other local government district in north west Wales (except Llangefni) and well above the Wales and national figures.[9] In building about 950 modern dwellings and demolishing in the region of 250 old, substandard properties, the council significantly ameliorated housing conditions in Bangor. Data relating to household amenities reveal that in 1971 a very high proportion of households possessed the exclusive use of a fixed bath or shower, an indoor W.C. and a hot water system (Table 8).

Some idea of the progress made in the provision of household amenities may be gathered from a comparison of the data relating to households having the exclusive use of a fixed bath (Table 9).

TABLE 8

*Availability of Household Amenities, 1971*

| Households with exclusive use of: | Number | % of total |
|---|---|---|
| fixed bath or shower | 3,890 | 89.1 |
| flush indoor W.C. | 3,655 | 83.7 |
| hot water system | 4,065 | 93.1 |
| all three amenities | 3,585 | 82.1 |
| Total households = 4,365 | | |

*Source: Census 1971*

TABLE 9

*Households having the exclusive use of a fixed bath*

| Year | Number | % of total |
|---|---|---|
| 1951 | 2,492 | 65.9 |
| 1961 | 3,291 | 82.3 |
| 1971 | 3,890 | 89.1 |

*Source: Census 1951, 1961 and 1971*

Overcrowding had been progressively reduced: the proportion of persons living at a density of more than 1½ persons per room decreased from 5 per cent in 1951 to 1.9 per cent in 1971.

Housing was only one aspect of urban development during the period. The Town and Country Planning Act 1947 vested in local authorities a far greater degree of control over the form of urban growth and the Town Plan produced by the County Planning Authority in 1961 unveiled the strategy for that growth. Prime consideration was given in the Plan to the comprehensive re-development of the city centre, a much needed objective if it was to maintain and consolidate its position as the major regional retail and commercial centre in north west Wales. The commercial core of the city is unique in that it is concentrated almost entirely along a three-quarter mile length of High Street, which had been for centuries the main thoroughfare. The street is narrow and despite the operation of a one-way traffic system, congestion was caused by street parking and by the loading and unloading of commercial vehicles. Until restrictions were enforced, the narrow streets leading off High Street were also used for parking, thereby compounding the congestion. Vehicles and pedestrians vied with each other and environmental standards were lowered by the constant noise of vehicles and exhaust fumes.

The Town Plan was intended to alleviate these problems by the following means. Firstly, shopping facilities were to be concentrated in a half mile stretch of High Street between the entrance to Kyffin Square and James Street. In this context it proposed the re-development of the Berllan Bach area, between the cathedral and town clock, as a multi-storey shopping precinct. Secondly, High Street between Lon-y-Popty and Glynne Road was to be pedestrian-ized. Thirdly, two distributor roads were to be constructed at the rear of existing High Street premises for the use of vehicles visiting the central area and for servicing the shops. Finally, the provision of adequate parking areas, some of which would have to be multi-storey, was planned. In response to the inevitable criticism of the proposals the County Planning Officer forecast ruin if the plans were not implemented and advised that the matter should be taken in hand soon, otherwise the city centre 'would be engulfed by the motor car'.[10]

In the last ten years of its life the council took tentative steps towards implementing what after all was a long term objective, Partial pedestrianization of High Street was inaugurated on 7 September 1973 and some land to the rear of the shops was purchased and cleared for parking. In November 1973 plans were revealed for the con-struction by a property development company of a fully covered multi-storey shopping mall at Berllan Bach but no visible developments have yet occurred.

Two further recommendations contained in the Town Plan require consideration, namely, the confinement of the expansion of the University and the development of the central area of Maesgeirchen. Throughout the post-war period the council actively supported the expansion plans of the city's colleges but it had reservations about the encroachment of university buildings south of Deiniol Road. In 1965, for example, the council earmarked a site off Dean Street for its new indoor swimming pool but it was the university's application for the site for the extension of the Department of Electronic Engineering which received the approval of the County Planning Authority. There were cries of 'land grabbing' and 'college buildings are strangling Bangor'.[11] Similar opposition greeted the decision of the University

College to purchase Deiniol Secondary School when it was vacated in 1971 but since the land was designated for educational use in the Town Plan the purchase was approved by the Planning Authority. In Upper Bangor the University College had bought property piecemeal as it became vacant for offices, lecture rooms and living accommodation; the Town Plan, however, restricted the college's encroachment to a specific area adjacent to the college itself.

Maesgeirchen was built with scant provision for urban services. Only four shops were included in the original scheme. In 1946 the Y.M.C.A. erected a pavilion which was put to a wide range of community uses, including religious and recreational ones. A Presbyterian Church was built in 1952 and the Church in Wales built Eglwys-y-Groes in 1958. Anticipating an increase in the population of Maesgeirchen to 3,000 when the Tan-y-Bryn extension was completed (1968) the council planned to provide more community facilities, including a post office, public house, health centre, sports hall, sheltered housing for the elderly and shops, but no start had been made on implementing this plan before 1974. A long-standing plan to build a primary school was consummated in 1969.

Matters relating to roads and traffic occupied much of the council's time. Streets and pavements had to be maintained, cleaned and lit and although the council had no statutory powers with regard to either the movement or street parking of vehicles, it acted as spokesman for the city in these matters. Immediately after the war the relief of traffic congestion in High Street became a controversial issue once again. In October 1946 the council, supported by the Chamber of Commerce, recommended a one way flow of traffic down the High Street with parking on the north side of the street only and, with Ministry of Transport approval, it was inaugurated in October 1948. Continued congestion five years later led the council to recommend a 'no parking' restriction between the Castle Hotel and Waterloo Street, the narrowest section of High Street. Subsequently parking was restricted to a period of twenty minutes between the entrance to Kyffin Square and the Castle Hotel, and between Waterloo Street and James Street. These restrictions constrained motorists to park on streets close to the High Street, thereby transferring the inconvenience to these streets and annoying the residents. The obvious solution to the problem was to provide parking grounds but there was little land available for this purpose. By developing land in the Dean Street area, in Berllan Bach, the Deanery grounds, Kyffin Square, behind the Castle Hotel and opposite Plas Llwyd Terrace small though inadequate car parks were created. Problems arose when shop and office workers parked their cars in the parks adjacent to High Street and left them there all day, thereby depriving shoppers of their use. In 1965 the council decided to charge for parking in some of their grounds. The intention was to channel long stay motorists to the park at the lower end of Dean Street where they could park for the whole day for a shilling; at parks nearer the High Street a charge of one shilling was levied for a stay of up to two hours. The implementation of this scheme caused a furore; motorists boycotted, albeit for a short while, the parks and created even greater congestion in streets near High Street. Chronic traffic congestion and inadequate car parking facilities led the County Planning Department to recommend the pedestrianization of High Street and the building of multi-storey car parks.

Similar problems faced the council in other parts of the city, notably Upper Bangor, through the centre of which passes the A5 trunk road. No-waiting restrictions were applied on this and tributary roads and the bowling green was converted into a car park. The whole length of the A5· passing though Bangor carried a heavy volume of traffic, especially in the summer months and a number of schemes were proposed to relieve the city of through traffic. However, it was not until after the reorganization of local government that the route of a by-pass for Bangor was approved. Work began in 1980 and the by-pass was opened in December 1983.

Several important schemes were implemented for improvements in recreational facilities and the environmental appearance of the city. Three interesting projects were completed near the city centre. Firstly, the old graveyard at Tan-y-Fynwent, which had not been used for burials since about 1870, was presented to the council by the Dean and Chapter of the Cathedral in 1939. A record of the inscriptions on the tombstones was made before they were removed and the ground was levelled and grassed over. Trees were preserved, flower borders and shrubs planted and paths laid down. Opened by the mayor in June 1951, it is a peaceful retreat from the bustle of the nearby town centre. Eight years later a section of the garden was designated a garden for the blind.

In 1958 the church authorities presented a portion of the cathedral close to the council with the stipulation that it should remain an open space in perpetuity. An attractive design was drawn up which incorporated a small open air theatre and a Bible Garden. The idea of a Bible Garden was conceived by Dr Tatham Whitehead, O.B.E., who had been Chief Plant Pathologist for Wales at the National Agricultural Advisory Service Centre at Bryn Adda, and who was a member of the council from 1959 until his death in 1964. On the upper side of a curved walkway, plants traditionally associated with the Christian festivals and the saints were planted while on the lower side trees, shrubs and flowers specifically mentioned in the Bible were arranged in chronological sequence, starting with a symbolic representation of the creation, passing through 'the fall of man' and 'the deluge' and ending with the Judas tree. When it was opened by the Bishop of Bangor on 4 May 1962 the garden was the only one of its kind in the world and it has attracted visitors from many countries.

Another church property, the former Canonry, lying between Tan-y-Fynwent and the Bible Garden was purchased by the University College in 1951. It was converted into an exhibition gallery and museum. Contents of the museum housed in the former Girls' Grammar School in Upper Bangor, among them many items which had been transferred there from the city's museum in 1940, were now assembled at this more central location in 1970.

Two attractive areas of open space were presented to the city during the period. In 1953, to commemorate the coronation of Queen Elizabeth II, Sir Michael Duff conveyed the freehold of Menai Woods, and in 1968 Mrs Wartski bought from the Vaynol Estate and donated a number of fields lying between the Look Out and the Strait in memory of her husband, Isidore Wartski. The fields formed a portion of Nantporth Farm, the whole of which is designated land of great landscape value and its scenic attractions are protected.

The council responded to demands for recreational facilities for citizens of all ages. In 1950 it finally completed laying out the surface of the old tip at Glanadda as a recreational park, incorporating a bowling green, tennis courts, a putting course and a children's play area, with funds derived from the King George V Playing Foundation. Playground equipment was installed at several sites throughout the city and in 1971 a children's paddling pool, landscaped gardens and rockeries were laid out on a site adjoining the indoor swimming baths.

The history of the Siliwen baths in the post-war period was one of declining receipts and escalating costs. Fears were raised in the mid 1950s about the safety of the baths in view of increased pollution in the Strait. Bacteriological tests conducted in 1958 confirmed the presence of pathogenic organisms in the water and the Medical Officer of Health was not prepared to issue a certificate of safety unless complete and effective chlorination could be undertaken. There was no means of ensuring this so in May 1958 the council closed the baths. Thus came to an end nearly one hundred years of sea bathing at Siliwen. The council was determined that the long tradition of bathing in Bangor should not be broken and decided to erect indoor swimming baths nearer the town centre. A site adjacent to Garth Road was finally designated and a tender for £150,000 (£840,000), submitted by Messrs. Pochins Ltd., was accepted in 1964. The baths were opened on 22 October 1966. The heated swimming pool, measuring 110 feet by 42 feet and having a depth varying from three feet six inches to twelve feet six inches at the diving end, complies with the standards of the Amateur Swimming Association and caters for international competitions. There is also a spectators' gallery which seats 200 people and a cafeteria overlooking the pool. The baths have proved an immensely popular venue for people of all ages from Bangor and the surrounding districts and an added attraction for holidaymakers. An annual average of nearly 200,000 bathers and 28,000 spectators were admitted in the years between 1968 and 1974. Various clubs were formed, swimming was put on the curriculum of the city's schools and trainee teachers at the city's three teacher training institutions were taught to instruct children in the skills of swimming and lifesaving. Control of the baths passed to the Arfon Borough Council in April 1974.

Books borrowed from the library increased from less than 70,000 a year in 1945 to over 200,000 in 1970. The library was remodelled in the late 1950s to give it a more welcoming appearance and a children's library was designated. A collection of music on records and cassettes was established in the mid 1960s.

Soon after the end of the war in Europe the decking which had been removed from the pier was replaced and the pier was re-opened in the autumn of 1945. Its future remained very uncertain, however. An attempt to sell it in 1947 failed and the Pier and Ferry Committee recommended to the council in 1949 that the pier should be dismantled. The council turned down this recommendation and instead voted £6,250 for essential repairs. Attempts were made to organize entertainments such as dances during the summer months but with little real success and the deficit on the pier amounted to about £6,000 a year in the late 1960s. In 1968 a subsidiary of the Forte organization, which had bought the piers at Llandudno and Colwyn Bay, was approached but it showed no interest in buying it. A company was eventually found which was interested in building an amusement arcade at the entrance to the pier. Several councillors opposed the project on the grounds that the development would intrude into the peace and scenic beauty of the spot. They thought that a development of this nature would mar the city's image and feared that the area around the pier might come to resemble 'one of Rhyl's slot machine dens'.[12] The council's decision to proceed with the project was greeted with a demand from ratepayers for a referendum. A poll of readers canvassed by the *North Wales Chronicle* revealed that 81 per cent of those who responded thought that a referendum should be held on the proposal to build an amusement arcade at the pier and 75 per cent thought that the council should retain control of the pier. The reaction of people to the project convinced the council that it was not in the best interests of the city whereupon it terminated discussions with the development company.

Deep concern about the deteriorating condition of the pier in the late 1960s led the council to commission a firm of consulting engineers to inspect the pier. Their report highlighted the serious state of decay and delapidation in which they had found it and estimated the cost of repairing and restoring it in the region of £300,000 (£1,290,000). In view of the dangerous condition of the pier the council had no option but to close it in April 1971. Undaunted by the situation, however, the council seized the initiative. It drew up a comprehensive development plan for Garth Point which included the repairing of part of the pier and the building of a hotel and yachting marina, thereby creating a new coastal environment at Garth which would blend with the town and its natural surroundings. Of course, the whole project was dependent on private capital and in the inflationary days of the early 1970s this was not forthcoming.

The next move on the council's part was the setting up of a Pier Development Committee under the chairmanship of Cllr. George Gibbs. Failing to attract private investment the council resolved in March 1973 to proceed itself with the repair and renovation work. The decision received a mixed reception. Petitions signed by several thousand people were presented to the council calling upon it to repair the pier. Opponents of the scheme pointed out that for the price of renovating the pier the council could build two community centres and two sports complexes, lay out half a dozen football pitches and grant free transport to senior citizens for years, all of which, they considered, would be more worthwhile than repairing the pier.

In view of the high cost of renovating the pier the council decided that a referendum should be held so that citizens might determine its future. This was only the second referendum the council had held in its history – the first, in 1896, was on whether or not the people of Bangor wanted a pier. The facts were laid before them: the cost of repairing and renovating a shortened pier and developing the immediate vicinity would be £360,000. Voting took place in June 1973 and although there were 10,000 people on the electoral roll only 1,419 troubled to vote; 625 persons were in favour of repairing the pier and 794 against, a majority of 169 against. Apart from highlighting the conspicuous apathy of the people the result was inconclusive. With reorganization of local government pending the council agreed not to proceed with its plan and the pier which had once been the centre of so much activity and fun was left forsaken, open only to the elements which continued their relentless attacks unhindered.

The council's own home, the town hall, was experiencing a slow, insidious attack from another source. A report presented in 1956 alerted the council to the dangerous condition of the roof and the external walls (portions of which were half timber work plastered over), due to worm and beetle attack. Since the building was designated one of 'historical and architectural interest' the council decided to preserve as far as practicable the style and character of the building in the reconstruction plans. Concern for the city's heritage in the post-war period contrasted with the decision taken in the 1930s, though not implemented, to demolish the building and construct a new town hall on the site. Additional office accommodation, built in harmony with the old building, was added to the east wing. Reconstruction cost £27,500 (£165,000) and the town hall was re-opened by Sir Michael Duff on 4 May 1962 [Plate 9 (i)].

Attacks on the council's property came too from another more reprehensible direction. Facilities it had provided for the benefit of citizens seemed to be a target for mindless vandalism. No period was free from such acts. In the period 1880 to 1914 the council's notice was frequently drawn to the wholesale and wanton damage done to its property on the Bangor Mountain recreation ground in particular. Street lamps were a prime target for young offenders, kiosks on the pier were damaged and disfigured and flowers planted in the cemetery were removed. Newly planted trees along Deiniol Road and new gates erected at the entrance to Roman Camp were additional items to be vandalized in the inter-war years. Incongruously, after 1945, growing affluence and rising standards of education were accompanied by a mounting wave of vandalism. Between 1948 and 1952 the cost of repairing damage to council property averaged £500 a year and it steadily increased after that time. The mayor, in his installation speech in 1952, referred to the wanton damage inflicted on council property: public conveniences were wrecked, plants uprooted, trees sawn down and seats in public places broken. From that time on, mayors frequently drew the public's attention to the upward trend in vandalism and to the resulting costs. The problem was compounded in the 1960s and 1970s by the activities of members of the Welsh Language Society who, in pursuit of their policies, systematically daubed paint over or removed English street name-plates.

No generation of councillors has been able to find a solution to the problem of vandalism. In November 1894 and in January 1901 the council asked the public to assist in the protection of council property and offered a reward for information leading to the conviction of any person wilfully damaging it. In the 1950s and 1960s mayors frequently called on the public to 'wage war on the wreckers' by forming volunteer warden groups to patrol parks and public places. Rewards were again offered to anyone reporting an act of vandalism leading to a prosecution but there is no evidence of any response from citizens.

While seemingly ineffective in countering the attacks of vandals on its property the council was totally incapable of withstanding the forces which led eventually to its own demise in 1974. Doubts had been raised in the late 1930s about the viability of small municipal councils in the face of increasing central government involvement and control (p. 161). Pessimism was rife in the early post-war years. Ithel Williams, in his installation speech in 1946, prophesied that 'we are on the verge of great social and economic changes (that) will inevitably affect the system of local government in this country'. He thought the changes would 'radically affect the status of the smaller authorities' and would strike at the very roots of healthy local government . . . It is a fundamental principle of democratic government in this country that the government should be as near as possible to the people who are being governed. 'The smaller local authorities', he considered, 'are the most democratic of all institutions and it would be a tragedy if we allow them to fall into decay'.[13] The mayor in 1947 was even more pessimistic: he saw a 'voracious Whitehall busily monopolizing civic work'[14] and despondently predicted that he might well be the last mayor of Bangor! Throughout the 1950s and 1960s the government regulated the activities of local authorities with greater rigour and contributed large sums to support the higher standards of services which they provided.

Pressures for reform culminated in the Local Government Act 1972. The Act created two tiers of local government at county and district level: both were to be larger and therefore better staffed and better equipped than most of their predecessors and would have more control over those public resources which would affect the development of their services. The new units were to accord more closely with the living and working patterns of modern society based on the interdependence of town and country created by the increase in personal mobility (see p. 26-7). To the large and powerful county councils was allocated the major share of local government activity. The three counties of north west Wales were amalgamated to form the county of Gwynedd with responsibility for, *inter alia*, education, the social services, fire service, traffic and highways and town and country and transport planning. Housing, development control, public health, and rate collection became the responsibility of district councils. The municipal boroughs of Bangor and Caernarfon, the urban district of Bethesda and the rural districts of Ogwen and Gwyrfai were amalgamated to form the Arfon district.

Bangor City Council protested vehemently against the lower tier proposals; the council in its present form would cease to exist and its major responsibilities would be transferred to the Arfon District Council which would administer an area stretching from Aber in the north to the Nantlle Valley in the south. Comprising two distinct natural regions traditionally focusing on Bangor and Caernarfon, it had no common centre or community of interest. In fact, Bangor's ties with southern Anglesey had always been very much closer than they were with Caernarfon and Gwyrfai and the principle that the new councils should reflect the interdependence of a centre and its sphere of interest was difficult to reconcile in this case. The mayor, Cllr. Vivian Lewis, in his installation speech in 1971, said that his council was determined not to be swamped in a massive mid-Caernarvonshire district authority and promised that it would 'fight any such proposals to the bitter end'.[15] This indeed it did, carrying the fight onto the floor of the House of Commons. As an alternative to the Arfon district the council proposed a district comprising the existing Bangor, Bethesda and Ogwen local government districts; a strong community of interest had matured between the slate quarrying area and its port of export. These districts persuaded the constituency M.P., Mr Wyn Roberts, to move an amendment to the Local Government Bill, when it was debated in the House of Commons, calling for a separate Nant Ffrancon Authority. Inevitably, the amendment was defeated on the grounds that the population of the proposed district (*c.* 24,000) did not reach the threshold of 40,000 people which was considered to be the minimum required to support the range of services prescribed for a district council and the council had to bow to the inevitable.[16]

The last two years of the council's life were overshadowed by its impending dissolution. Important projects such as a new sewerage system, the redevelopment of the Berllan Bach area, the development of the central area of Maesgeirchen and the scheme for improving scores of the council's pre-war houses were shelved. In the final year much time was taken up in arranging the transfer of powers to the Arfon authority.

Two events brightened its last months, however. The first was the signing on 28 September 1973 of twinning charters by the representatives of Bangor and those of Soest, an ancient cathedral city situated in the state of North Rhine-Westphalia in the German Federal Republic. The two cities solemnly committed themselves to keep in touch with one another constantly and to provide exchanges among their citizens in order to develop a true feeling of unity. Soon, mutual exchanges and visits became a common occurrence.

The second event, on the last Saturday of the council's existence, was a ceremony to confer upon several persons and institutions who had served the city well over the years the honorary freedom of the ·city. The persons honoured were: six aldermen, who had also been mayors of the borough and who had served the council for an aggregate of 173 years; Sir Michael Duff, for his faithful association with the civic life of Bangor and Angus Macdermid, a native of Bangor who had been the B.B.C.'s correspondent in South Africa and Washington and who had started his career on the staff of the *North Wales Chronicle* reporting, among other events, council meetings. Representative personalities received the honour on behalf of the C. and A. Infirmary, the University College and the B.B.C., three institutions which had played a significant role in the development of the city. The leader of the Deiniolen Silver Band was honoured for the contribution the band had made to the public life of the city. The previous Saturday the city had similarly honoured the R.A.F. Station, Valley. After that ceremony in the grounds of the University College a procession marched through the streets of the city to the town hall. These ceremonies were a fitting climax to over ninety years of administration by the city council and mark the end of a chapter in the civic history of Bangor.

*Notes*

1. Words spoken by the Mayor, Ald. Glynne Owen, at his installation ceremony in 1947, NWC, 14 November 1947.
2. Royal Commission on Local Government in England, Report, Cmnd. 4040.
3. NWC, 19 December 1947.
4. NWC, 1 August 1947.
5. NWC, 2 November 1945.
6. Since the passing of the Housing Act 1980 sixty-one houses at Coed Mawr, *c.* 23 per cent of the total, have been sold to tenants.
   By 31 December 1983, 11.6 per cent of council houses in Bangor had been sold. *Source:* Arfon Borough Council.
7. Houses and flats were built facing Ambrose Street and Edmund Street.
8. The Council accepted the principle of the sale of its houses in November 1972 but it rescinded its decision the following February.
9. Per cent of households living in council property: Llangefni 64, Bangor 45, Caernarvonshire 24, England & Wales 29.
10. NWC, 9 May 1970.
11. NWC, 5 November 1965.
12. NWC, 10 April 1969.
13. NWC, 15 November 1946.
14. NWC, 14 November 1947.
15. NWC, 27 May 1971.
16. Fourteen of the 296 districts created had a population below 40,000; the smallest, Teesdale in Co. Durham, had fewer than 25,000 people.

*Plate 6.* (i) Mrs Elsie Chamberlain, J.P.; Mayor 1941-43.
(ii) Price F. White, Electrical and Gas Engineer, 1899-1941.
(iii) B. Price Davies, Surveyor, 1929-44.
(iv) W. Elwyn Jones, B.A., Ll.B.; Town Clerk, 1939-68.

*Plate 7.* Bangor City Council, 1953.

*Back row, from left to right:* Norman Gibbons (Deputy Town Clerk), G. W. Outram (Sanitary Inspector), Angus McDermid (N. W. Chronical Reporter), Caradog Jones, Iorwerth Hughes, Mervyn O. Hughes, L. O. Arridge (Librarian), Vivian Lewis, Ungoed Evans, R. J. Buckland, R. T. Williams, O. E. Griffiths.

*Middle row:* Cyril Richard (Surveyor), Eirwyn Owen, O. T. Pritchard, James Fielding, G. H. Burgess, Patrick Hogan, Pat Burgess, Eric Whitworth, Robert Owen, Stanley Davis, Mrs M. L. Brambell, W. H. Edwards, W. Stake (Treasurer).

*Front row:* William Owen, Ithel Williams, Rev. Gerallt Davies (Mayor's Chaplain), W. Elwyn Jones (Town Clerk), Hugh J. Jones (Mayor), Mrs Jones (Mayoress), Emrys W. Edwards (Deputy Mayor), O. Glynne Owen, F. W. Pozzi, Ioan Y. Glynne.

*Absent:* W. S. Williams, O. P. Rowlands.

# CHAPTER 8

# 1945 — 1974

### 'Bangor people have lost interest in Local Government.'[1]

THE WAR years and those that followed saw the inexorable integration of Bangor into the national and global society. Radio, and eventually television, brought national and international events live into people's homes and a growing number were spending their annual holidays on the continent of Europe and further afield. People became more involved in, and identified with, the wider scene in the fields of politics, sport, and entertainment and local events and issues seemed less important and certainly less exciting. The functions and affairs of the council came to be dominated by outside influences as national norms were applied to the services it provided. Few issues excited controversy; an efficient administration came to be expected, and, on the whole the council provided it.

After a period of austerity for eight years or so after the war, the economy gradually expanded. From the mid-1950s society changed in the wake of greater affluence, the emancipation of women, the loosening of religious and moral standards and the development of a youth culture, which often expressed itself in rebellion against authority and traditional values. Among Welsh speakers in particular there was a deeper awareness of the distinctive language and culture of Wales. Better employment opportunities together with rising real incomes led to a consumer orientated growth in economic activity which induced Prime Minister Harold MacMillan to remind the electorate in 1959 that we had 'never had it so good'. The housing situation had greatly improved by this time and by the early 1970s a high percentage of houses had the basic amenities, improved kitchen layouts and fittings, washing machines and refrigerators, modern furniture and wall to wall carpeting. In 1971, 50.3 per cent of households (58.2 per cent of the population) in Bangor possessed at least one car and an increasing number of houses were having central heating systems installed. Educational opportunities and standards had improved, more children were staying on in school beyond the statutory school leaving age and more were proceeding to higher education. For everyone the National Health Service provided a comprehensive and efficient health care system and for those whom affluence passed by there was support from various state agencies, funds and institutions.

In the more comfortable, secure and meritocratic society of the 1960s and early 1970s the distinctions between rich and poor had been further narrowed. When the fourth Baron Penrhyn died without an heir in 1947, the ancestral home of the family, Penrhyn Castle, was transferred to the National Trust and the shadow of the castle and of the aristocratic tradition which it had maintained was lifted from the city. By 1950, the estate owned little land and few houses in the city, Port Penrhyn was virtually defunct and the slate industry was in progressive decline. Sir Michael Duff of Vaynol now undertook many of the ceremonial duties which had traditionally been performed by members of the Penrhyn family.

The post-war period is notable for the steady increase which occurred in the number of people in middle class occupations. At the time of the 1971 Census, on the basis of the Registrar General's classification, 36 per cent of those gainfully employed in Bangor were middle class. A rise was particularly evident in the number of professional, managerial and clerical workers which was the natural corollary to rising employment opportunites in the field of education and hospital services, national agencies and local government and in banking, financial and other professional services. Opportunities for local entrepreneurs and business men declined, however, as national multiple stores and building societies bought premises along High Street when they became vacant. In a more mobile society members of this class were not generally natives of Bangor and were invariably on the promotion ladder which would take them away again. Furthermore, with the rise in car ownership increasing numbers of middle class incomers chose to live along the attractive northern shore of the Menai Strait rather than in Bangor (see p. 26). Consequently the commitment of many members of this class to the municipal affairs of Bangor was minimal.

Large reductions occurred during the period in the workforce at the port, the railway station, the bus depot and in some of the traditional industries such as slate manufacture and foundry work. New opportunities were created, however, for a range of manual skills in the construction and manufacturing industries, for public works projects and for maintenance personnel, porters, cleaners, etc., in the hospitals, schools and colleges. Across the occupational range, women found it easier to obtain employment and there was a degree of affluence in those households in which two incomes were earned.

The working class had improved its living standards markedly by the early 1970s and the differentiation in terms of remuneration between professional and manual workers had narrowed as, indeed, it had between skilled and unskilled workers and between men and women. The narrowing in the economic differential between the classes was accompanied by a convergence in the size and amenities within houses built by private builders and those built by the council, although with their more varied designs and embellishments, integral or free standing garages, larger plot sizes and better cared for front gardens, private estates were easily distinguishable from council estates. Living in an area of owner occupied housing or on a council estate became an indication of social status in post-war society. To become a house owner, albeit with a massive mortgage to finance, was a mark of success and conferred upon the owner a degree of independence. Council house tenants, on the other hand, were generally in receipt of lower incomes or they were too old to embark on the mortgage cycle. A legacy of the slum clearance and council house building programme of the 1930s was the creation of an unfortunate image of the council estate which has proved difficult to eradicate over time and which has helped to fuel the social polarization which existed between the owner occupier and the council house tenant. Two groups of people did not share in the general affluence of the period, the unemployed and the elderly. Unemployment persisted stubbornly around 5 to 7 per cent and the number of pensioners in the population rose steadily to 19 per cent in 1971, both figures well above the national average. For the elderly in particular the council provided dwellings in the form of flats; 22 per cent of the dwellings it built in the post-war period were flats.

The political background against which the council operated must be viewed in relation to the national scene. The most conspicuous features of the period were the landslide victory of the Labour Party in the 1945 General Election and the social changes which the Attlee government set in motion. In each of the general elections between 1950 and 1970, inclusive, the Party gained between twenty-seven and thirty-two of the thirty-six parliamentary seats in the Principality and its share of the poll exceeded 50 per cent on each occasion. The

Labour Party exercised its hegemony over Welsh political life generally as surely as did the Liberal Party between 1880 and 1914. The Party did not, however, exert that dominance over the constituency of which Bangor formed part. Against the national trend in 1945, Caernarvon Boroughs returned a Conservative member to Westminster. The 1950 election, which was fought on revised constituency boundaries, saw the return of the Labour candidate, W. Elwyn Jones, the Town Clerk of Bangor. He was defeated in the 1951 general election and the Conservatives held the seat until 1966; the seat returned to the Conservatives again in 1974. Two members of the city council contested, unsuccessfully, parliamentary seats for the Conservative Party: Cllr. Owen Meurig Roberts (Anglesey, 1951 and 1959, and Caernarfon, 1955) and Cllr. Vivian Lewis (Anglesey, in the two elections of 1974).

After the war the influence of the Liberal Party continued to decline, it lost both the Caernarvonshire seats in 1945 and both Anglesey and Merioneth in 1951. Thereafter, its influence on Welsh politics was negligible. Two stalwarts of Plaid Cymru in Caernarvonshire, Ambrose Bebb and J. E. Daniel, contested the two county constituencies in 1945 but both were heavily defeated and for the next twenty years the Party made little headway either in Caernarvonshire or on the Welsh national stage.

A transformation in Welsh political and cultural life occurred in the early 1960s. The catalyst for change was the sudden realization that the Welsh language was in danger of extinction. A report from the Welsh Joint Education Committee in 1961 showed that only 17.6 per cent of children in schools in Wales could speak Welsh. Census data for 1961, when published in 1963, confirmed the decline of the Welsh language. Of special concern was the fact that, according to the census, only 14.7 per cent of children between five and nine years of age could speak Welsh. When Saunders Lewis, one of the founders of Plaid Cymru, was invited to deliver the B.B.C.'s annual radio lecture in February 1962, he took as his theme the fate of the language, 'Tynged yr Iaith'. He asserted that the future of the language was more important than self government and that more agressive and possibly revolutionary methods should be applied to ensure that the language be given at least equal, if not superior, status in Wales. The lecture fired the imagination of Welsh language activists, particularly among the younger generation, and in the summer of 1962 a new society, Cymdeithas yr Iaith Gymraeg, the Welsh Language Society, was formed to campaign for the rightful place and dignity of the language in Wales. Petitions and peaceful persuasion were replaced by often noisy, angry, demonstrations and sit-ins and sometimes acts of vandalism and sabotage were performed in a campaign to persuade departments of central and local government to print forms, licences, notices, street names, road signs, etc., in Welsh and to conduct more of their business through the medium of the Welsh language. The apparent legitimacy of the movement was under-pinned by the Welsh Language Act 1967 which gave Welsh equal validity with English in Wales and over the years many public bodies in Wales acceded to the Society's demands. Plaid Cymru profited from the upsurge in Welsh national identity and gained its first Parliamentary seat at a by-election in Carmarthen in 1966. The Society found support among staff and students of the colleges in Bangor where a branch was formed in 1963. Expansion at the city's colleges had led to the inevitable decline in the proportion of students who came from Wales and who were Welsh speaking and in the city itself the proportion of the population able to speak Welsh had fallen from 76 per cent in 1931 to 65 per cent in 1961. The branch was active in promoting the use of Welsh in many spheres of life in Bangor.

In the post-war period the influence which the churches and chapels exerted on the life of the community progressively declined. Congregations dwindled especially in the Welsh nonconformist chapels where the effect of language decline was most marked. Membership of the Presbyterian Church of Wales, the strongest denomination in Bangor, decreased by nearly a half between 1945 and 1974; there was a steeper fall in the number of children who attended chapels and Sunday Schools. Five nonconformist chapels were closed but a Welsh Presbyterian church and an Anglican church were opened at Maesgeirchen. With fewer members it was difficult to sustain those social activities which centred upon the churches and chapels. Social norms and standards of morality were now being learnt from the media in its widest sense rather than from the pulpit and the distinctive Welsh nonconformist culture of the city was severely eroded.

The period also witnessed changes in the constitution of the council and the electorate. From 1945 the electorate was no longer confined to ratepayers but comprised all persons over the age of twenty-one. When the age of majority was reduced to eighteen in 1970 young people, including students at the city's colleges, were eligible to vote. In 1946 the Home Office agreed that since the population of West Ward had increased considerably it should have another three seats on the council and that the number of aldermen should be increased to seven. Finally, in 1947, the Home Office changed the date on which municipal elections were to be held from 1 November to the third Thursday in May; there was no municipal election in 1948.

The first post-war municipal election in 1945 generated a great deal of interest. Twenty-two candidates were nominated to contest eleven seats; thirteen stood as Independents. The local Labour Party nominated eight candidates and W. J. Holland, a railway guard, stood as a member of the Communist Party. Cars with amplifiers were used for the first time in a municipal election and a large crowd gathered outside the town hall to hear the declaration of the results. Independents won eight seats, thereby retaining the comfortable majority they had held since the First World War. Throughout the period 1945 to 1974, Independents were in the majority though in the last two years it was by virtue of the fact that they held six of the seven aldermanic seats (Appendix, Table 18). The result was a disappointing one for the Labour Party, which won only three seats, particularly in view of the success the Party had achieved in the national poll six months earlier. The Party's chagrin was intensified by the unexpected defeat of Mrs Chamberlain in West Ward.

There was no outstanding issue before the electors in November 1946 and only 40 per cent of them turned out to vote. Attention was focused in West Ward where there were three additional seats to be contested. In this ward where there were large numbers of railwaymen, the Labour Party won two seats and Mrs Chamberlain topped the poll. A Communist stood for the more conservative North Ward and surprised everyone by polling 259 votes. Ambrose Bebb did not seek re-election and with his departure the voice of Plaid Cymru was absent from the council chamber for the next twenty years.

The Labour Party gained another two seats in the election of 1947 bringing the number of Labour councillors up to seven, a figure which was not reached again for another twenty years. One of their victors was the erstwhile Communist, W. J. Holland who, in a speech at the declaration of the poll, said that he hoped that his advent to the council would be for the betterment of the city and all sections of the community.[2] Within eighteen months, however, Holland had left socialist Britain for Australia and handed over the betterment of the city to others. Disillusionment with the first post-war Labour government was general, and by 1951 only two Labour councillors were still in office. When W. S. Williams, the Party's only alderman died in 1958, it was not represented on the aldermanic bench again for thirteen years.

During the late 1940s and early 1950s Liberal candidates once again contested seats and in 1951 and 1952 the Party had six members. Under the capable leadership of G. H. Burgess, a Londoner and an upholsterer by trade, they formed an articulate and effective force within the council. Two of their number, schoolteacher Pat Burgess (G. H. Burgess' daughter) and Vivian Lewis, a solicitor, were Young Liberals in their twenties and they injected spice into council discussions. In the 1960s their number and influence waned and by 1968 only Lewis remained.

The Labour Party renewed its challenge in the 1960s; it doubled its membership from four in 1963 to eight in 1967 and by 1972 it had thirteen members, giving it numerical equality with the Independents. Railwaymen, who had formed the majority of Labour members on the council in the inter-war and immediate post-war period had declined in numbers and no railwaymen stood for election after 1957.[3] Among the new members were well educated and articulate professional men, including Ungoed Evans, a secondary school headmaster, Colin Trask and D. Machin, University lecturers, and members of the highly unionized Post Office staff such as Charles McDonagh, local secretary of the Union of Post Office Workers, Frank Woodcock, local chairman of the same union and of the Bangor Labour Party and Harri Gwyn Jones, local chairman of the Post Office Engineering Union. Nevertheless, Party members could not achieve the unity which might have made them an effective force within the council. In November 1972, for example, a motion that the council should sell its houses to sitting tenants, as sanctioned by the Housing Finance Act, 1972, was proposed by Harry Cozens a Labour councillor, yet all his Party colleagues voted against it. When Wyn Roberts M.P. agreed to move an amendment to the Local Government Bill 1972 calling for the creation of a Nant Ffrancon district authority, a delegation of Labour councillors lobbied members of the Labour Party, then in opposition, to support Roberts' amendment. The delegation, however, received short shrift from George Thomas M.P. and other Welsh Labour Party members and in a fit of pique five of the Bangor councillors resigned from the local Labour Party, 'putting conscience before politics and duty above pride'.[4] Three members eventually rejoined the Party but the rift had not been healed at the reorganization of local government in 1974.

Revival of Labour Party activity in the late 1960s generated a

Conservative backlash and, in the municipal elections of 1968, the Party fielded five candidates. Three were successful and they joined C. W. Foster, who had won a seat in a by-election the previous July. The Party lost two of these seats in the 1971 election.

In the mid-1960s another pressure group sought to influence certain aspects of the council's work. Members of the local branch of the Welsh Language Society took positive steps to ensure that Welsh was given a prominent place in local government administration. In June 1963 the council received a petition organized by the Society and containing 600 signatures requesting that the rate demand notices should be issued in both English and Welsh. At this early stage the council paid little heed to the Society's demands. However, influenced by a group of earnest Welshmen on the council itself it did agree in 1964 to print in English and Welsh certain forms and notices to do with the administration of local elections. The council was pressed in 1965 to erect bilingual street name-plates. For over fifty years it had adopted a policy of giving new streets Welsh names; it considered that it would be inappropriate to translate these names into English and equally so to translate into Welsh English names, which had been in common use for over a century, Soon there began a campaign to disfigure and remove English name-plates. When the council did decide to substitute bilingual plates for the English ones there was overt disgust in the council chamber when councillors were told that even these plates had been vandalized or removed altogether by Welsh extremists. Inevitably, in the charged atmosphere of the time there was a backlash which manifested itself in the daubing with paint of Welsh name-plates.

During a discussion in January 1966 which followed the reading of a letter written in Welsh asking the council to support a petition calling on the B.B.C to establish a television studio in Bangor, Cllr. McDonagh asked under what rule in standing orders Cllr. G. W. Smith had been allowed to speak in Welsh. Welsh speaking members of the council were accustomed to express their views in Welsh from time to time especially in committees of the council whose membership was entirely Welsh. McDonagh's interruption brought forth a sharp retort from Ald. H. J. Jones. 'Everyone here has the right to speak in Welsh if he wants to' he said, and others were heard to remark, 'This is our language' and 'This is Wales after all'.[5] The incident highlights the sensitive nature of the language issue in the mid-sixties and the strong emotions which were aroused on both sides of the language divide. Later that year Cllr. Smith presented a motion calling on the council to adopt the principle of equal status for the English and Welsh language at all council meetings and to apply it also to minutes, notices, etc. Smith was prevailed upon to withdraw his motion because of the extra expense that would be incurred in printing costs, etc. and the fear that monoglot English persons would not be able to follow discussions in council.

At the municipal election of 1965, the first post-war challenge by persons sympathetic to the aims of Plaid Cymru and the Welsh Language Society was made. A candidate stood in north and west wards but both were decisively defeated. The next year the same candidates contested the same wards and this time one of them, Mrs Bebb-Jones, a former school teacher and college lecturer, was returned for north ward. She lost no opportunity to advance the cause of the Welsh Language movement. When the indoor swimming baths were to be opened in October 1966 she strongly objected to the fact that the plaque commemorating the opening and the designation and direction signs were in English only. Predictably the opening ceremony itself was accompanied by a demonstration organized by the Welsh Language Society demanding the erection of Welsh notices and signs. A month later the council agreed to erect designation and direction signs and a second commemoration plaque in Welsh. A Welsh sign 'NOFIO' was discreetly erected on the exterior of the building just before the Royal National Eisteddfod was held in Bangor in 1971. Bilingual signs were erected at the outset at the crematorium built in 1973.

Mrs Bebb-Jones resigned her seat in 1968. Although several further attempts were made by Plaid Cymru to win seats on the council none was successful; the Party received little support from the voters of Bangor. Meanwhile, patriotic Welshmen within the council succeeded over the years in persuading fellow members to support the Welsh language wherever possible. Rate demand notices were first printed bilingually in 1967, yet English remained the medium of council minutes and, essentially, of council meetings until reorganization of local government in 1974.

The foregoing analysis of the political composition of the council during the period suggests that there was more political activity in municipal affairs than at any time since the first decade of the century. When the Liberal Party joined with the Labour Party in challenging the hegemony of Independent members in 1951, Cllr. H. J. Jones (Independent), at the mayor's installation ceremony condemned the introduction of party politics into local government. 'What connection', he asked, 'have the parties in Westminster and their differences to do with roads, rates and rubbish?' He was convinced that citizens realized 'that the task of a local authority was to conduct the practical affairs of the district under its control and not to act as a sounding board for Westminster. They are bored', he said, 'by faction fights in the council chamber (and) they want to see things done. Local bodies should be purged of politics so that the confidence of the electorate might be restored'.[6] Jones's magisterial remarks went unheeded. In the following election, Independent, Labour and Liberal nominees again contested seats.

Clearly not everybody subscribed to H. T. Jones's views. A Leader in the *North Wales Chronicle* in September 1964 stated: 'Since central government provides more money towards the cost of local government than is obtained from the rates, it is important that the electorate should know the political views held by candidates at local elections because these views reflect a candidate's approach to both the lives and purses of the ratepayers'. Whilst conceding that most of the members of the council were Independents the leader contended that '. . . that did not mean they did not have political views'.[7]

The election of 1971 was one of the most political, in a Party sense, ever fought in Bangor. Thirteen candidates contested eight seats: four Labour, four Conservative, two Plaid Cymru and three Independent. Even the long standing tradition that a sitting mayor should not be opposed at an election was broken when a Conservative contested the seat held by Cllr. Vivian Lewis. An article in the *North Wales Chronicle* supported the intrusion of party politics into local government. 'Few councillors', it stated, 'do not have an allegiance to one of the political parties and the decisions they make on local issues must be coloured by the political philosophy they hold. Independents', the article stressed, 'wish to be all things to all men, but this stance is no longer viable since electors want to know what ideals and beliefs a candidate holds in matters of policy. After all, local government is political, it handles public money and councillors are responsible for allocating and spending that money'.[8]

Candidates who are members of a party have some advantages; they can be identified by the public with the ideology of the party for which they stand and with that Party's programme for coping with the problems of local government; they can count on the support of Party members at election time and, once in the council, they can rely on the broad support of Party colleagues. Yet, those who used a Party label were not always disposed to follow a Party line. Only among members of the Labour Party was there some attempt to obtain a consensus view but this was not always achieved.

The tendency towards the greater involvement of political parties in local government must be due to the greater publicity which local government elections received from the national media. Local government elections became the testing ground for the popularity of the rival parliamentary parties and their results normally mirrored national trends. People tended to vote for candidates of the Party they normally supported in general elections rather than for the individual and local issues. Electors could not be blamed for giving priority to a wider focus. In the more open, less personalized society of the post-war period local candidates were by and large unknown to the majority of the electorate. They were often newcomers to the city, had a minimal involvement in community affairs and, apart from the Independents, relied heavily on their Party for nomination and support. A large number did not attend a place of worship, the milieu in which, traditionally, people had learnt the qualities of service, responsibility and public discussion.

There were few outstandingly contentious issues to place before the electorate. National standards were laid down for the services the council provided and money was forthcoming from the Treasury to pay for them. There was little controversy over either the scale or the location of the council's housing projects as there had been in the inter-war years. Where the council did exercise its discretion in the commitment of large sums of money, for example the building of an indoor heated swimming pool and a crematorium, support, if grudging, was not overtly hostile. Only on the issue of the future of the pier did the council feel that it needed to consult the electorate at large (p. 207-08).

Public apathy towards the affairs of the city and the council which administered them, was starkly revealed in the pier referendum of June 1973. Little had changed over the years. Alderman H. J. Jones lamenting the apathy which people were showing towards local government said in 1951 'Bangor people have lost interest in local government. It is a deplorable commentary on the attitude of the public towards public administration'.[9] The turn out at elections varied between 30 and 66 per cent but in by-elections it was very much lower, e.g. 10.5 per cent in West Ward in 1971. All seats were contested between 1945 and 1951 (inclusive) but in 1956 and in 1967 there was no contest. With one-third of councillors retiring each year the maximum number of seats becoming vacant at the May elections in the period 1952 to 1972 (inclusive) was 147 yet only fifty-nine of these (40 per cent) were contested.

Throughout the post-war period a high percentage of council members was drawn from the middle class; in the 1950s and early 1960s over 80 per cent of members were so drawn but the percentage fell below seventy in the early 1970s as Labour Party members made inroads into the council (Appendix, Table 18). Reflecting the changing employment opportunities within the city, there was an increase during the period in the number of members who were fee and salary earners and a decline in the number of members who worked on their own account. This trend is illustrated in the analysis of data relating to the occupations of mayors (Appendix, Table 16). Middle class members invariably lived in owner occupied houses. In the Council of 1972-73 nearly two-thirds of members were owner occupiers and 28 per cent were council tenants.

Despite the fact that women in greater numbers were entering a wider range of occupational fields, they appeared to be reluctant to stand for election onto the city council. Elsie Chamberlain retired from the council in 1950 and the absence of women on it led the Bangor Branch of the British Council of Women, a non-political organization, to sponsor two candidates at the 1952 election. Only one candidate actually stood and she, Mrs Rogers Brambell, the wife of a University Professor, topped the poll in North Ward. Nine women were elected during the period, but apart from Mrs Christie, who served an unbroken term of twenty years, the average length of service of each woman was three years. In four years only (1954, 1956, 1970 and 1971) were there as many as three women on the council. By occupation, or marriage, they were all middle class and six of them were, or had been, schoolteachers.

Although there was a general decline in church and chapel membership and in the influence of religion in society generally, a high proportion of council members were still regular and active members of their places of worship. In 1963, for example, nine members were chapel deacons, one was a lay reader and another was the secretary of his Parochial Church Council; several were Sunday School teachers. In the late sixties, however, there was a marked decline in the number of active church members. One of the first initiatives taken by Ioan Glynne on being elected mayor in 1950 was to persuade the council to implement the suggestion made by the Dean of Bangor, the Rev. J. T. Davies, in a sermon he delivered at the annual civic service, that the council should commence its meetings with prayers. It became the custom for the mayor to choose a chaplain for the period of his mayoralty who would be invited to offer prayers at the commencement of meetings. Although nonconformists were always in the majority on the council, the traditional procession to and service at the cathedral on Mayor's Sunday had become firmly established in the council's calendar.

Strong sabbatarian attitudes persisted long after they had been abandoned by the population at large. These came to the fore whenever discussion took place concerning the opening of municipal recreation facilities on Sundays. Moves to open playgrounds on Sundays were regularly defeated throughout the 1950s; in 1958, for example, by twenty votes to five. In 1961 it was agreed by two votes to open the Heol Dewi ground between the hours of one and five p.m. for a trial period of two months for the purpose of walking and sitting. Although all the children's playground equipment would continue to be chained and the bowling green and tennis courts would remain closed on Sundays, this decision was the thin edge of the wedge. Cllr. Gwenda Williams objected to the proposal on the grounds that the opening of parks would lead to a decline in Sunday School attendance. Five years later the council bowed to the inevitable by removing all restraints on the use of children's playgrounds on Sundays. Logically, it could not resist the pressure any longer, particularly in view of the fact that it allowed the new indoor swimming pool to open on Sundays. Many councillors were uneasy about the decision, however, and Cllr. Trefor Hughes expressed their feelings when he said that 'the sanctity of the Sabbath was part of our (Welsh) heritage and should be preserved'.[10] The council drew the line, however, when it came to holding competitive matches on Sundays; it refused to sanction the holding of a competitive bowls match on the Heol Dewi Green in the summer of 1972, an idiosyncratic decision in view of the fact that competitive cricket and golf matches were being played on other grounds on Sundays.

Up to the mid-60s, 80 per cent of members were native Welsh speakers who used the language naturally in their daily lives; many were deeply immersed in Welsh culture and promoted the use of Welsh wherever practicable. The council gave generous support to the Royal National Eisteddfod held in Penrhyn Park in 1971. The proportion of Welsh speakers fell to below 60 per cent in the early 1970s; several of the Labour members in 1972, for example, had only recently moved to the city to live.

Leadership of the community had passed from the aristocracy and wealthy, well-educated élite to a broader based middle class group at the time of incorporation of the city. From that time up to the early 1970s the council was dominated by men who were conservative in outlook, middle class in social rank, engaged in professional and business occupations, actively non-conformist in religion and Welsh in speech. This was so despite the recruitment of some working class representatives, of women and, in the last decade or so of the council's life, of non-Welsh speaking migrants without strong religious affiliations. Since changes had occurred in society during the present century the foregoing attributes were no longer characteristic of the people of Bangor at large, therefore councillors could not be said to be representative of them.

One reason for this apparent anachronism lies in the character of the Municipal Corporations Act 1835, which was the blueprint for municipal government. Conceived at a time of great social unrest the Act was deliberately engineered to produce a system which would not respond quickly to change. The breaking mechanism was particularly apparent in the aldermanic system. Aldermen, who comprised a quarter of the council, were elected by members of the council and held office for six years, half their number retiring every three years. On the Bangor council long service became the criterion for election onto the aldermanic bench. An analysis of the aldermanic bench in 1963 and 1973 shows that it epitomized the city's 'establishment' (Table 10), but differed markedly from the remainder of the council. In 1972 the seven aldermen had an aggregate of 206 years of service on the council whereas ten of the twenty-one councillors each had less than two years.

TABLE 10

*Some characteristics of Aldermen, 1963 and 1973*

|  | 1963 | 1973 |
|---|---|---|
| Per cent male | 100 | 100 |
| Average age | 68 | 75 |
| Average length of service on the council (in years) | 23 | 27 |
| Per cent middle class | 100 | 86 |
| Per cent Welsh speaking | 100 | 100 |
| Per cent nonconformist | 86 | 100 |
| Per cent holding office in church or chapel | 100 | 86 |
| Per cent born within 5 miles of Bangor | 71 | 71 |

The aldermanic system, also ensured that there was a pool of experience to guide the council in its deliberations. Having served for many years on the council, often as chairmen of committees, the aldermen gained immense knowledge of the workings of local government and became undoubted experts in their fields of interest. Long service, knowledge, expertise and the purple robe combined to invest them with considerable prestige and power. They tended to stick together and to work closely with the council's officers. Masonic ties frequently cemented the bond between them. A bid to shake up the aldermanic bench was attempted by a group of young, progressive members at the time of the aldermanic elections of 1970. A plot was hatched to unseat three aldermen whose seats came up for election that year; it failed because a number of conservative members feared that more radical members would gain access to the aldermanic bench and, in any event, most councillors were loathe to hurt the feelings of men who had given long and honourable service to the council.

Eight of the fourteen mayors elected during the period were drawn from the aldermanic bench. Length of service was the principal criterion for election to the office and the custom that each mayor should serve a two year term was strictly adhered to. Without exception they filled the office with dignity and with untiring devotion to duty. Eight of their number received the freedom of the borough in recognition of their loyal service.

The first post-war mayor, Ald. Ithel Williams (1883-1966), was a native of Llanllechid. He was educated at Bethesda County School and U.C.N.W. Bangor and entered the teaching profession. After serving in the First World War he was appointed headmaster of St Mary's School in 1919 and remained there until he retired in 1943. During the Second World War he enlisted as a member of the Special Constabulary and the Royal Observer Corps and became the Head Observer in Bangor. For twenty-seven years he was Secretary of St Mary's Parochial Church Council. During his mayoralty King George VI and Queen Elizabeth visited Bangor.

Alderman O. Glynne Owen (1891-1975) was the son of John Owen who had established livery stables at the bottom end of High Street in the last century. John Owen soon realized the potential of the motor car and turned his business into one of car hiring, consequently he branched out into car repair work and built a garage at the junction of High Street and Glynne Road. Glynne was educated at Bethesda County School and trained as a marine engineer in Liverpool. After service in the R.A.S.C. during the First World War he returned to the business founded by his father and built it up into a thriving one, employing many men. For about ten years before he joined the council in 1933 he was Captain of the City's Fire Brigade. He served on most of the council's committees and was chairman of the Finance Committee for many years. He was an elder at Tabernacl C.M. Chapel.

Alderman Ioan Ynyr Glynne (1897-1979) was a native of Bangor and the son of a member of the first city council, J. Glynne Jones. Ioan was educated in Friars School and enlisted in the West Yorkshire Regiment in 1916. He rose to the rank of captain and was awarded the M.C. After serving his articles in his father's firm he joined the practice and became a partner and later principal of the firm. In 1937 he relinquished the post of Deputy Town Clerk which he had held since 1923 and was elected onto the council in 1938. He made the water service his main sphere of interest, becoming chairman of the Water Committee. He was one of Wales' two representatives on the British Waterworks Association and became chairman of the Eryri Water Board on its formation in 1967. For his public services he was awarded the O.B.E. in 1957. He was an elder at Princes Road Presbyterian Church.

One of the most able men on the council was Ald. Hugh J. Jones (nat. 1899). A native of Bodorgan, Anglesey, he was educated at Holyhead County School and Manchester University. He served with the South Wales Borderers in Belgium and France during the First World War and with the Royal Observer Corps in the Second World War. Joining the District Bank in 1920 he was appointed Manager of its Bangor Branch in 1935, a post he held until his retirement. He joined the council in 1943 and for the next thirty years immersed himself in public life serving on most of the council's committees, in the capacity of chairman of several of them, including the Finance Committee. In 1959 he was elected onto Caernarvonshire County Council and became Chairman of the Youth Services Committee and Vice-Chairman of the Finance Committee. Nationally he served on both the Electricity and Gas Consultative Committees for Wales. A keen supporter of the Scout movement, he was County Commissioner from 1950 to 1971. He gave unstinting service to his chapel, Ebenezer Congregational, where he was a deacon, and to the Welsh Congregational Union's Central Fund, of which he was Treasurer. During his mayoralty he visited the former slate quarrying town of Bangor, Pennsylvania, U.S.A., and forged links between the two Bangors.

Alderman Frederick W. Pozzi (1893-1971) served on the council for twenty-two years before accepting the mayoralty in 1954; since he practised as a solicitor in the local Magistrates Court he would not accept the mayoralty until after his retirement because that also brought with it, *ex officio*, a seat on the bench of magistrates. His father, the son of an Italian *émigré*, had established a successful business in Bangor and had sat on the council from 1915 to 1918. Charles was educated at Ampleforth College, Yorkshire. He served throughout the First World War, was commissioned in the RWF in 1916 and was wounded at Cambrai and again at Loos on the Western Front. After the war he served his articles in Bangor and after practising in a firm of solicitors in Holyhead and Llangefni he returned to Bangor and set up his own practice in 1938. He joined the council in 1932 and his main contribution was to the Pier and Ferries Committee. Pozzi was a Catholic in religion, the only Catholic to hold the mayoralty, and a Conservative in politics.

Another native of Bangor and son of a former councillor was Ald. Eirwyn Owen (1901-84). His father, the Rev. W. J. Owen (Afallen), a Presbyterian minister, had held pastorates in the U.S.A. and Wales and had been a member of the council from 1933 to 1941. Eirwyn was educated at Hirael and Garth schools and Beaumaris Grammar School. On qualifying as a pharmacist in 1929 he set up his own business at 345 High Street. Joining the council in 1945 he made health matters his particular interest. He was chairman of the council's Health Committee, of the Beaumaris Port Health Authority and of the Caernarvonshire Joint Sanitary Authority. During the Second World War he was Chief Air Raid Warning Officer for Caernarvonshire and was awarded the Civil Defence Medal for his services. He was an active member and chairman of the Bangor Chamber of Commerce and gave long and devoted service to the Bangor and District Branch of the Presbyterian Church of Wales' Sunday School Union.

Alderman Caradog R. Jones (1906-71) was born in Orme Road, Hirael, and was educated at Bethesda County School. He intended entering the ministry of the Presbyterian Church of Wales but, after a year at the University College, Bangor, had to give up his course on account of ill health. In 1923, he established a milk retailing business in Bangor which sustained him until his retirement. He joined the council in 1945 and was a faithful and conscientious member of several committees. The affairs of Salem Chapel, Hirael, were one of his main interests; he was an elder there and he fulfilled his desire to preach the gospel by becoming a lay preacher.

The second headmaster to become mayor in this period was Ald. Owen T. Pritchard (1900-79). Born in Nebo, he was educated at Penygroes County School and the Normal College, Bangor. At the age of twenty-three he was appointed to the headship of Sarn Primary School, Lleyn, and in 1945 he was appointed to that of Glanadda Primary School. Elected onto the council in 1946, he played a prominent part in establishing a separate Parks and Open Spaces Committee in the late 1940s and was its chairman for many years. He was the driving force behind the building of the indoor swimming pool (1966) and the crematorium (1973). As a headmaster he took a particular interest in the Road Safety Movement; he was chairman of the North Wales Federation of Road Safety Committees and translated the Highway Code into Welsh. For his work for the National Playing Fields Association he was awarded the President's Certificate in 1973. Pritchard was a keen member of the St John's Ambulance Brigade and a deacon at Pendref Congregational Chapel.

Another native of Bangor to follow his father into the council chamber was Cllr. Emrys Edwards (*nat.* 1906). Evan Edwards, who served on the council from 1928 to 1939, had gained employment with a Liverpool firm of tea merchants, Robert Roberts & Co., in 1891. Soon he was appointed manager of their grocery and provisions business in Bangor and became a director of the company in 1917. In 1925 he bought the Bangor business and was allowed by the company to retain the original name. Under his enterprising direction, bakery and confectionary departments and a café were added and 'Bobby Bobs' become one of the best known cafés in North Wales and was a popular venue for generations of students at the city's colleges. Emrys, who was educated at Hirael, Garth and Friars Schools, entered his father's business and became a master confectioner. He was elected onto the council in 1946. Principal among his many business and sporting interests was the Bangor City Football Club. He was chairman of the directors of the club when it reached the peak of its success in the early 1960s, winning the Welsh Cup (1961-62) and representing Wales in the European Cup Winners Cup in 1963.

Councillor Robert Owen (1905-73) was the only member of the Labour Party to hold the mayoralty in the post-war period. Born in Rhiwlas and educated at Bethesda County School, he worked for twenty years at the Penrhyn Quarry. When war broke out he obtained employment on the railway first as a signalman and then as a guard.

He entered the council in 1947 and was chairman of the Housing Committee for a number of years. Members at Berea Welsh Presbyterian Chapel, Glanadda, appointed him an elder.

Councillor Eric Whitworth (1907-77) was born in Southport and in 1928 joined the staff of the King Flour Mills Ltd. Ellesmere Port, as their sales representative in North Wales, a position he held until his retirement in 1972. He entered the council in 1949 and his main contribution to its work was as Chairman of the Library Committee for over twenty years.

Councillor Iorwerth Hughes (1905-81) started work as an errand boy at the Star Supply Stores in his native Penmaenmawr. He was promoted via the Bangor branch to be manager of the Caernarfon branch; he then became inspector of the firm's stores in North Wales, Shropshire and Cheshire. In 1938 he established his own bakery and grocery business in West End, Bangor, and eventually opened shops in Upper Bangor and Bethesda. Hughes entered the council in 1952 and became mayor in 1968. At his chapel, Berea C.M., Glanadda, he was an elder, the treasurer and Sunday School Superintendent.

Public service for the people of Bangor would seem to have been the natural course of action for Cllr. Vivian Lewis (*nat.* 1930). His great grandfather was Thomas Lewis, the second mayor of Bangor, and his grandfather, T. C. Lewis, was a city alderman (1889-1908) and alderman of Caernarvonshire County Council (1889-1943). Lewis was educated at Friars School and Liverpool University and, after graduating in Law and serving his articles, he established a solicitor's practice in Bangor. Steeped in the Liberal traditions of his family, he entered the council in 1953 to join a small group of active Liberal councillors. Housing and town planning were his particular interests. He launched the twinning arrangement with Soest, leading a delegation to the West German city in September 1970. He also originated the link with R.A.F. Valley which culminated in the freedom of the city being conferred on the Station. His mayoralty was overshadowed by the impending demise of the council but he led a spirited campaign for the creation of a separate Nant Ffrancon District authority. Lewis was a member of Caernarvonshire County Council, 1963-66 and 1970-74, and was Conservative candidate in Anglesey in both the 1974 parliamentary elections.

The last mayor before local government reorganization in 1974 was Mrs Jean Dowling Christie (1920-84). She was only the second woman to hold the post in the council's ninety year history. Born in the Wirral, Cheshire, she entered the nursing profession in the

Second World War and at this time met her future husband, Dr David Christie, who was then a House Surgeon in the St Helens Hospital. After service in the R.A.F. Dr Christie came to Bangor in 1946 to take up general practice. Mrs Christie was the founder secretary in 1952 of the Bangor Townswomen's Guild and interested herself in the Guild's Drama productions. From acting in and producing plays she moved on to writing plays and she obtained considerable success as a playwright. She entered the council in 1954 and was a vice-chairman of the Health Committee. She was passionately committed to the preservation of the customs and traditions of the city and the enhancement of the urban environment. She was chairman of the Bangor branch of the Council for the Preservation of Rural Wales and of the Bangor Civic Society. After local government reorganization she was elected the first mayor of the Community Council and she also won a seat on the Arfon District Council.

Throughout the period the council was served by able and loyal officers. The administrative structure was controlled by the town clerk, who between 1939 and 1969 was W. Elwyn Jones. Born in 1904, the son of a Welsh Wesleyan minister, he was educated at Ffestiniog County School and at U.C.N.W. Bangor. After graduating he was articled to Pentir Williams, solicitor and town clerk of Bangor, and in 1927 he was awarded the LL.B. degree of the University of London. He then entered into partnership with Pentir Williams and in 1934 became Clerk to the Bangor Magistrates, a post he held until 1950. In 1937 he was appointed deputy town clerk and when Pentir Williams died in 1939 he succeeded him to his post. Elwyn Jones was active in politics: he was Labour candidate for the Caernarvon County constituency in the 1931 and 1935 elections and for the Caernarvon Boroughs constituency in 1945. In 1950 he won the Conwy constituency of the county but his membership of Parliament was shortlived since the second Attlee administration lasted only twenty months and he was defeated at the 1951 election. For many years he represented North Ward on Caernarvonshire County Council. Among Elwyn Jones's many interests are the National Eisteddfod and the University College at Bangor. He was chairman of the executive committee of the eisteddfodau held in Bangor in 1931 and 1971 and is an honorary member of the Gorsedd of Bards. He has served on the Council of the University College since 1943 and was appointed Treasurer in 1970. Shortly, after his retirement from the office of town clerk in 1969, he was made an honorary freeman of the borough in recognition of his outstanding service to the council for a period of thirty years. The final accolade to a long and distinguished public career was the award of a knighthood in 1978 [Plate 6(iv)].

When Elwyn Jones retired in 1968 the council decided to appoint its first full time town clerk. This decision was necessary because of increasing regulation by central government and the complexity of modern administration. The person appointed, Edward J. Lloyd (*nat.* 1928), was a native of the Vale of Clwyd and had spent his working life in local government. His appointment was followed by major changes in the town hall but, with the reorganization of local government pending, he resigned at the end of 1973.

Both the greater involvement of central government in the affairs of local councils and the uncertainty which shrouded local government over much of the post-war period undoubtedly had an effect on the recruitment of members to serve on the council. The failure of local government to attract talent was recognized at the highest level; for example, Dame Evelyn Sharp, Permanent Secretary to the Ministry of Housing and Local Government said in 1962 that she 'did not think that enough really able people are interested today in taking part in local government . . . not enough good recruits are coming forward'.[11] The Maud Report revealed that the recruitment of an adequate number of people for service in local government was felt to be a problem of almost all the authorities consulted.[12] With more uncontested than contested elections for seats of the Bangor council and with rarely a majority of electors turning out at the polls, Hugh J. Jones's conclusion in 1951 that the people of Bangor had lost interest in local government still applied for most of the period. Yet, this was only a symptom of the general malaise which afflicted local government in Britain in the post-war period.

*Notes*

1. Words spoken by Cllr. H. J. Jones, Deputy Mayor, on the occasion of the installation of Mayor Glynne in 1951. NWC, 4 May 1951.
2. NWC, 7 November 1947.
3. Two-thirds of the Labour councillors elected before 1957 were railwaymen.
4. NWC, 27 July 1972.
5. NWC, 7 January 1966.
6. NWC, 4 May 1951.
7. NWC, 11 September 1964.
8. NWC, 13 May 1971.
9. NWC, 4 May 1971.
10. NWC, 9 December 1966.
11. Quoted in the Municipal Review, August 1962, p. 516.
12. Maud Report, 1, Cmnd. 4040, p. 474.

# CHAPTER 9

## 1974 — 1983

'. . . we must keep the dignity'.[1]

THE LOCAL GOVERNMENT ACT 1972 replaced the existing structure of local government by a two-tier system based on the county and the district. Whilst recommending larger and more powerful units the Maud Commission Report, however, expressed the view that 'there must be a level of local government which fosters pride and interest of local communities (otherwise) a vital element will be missing from the democratic pattern'.[2] It prosposed, therefore, that 'local councils' should be elected for each of the old boroughs, urban districts and parishes whose functions were to give a focus to community identity and to articulate community aspirations and needs. The Act accepted the need for community involvement in the local government process and enacted that all former boroughs, urban districts and parishes should be redesignated parishes in England and communities in Wales and that each parish or community should elect a council whose principal function would be to voice its views rather than exercise any executive functions.

Such a radical reorganization of local government was a traumatic blow to the status and pride of the city and to the council which had served the city well for ninety years. No longer would the citizens of Bangor be masters in their own city and their voice on the new district council would be a minority one. There must have been a feeling of despondency among members of the council as they walked in procession through the streets of the city to attend their last civic service at the cathedral on 10 June 1973. The Bishop of Bangor in his address, however, struck a cheerful note. He assured the congregation that it was not a day of sadness, and, drawing an analogy with the events of Whitsun in the Christian calendar, he perceived it as 'a day of optimism and hope for the future'.[3]

It is in this spirit that the new community council in Bangor has approached its task since 1974.

From the outset it resolved to retain elements of the status of the 'old' council. This determination was expressed by Mrs Christie, the first mayor of the new council, in her installation speech: 'Although the new council is not going to have a lot of power we must keep the dignity . . . The city was proud of its city status and of its civic ceremonial and these characteristics should be maintained'.[4] Accordingly the council exercised its right to adopt the title of town council which carried for its chairman the privilege of assuming the title of mayor. It also petitioned the Home Secretary to advise the Queen to grant Letters Patent, conferring upon it the title of city. Constituted as a body corporate under the Act and assuming the title of the City of Bangor Council, the council has become the natural successor of the old council. The council was also authorized to use the existing Coat of Arms and Common Seal and to recognize eminent local service by granting the honorary freedom of the city. At its first meeting the council resolved that robes should be worn by members at council meetings and on public occasions. Later it decided that past mayors should wear the gowns formerly worn by aldermen as a mark of respect for their service and status within the council. The tradition that council meetings should open with prayers was adhered to as was the annual civic service at the cathedral. The mayor is recognized to be the city's first citizen and as such welcomes visiting dignitaries on its behalf and represents the city on public occasions, in particular at the cenotaph on Remembrance Sunday. In several respects, therefore, a degree of continuity between the two councils has been achieved.

The 1972 Act abolished the aldermanic system in local government but enacted that the number of councillors should equal the number elected onto the 'old' councils; where a borough had been divided into wards, these wards were to be retained and each ward was to have the same representation on the council as previously. A city council of twenty-one members was therefore constituted. The Act laid down that elections to the council should be held in 1974, 1979 and every fourth year thereafter and that the whole number of councillors must retire together at the end of their term of office. The mayor is elected annually from among the councillors and the Bangor Council has exercised its discretion under the Act to appoint a member of the council to be vice-chairman.

Under pressure from Plaid Cymru councillors the council adopted a bilingual policy with precedence being given to Welsh. All agendas and minutes, public notices and orders and stationery headings are printed in both languages. Councillors are free to speak in either

Welsh or English at meetings but since there is no simultaneous translation system available, members who speak in Welsh are requested either to translate what they say or ask the town clerk to do so. Thus the council has consummated a policy which the 'old' council had begun ten years earlier.

Functions specifically prescribed in the Act were, broadly speaking, those already undertaken by parish councils. These included the maintenance of footpaths and bridleways and litter bins and seats alongside them; certain responsibilities connected with footway lighting, bus shelters and off-street parking; the provision and administration of allotments and the care and maintenance of parks and open space. Bangor Council insisted that all gifts made to the citizens of Bangor and which had been in the care of the 'old' council should be in its own keeping. These gifts included the town clock, the Penrhyn Hall and areas of open space comprising Menai Woods, the 'Look Out', the Dargie Playing Field, the Ashley Jones and Isidore Wartski Fields and Roman Camp. The Penrhyn Arms Wood, a small area of natural woodland at the eastern entrance to the city was purchased from the Penrhyn Estate in 1976 so that it might be preserved as a visual amenity. The council also purchased a triangular plot of land along Caernarfon Road, from which several houses unfit for human habitation had been cleared, and laid it out as a garden to commemorate the wedding of Prince Charles and Princess Diana in 1981. The council now owns over 100 acres of open space within the city. Finally, the Act provides community councils with a right to be consulted about planning applications affecting land and buildings in their areas and the Bangor Council has conscientiously exercised this right.

Yet it is not so much in the sphere of executive duties as in the social and ceremonial scene that the role of community councils was envisaged by the authors of the 1972 Act. They were influenced, of course, by the Maud Commission Report which stressed that 'the most important function of the local councils . . . will be the duty to voice the opinions and wishes of the local community . . . It will be their responsibility to see that the views and wishes of their inhabitants about any local government service, or any other matter of concern to the local community are made known to the responsible authorities'.[5]

As watchdog and spokesman for the community the council has taken up with the county authority issues relating to traffic control, parking and street lighting. Proposals for the creation of separate

English and Welsh medium secondary schools in Bangor were strenuously opposed on the grounds that the whole concept was divisive and alien to the council's own ethos of community harmony. Issues of council house repairs, street cleaning, conditions of the grounds at the cemetery and the crematorium, the general state of the swimming pool and recreation grounds have been brought to the attention of the district council. The proposed and controversial continued expansion of the University College in the mid 1970s was supported on the grounds that it was in the best interests of the community.

Frequent complaints from citizens concerning the unkempt condition of the streets and from council house tenants about the lack of attention paid to their grievances are symptomatic of the decline in standards of some local government services since the re-organization of local government and of a failure to gain satisfaction from a more remote and impersonal authority. Many citizens are confused about which reponsibilites are allocated to the district council and which to the community council; the number of district councillors they can approach is less than half the number of 'old' city councillors and the district council offices are scattered in various locations not only in Bangor but in Caernarfon also.

Frustration at the inability of the larger authority to maintain standards and to respond expeditiously to complaints has led the council on a number of occasions to seek to have certain functions transferred to it. In 1976, for example, the council passed the following resolution: 'Whilst the members and officers of Arfon Borough Council and Gwynedd County Council have striven to overcome the shortcomings of local government reorganization . . . the new and larger District Council has proved to be more costly and less efficient than the previous administration with a consequent deterioration in standards of services to the local community. Accordingly, the City of Bangor Council calls upon the Secretary of State for Wales to initiate new legislation so as to enable towns the size of Bangor to revert to their former independent status'.[6] No new initiatives from central government were expected so soon after the major reorganization but at least the matter has been referred to the highest authority. The issue surfaced again in a plea made by Cllr. Frank Woodcock at his installation as mayor in May 1983 for the return to the council of its former powers. He hoped that the government soon to be elected would reorganize local government so that authorities like Bangor City Council would once again be masters in their own city. He expressed a general feeling that street cleaning and municipal housing affairs should be under the control of the City Council.[7]

The Maud Commission also recommended that local councils should on their own initiative do anything which they considered might be beneficial to their locality as long as it did not come within the statutory ambit of either the county or district council. A leisure and amenities fund was established by the council and sums of money are granted each year to local sports clubs, including the tennis, swimming and gymnastics clubs, and to cultural organizations such as the *Cwmni Theatr Cymru* and the Art Gallery. In co-operation with the University College the council helped to finance the building of a gymnastics hall, it has supported a wide range of activities connected with the annual Festival Week which is held in the month of July and it has sought to maintain and strengthen the link which the 'old' council had forged with the city of Soest in West Germany.

Elderly people constitute a high percentage of the population of Bangor; according to the 1981 census, nearly one in five of the population is of pensionable age. Financial support has been given to pensioners' clubs at Minafon and Glanadda, for example, and in 1981-82 the council converted the former Crosville Information centre on Garth Road into a comfortable rest centre for the elderly and disabled. The needs of the large number of unemployed in the community, particularly young people, have not been overlooked; for many of its improvement projects the council has employed labour drawn from among the unemployed under the auspices of various Job Creation Schemes. Among these projects have been improvements at the Library Hall and at Bron Castell.

The hall adjoining the library, formerly the museum, had been used as a meeting place ever since the contents of the museum had been transferred to the University College in 1940. After reorganization of local government in 1974 the County Council handed over the hall to the council which has since installed kitchen and toilet facilities to make it a more attractive venue for community events. Perceiving the need for a community centre and for a meeting place and offices for itself, the council purchased Bron Castell from the B.B.C. in 1976. Recently, a meeting hall, a play centre for young children, a functions centre and a suite of rooms comprising a council chamber, mayor's parlour and council offices, have been created. A new civic centre has thus been established to replace the town hall which became the administrative centre of the Arfon District Council in 1974 [Plate 9 (ii)].

Undoubtedly, the most ambitious project which the council has undertaken for the benefit of the local community is the restoration of the pier. When Arfon District Council took possession of the pier in 1974 it inherited the same intractable problem which had plagued the 'old' council for years. Another attempt was made to interest a private developer but it did not meet with any success. Bangor Civic Society, whose chairman, Mrs Christie had for many years championed the restoration of the pier, then suggested that its renovation might be a suitable project for the council itself to undertake as a Job Creation Scheme. Hopes were raised in December 1974 when the Welsh Office listed the pier as a structure of historical interest and this prompted the city council to seek from the Arfon District Council the return of the pier. For the consideration of one penny the District Council agreed to hand over the pier and the adjoining land, including the car park, pier house and Garth gardens.

Three years were spent in exploring means of raising the money that would be required to restore the pier to its former splendour. A firm of consulting engineers, which had been commissioned to report on the viability of the project estimated the cost of restoration to be in the region of £750,000. By the summer of 1982 the following bodies had promised sums of money: the Welsh Development Agency (£100,000), the National Heritage Memorial Fund (£75,000), the Welsh Office (£15,000), City of Bangor Council (£15,000). A Pier Restoration Committee, an *ad hoc* committee of the council, was formed in order to launch a public appeal for a sum of £50,000 towards the cost of restoration. Further grants of money from the Welsh Office, the E.E.C. Development Fund and the Welsh Tourist Board were confidently expected. Finally, a massive sum of £406,000, promised by the Manpower Services Commission to finance the labour costs involved, encouraged the council to proceed with the restoration. Work commenced in November 1982 and it is calculated to take three years.

Bearing in mind the state of the nation's economy in the early 1980s, the ability of the council to attract such large sums of money for financing the restoration of its Victorian pier has been phenomenal. Even more remarkable is the fact that the council's own financial commitment has needed to be so small. Tribute must be paid to the vision and persistance of council members and in particular to George Gibbs who, as a councillor and later as town clerk, has worked unremittingly over a period of ten years to resolve the problem of the pier. Hopefully, the pier will once again give pleasure to the people of

(i)

(ii)

*Plate 8*.  (i) The Council's first houses, Minafon, 1905.
(ii) The last Council Estate, Tan-y-bryn, 1968.

*Plate 9.* (i) The Town Hall, 1903-1974 (Reconstructed 1963).
The main University College building is in the background.
(ii) Bron Castell Community Centre and Council Offices, 1976-

*Plate 10.* The Community Council, 1983.

*Back row from left to right:* E. Halliday, J. M. Williams, Mrs C. Norris, Alfred Jones, Mrs J. Knight, Mrs A. E. Elliot, A. Edmunds (Mace Bearer), Tony Eccles, Mrs D. Murray, Llewelyn Davies, Mrs M. Jones, R. K. Marshall, Mrs B. Roberts, George Naylor.

*Front row:* Edward T. Doggan, Mrs J. D. Christie, Miss Iris Parry J.P. (Deputy Mayor), Frank Woodcock (Mayor), C. G. Gibbs (Town Clerk and Financial Officer), J. Haydn Jones, G. Buckley-Jones.

Bangor, will attract tourists and at the same time make a contribution to the local economy.

Little enthusiasm for the new council was evident at the time of the first election in January 1974. There was no contest in East and West Wards; neither was there one in South Ward, but here only four persons were nominated for the six seats. In the only contest, in North Ward, eight candidates stood for six seats and only 26 per cent of the electorate voted. This lack of participation eclipsed even the poor turn out at the County and District Council elections the previous year when the percentage poll for the County elections ranged from 34 to 43 per cent and averaged 44 per cent for the District elections.

Although it was not envisaged that party politics would intrude into community council elections, in the event all but five of the twenty-one candidates carried a political label. When the council was finally constituted there were twelve Labour Party members, four Plaid Cymru members and five Independents. The result reflected the trend which had been evident since the late 1960s of greater Labour Party participation in local affairs and the determination of Plaid Cymru to make its presence felt on the councils formed in consequence of reorganization. It is interesting to note that three of the four Plaid Cymru members lived in the same street on an estate which lies outside the city's boundaries and the fourth was a University student. Within two years all four had resigned but not before they had ensured that the council had adopted a bilingual policy. After five years the position had already changed with ten Labour Party, one Plaid Cymru and ten Independent members. The 1983 election, which was held just before the General Election of that year, saw the return of six Liberal/S.D.P. Alliance members but no Plaid Cymru member. The new electoral system and the elimination of aldermen had resulted in a council which had responded quickly to changes in the mood of the electorate.

Besides that of political composition there are five further contrasts between the two councils. Only 43 per cent of members of the council of 1974 were drawn from the middle class, yet by 1983 the middle class was again in the majority (71 per cent). Possibly the council has now attained sufficient stature for the middle class to take an interest in it once again. Most of the middle class group was drawn from professional occupations, there being only two self-employed members. Secondly, members of the council do not have the same commitment to organized religion as did members of the 'old' council. In 1975 and in 1983 only two members held office in a church or chapel. Thirdly, women are playing a more prominent role in the council than they did in the 'old' one. Their number has increased from three in 1974 to eight in 1983 and three of the eight mayors to date have been women. Most of the women elected since 1974 either hold professional posts themselves or their husbands are in professional occupations.

Just as the percentage of women on the council accords more closely to their proportion of the population, so does the proportion of those able to speak Welsh. Census data for 1981 show that 56 per cent of the population of Bangor was able to speak Welsh; on the council 57 per cent of members were Welsh speaking in 1978 but the percentage dropped to 48 after the 1983 election.

Finally, the turn over of members of the council has been much more rapid than was the case in the 'old' council. At the opening of its tenth year only four members of the original council had served for the whole period. Excluding these four members, the average length of service of councillors is 3.2 years. Nearly half the fifty elected councillors have served for less than three years, which is hardly sufficient time for them to become immersed in the council's procedures and affairs. The continuity and fund of experience provided by aldermen in the 'old' council has been missed.

The council was fortunate initially in attracting eleven members of the 'old' council who handed down its working patterns and traditions. It was particularly appropriate that the last mayor of the 'old' council, Mrs Jean Christie, should be elected the first mayor of the new one, thereby identifying it with the 'old' one. Five of the mayors elected since 1974 served on the 'old' council and two of them, Jean Christie and Frank Woodcock have served two terms.

Mrs Christie's successor as mayor was Frank Woodcock, a native of Nottinghamshire. A postman by occupation, he is a keen sportsman, having played football for Bangor City and refereed boxing matches. He was chairman of the local branch of the Labour Party and sat as a Labour member for South Ward on the 'old' council between 1966 and 1974. In 1974 he was also elected a member of the Arfon District Council.

The third mayor, Miss Iris Parry, is a native of Bangor. Trained as a teacher at Cartrefle Training College, Wrexham, she was appointed to a post at a primary school in Llandudno. After a period as Youth Organizer in Caernarvonshire she obtained a teaching post at Hirael Infants' School. She was elected to the 'old' council in 1970 and to the Arfon District Council in 1974 and was mayor of that council in

1980-81. Iris Parry is an elder and Sunday School teacher at Park Hill C.M. Chapel and was the first member of the city council to be appointed a J.P. for over forty years.

The mayor during the Queen's Jubilee Year was Charles Hainge, a native of Birmingham. Employed as a commercial traveller, he came to Bangor in 1953 and took an active part in the affairs of the local Labour Party. He entered the 'old' council in 1966 and took a keen interest in the welfare of young people, the elderly and disabled. He represented South Ward on Gwynedd County Council from 1974 until his death in 1980.

Gareth Buckley-Jones, mayor 1979-80, served for many years in the police force. After retiring from the force he set up his own School of Motoring business in Bangor. A popular personality, he won seats on the Arfon District Council (1974), the City Council (1976) and Gwynedd County Council (1977) as an Independent candidate.

Two natives of Bangor held the mayoralty between 1980 and 1982. Mrs Glenda Jones was educated at the Grammar School for Girls and worked as a shop assistant before she married Glanville Jones, a carpenter by trade. In recent years she has been actively involved in the Bangor Awake Group, the Bangor Festival and the Amateur Pantomime Group. Edward T. Dogan, a mechanical engineer, was active in the local Labour Party and was its chairman for a number of years. He was only the second Roman Catholic to become mayor of Bangor.

The mayor for 1982-83 was Haydn Jones who had served for brief periods on the 'old' council. A native of Portmadoc, he trained as a teacher at the Normal College and after several appointments with Caernarvonshire Education Authority he was appointed headmaster of Garth Primary School; when the school was replaced in 1968 by a new school in Maesgeirchen, Haydn Jones became its first headmaster. Being the fifth primary school headmaster to become mayor, he followed a long tradition of service to the city rendered by local headmasters and members of the teaching profession generally.

George Gibbs, a printer by trade and a member of both councils was appointed part-time town clerk in 1974. As the work load of the office had increased he was appointed full-time town clerk and financial officer in 1977 and is now responsible for a staff of thirteen.

In taking over some of the civic and ceremonial duties of the former council, the community council has given a focus to community identity at a time when the management of local affairs has passed to larger, more impersonal authorities. It has articulated the community's views on a number of important issues and has, by its initiative and perception of local needs, enriched the lives of large sections of the community.

*Notes*

1. Words spoken by the Mayor, Mrs J. D. Christie at the first meeting of the Council, April 1974. NWC, 18 April 1974.
2. Royal Commission on Local Government in England, Report, Cmnd. 4040, para. 282.
3. NWC, 14 June 1973.
4. NWC, 18 April 1974.
5. Royal Commission on Local Government in England, Report, Cmnd. 4040, para. 381.
6. City of Bangor Council Minutes, September 1976.
7. NWC, 12 May 1983.

# CONCLUSION

BASICALLY the rationale for local government in this country is the provision of services for the advancement and well-being of the locality through a council elected by the inhabitants of that locality. It is incumbent on such a council to employ professional officers and a staff to carry out its decisions. An attempt has been made in this book to record the history of the council which governed the cathedral city of Bangor over a period of one hundred years from its formation in 1883.

Although its genesis may be traced to medieval times, Bangor's growth as a town dates from the period of intensive commercial and industrial activity which transformed the economy and society of north-west Wales in the early nineteenth century. Not having been granted borough status in medieval times Bangor had no effective governing body able to cope with the rapid growth of the city in that period and conditions of unmitigated urban squalor were allowed to develop and proliferate. The scale of the problem was so great that only by collective action and public finance could it be solved. An administrative structure capable of tackling urban sanitary problems was created by the Public Health Act 1848 and the inhabitants of Bangor wasted no time in petitioning for the Act to apply to the city. During the thirty-three years the Board of Health governed the city not only did it go a long way towards remedying the worst of urban squalor but it also undertook a broader ameliorative and developmental role, thereby enhancing the quality of life. Although it was the first effective public body to attend to the city's affairs, it was not a truly representative body: Board members were elected on a narrow franchise, membership was restricted to the economic and social élite of the city and the Board was dominated for twenty years by its chairman, Lord Penrhyn, the local lord of the manor.

Growth in representative democracy nationwide during the middle Victorian period encouraged local activists to agitate for a more representative and responsive body to manage the city's affairs. They had in mind the model of urban government fashioned by the Municipal Corporations Act 1835, a more prestigious body than a

Local Board and one which would be more appropriate for the image of the largest town in north west Wales. The Local Board's incompetence in handling the traumatic typhoid epidemic of 1882 led to positive steps being taken to petition for a charter of incorporation under the 1835 Act, and this was granted in 1883.

Assuming the functions of the Local Board of Health in both its narrow sanitary field and in its broader community obligations the council, set up under the charter, greatly improved and extended the services which the Board had provided. It did so by exercising its initiative based on its perception of the city's needs, which sometimes involved administering mandatory and permissive government legislation and presenting private bills to gain parliamentary approval for major development schemes. Inevitably, the council's collectivist approach to municipal development led to its playing a significant role in the daily lives of its citizens. In no sphere was the council's march towards municipal socialism more apparent than in its welfare role as a provider of houses. Early in the present century the building of houses on a non-profit basis for lower income groups was a contentious and sensitive issue. Yet, by the early 1970s, the council had demolished nearly a thousand houses and had become the greatest landlord the city had ever known; half the households in Bangor rented council property and looked to the council for the repair and maintenance of their dwellings.

Progress in the development of the council's services was, however, constrained by the finance that it could realistically raise from the levy of a rate on property and from loans sanctioned by the government. By the early years of the century the council had, in the eyes of many, overstretched itself by indulging in expensive improvement schemes and there followed a period of civic economy. Problems of financing the council's activities were exacerbated in the inter-war period by a downturn in the local economy which was a manifestation of a wide national and international depression. The growing popularity of Keynesian economics in the 1930s, however, induced the government to adopt interventionist policies to stimulate the economy and these were particularly apparent in the housing field where local authorities were encouraged to become major providers of houses.

The concept of the welfare state, subscribed to by both Labour and Conservative governments after the Second World War, led inevitably to central government taking greater control of the management of the nation's economic and social life. This concept applied to services administered by local authorities as well as those under the direction of national bodies and in order to ensure equality of treatment across the country and to raise standards uniformly, central guidance and surveillance were necessary. Central government came to determine the type, quantity and quality of service administered by local authorities and to attain its objectives it gave generous financial support. By the 1950s more of the council's revenues came from Exchequer grants than from the local rates. Greater financial control and supervision led to local councils becoming, to a large extent, agents of central government, a fact which became painfully apparent in 1972 when the Housing Finance Act of that year established central control even over the rents councils charged for their houses. Sceptical of the ability of local authorities to administer certain services efficiently and effectively, the government after 1945 transferred hospital, gas, electricity and water services to regional bodies, and urban planning and fire services to a higher tier of local government. Thus, the services now provided by the city council were mere items in a basket of services supplied by various local, regional and national agencies; these were financed largely from government funds towards which individuals contributed by paying rates and taxes.

Shifts in the functions and status of the council occurred against a background of continual change in the economic and social life of the community as it emerged from the parochialism of the closing decades of the nineteenth century to undergo complete integration with the national and international scene during the present century. The Charter of Incorporation was granted at the high noon of Victorian growth and prosperity. Trade and small industries flourished and those who were successful in business or professional enterprises attained high standing in the closed community. Leadership in the milieu of church and chapel gave a further badge of respectability and status. As a self governing body, the council, in its early years needed men of initiative and proven success in their working lives to establish its credibility in the eyes of the small community. The social élite of the city responded to the challenge and by their involvement secured for the council a high degree of authority and social acceptance. Even so, this middle class élite was rent by political and religious divisions which, on some occasions, paralysed the work of the council for months and frequently led to bitter exchanges between members.

The revolution in transport and mass communications during the present century broadened the social and intellectual horizons of the city's middle class. Their interests were diverted from the local scene and there were alternative calls on their loyalty; leisure time was spent with their families and they satisfied their social aspirations by joining the golf and rotary clubs and professional associations. From the 1930s, too, there was a steady decline in small businesses as commercial and financial institutions extended their colonization of High Street. Salaried employees managed these enterprises and, being newcomers to the area and often seeking further promotion, they did not have deep roots in the local community. Lack of opportunities in the city itself for the potential leaders who had benefited from grammar school education led to their migration to other parts of the country to the detriment of the local community.

Events following the end of the First World War, however, conspired to give the middle class a degree of unity which had eluded it in pre-war days. The disestablishment of the Welsh Church (1918) paved the way for greater religious toleration and the decimation of the Liberal Party (1923), together with the realization that the Labour Party was a powerful force in British politics, induced Conservatives and Liberals to sink their political differences. Under the guise of Independents, middle class Conservatives and Liberals established their hegemony in the council which was to last until the council's demise in 1974. As it transpired, the challenge of the Labour Party was ineffective.

After 1945 the economy of the city came to be dominated by large educational, medical, commercial and financial institutions. Senior staff of these institutions had interests in the broader national and international field and had no particular attachment to the city itself (indeed, large numbers of them were newcomers and lived beyond the boundaries of the borough). Neither, in the more open and cosmopolitan society of the mid-twentieth century, did leadership among the dwindling congregations of church and chapel confer the same social status as it did in earlier times. Service on the council was not so attractive to the city's new professional and commercial leaders since the council had lost much of the initiative it once possessed for propelling the city forward; it had, in large measure, become the tool of central government. Although less socially conspicuous, those who replaced the social élite were nevertheless still drawn predominantly from a higher social class than the majority they represented. The working class was not well represented until the late 1960s and several Labour Party councillors were upwardly mobile middle class radicals rather than representatives of the working class.

The problem of attracting able persons onto the council was not a

recent one. Misgivings about the calibre of candidates who sought seats were raised in the period immediately after the First World War (p. 176) and Henry Lewis at the time appealed to men in business and the professions to come forward. Whether the calibre of members did decline after 1945 would be difficult to prove. No apparent correlation exists between a person's occupation and his effectiveness or success as a city councillor. Intangible personal qualities of judgement, integrity, political awareness, determination and knowledge of the local scene are probably more important qualifications for the office of councillor than high attainment and success in daily employment.

At the level of the small borough council politics would seem to be inappropriate since decisions, particularly in more recent times, have been more concerned with matters of administration than of policy and the work of councillors is primarily to further the aspirations of the community as a whole rather than sections of it. Yet, in so far as issues and policies presented to the council were subjects for discussion and debate, it would be disingenuous to pretend that members' decisions on these matters were not influenced by their political predispositions which were themselves influenced by position in the class structure and social and religious norms and values. Membership of a party identified a person with the philosophy of that party and, moreover, was a great help to those, many of whom were strangers to the electorate at large, who counted upon party workers for support at election times. Political activity was keen in the early decades when deep-seated politico-religious feelings separated the parties. When party rivalry reappeared in 1945 after a period of relative quiescence between the wars, it tended to reflect party struggles on the wider national scene rather than local issues and personalities. Whatever their politics, however, it would appear that most members of the city council considered issues on their merits and gave due consideration to their likely effects on the local community; there is little evidence of the presence of party caucuses and formulation and toeing of a party line.

The model of urban government created in 1835 remained unchanged in its basic characteristics until the reform of local government in 1974. There was little appreciable change either in the characteristics of the members of the council for the council was dominated by Welsh speaking, middle class males who were middle aged and conservative in outlook. In these respects the council was not representative of the electorate at large: women, manual workers and young people, in particular, were grossly under-represented.

However, even in the most democratic society, not every section of that society is represented, be it at local or parliamentary level, and the concept of a council being a microcosm of an electorate is unattainable in practice. The office of alderman which was built into the 1835 model, effectively ensured the stability of the council and the continuity of its policies. In a number of characteristics, though, the influential aldermanic bench assumed an identity over the years which was markedly divergent from that of the remainder of the council.

For its part, the electorate has not shown any great enthusiasm for its democratically elected local council. Once the novelty of having their own 'little Parliament' faded, the majority have been somewhat indifferent to civic affairs. A high percentage of seats have not been contested and the turnout at elections has been disappointingly low. These responses may be interpreted in two ways: either there was general contentment with the way the city's affairs were being managed and a desire that those who were fascinated by civic service and prepared to engage in it should be allowed to carry on with it, or, the electorate had come to take the administration of services for granted.

Any assessment of the city council from 1883 to 1974 must be couched in general terms since there was no study of a similar council in a small Welsh town with which it may be compared. The abiding impression is that high standards of competence and integrity were attained by most council members and officers and the whole system has been free from corruption. At most times the council was sensitive to the city's needs and carried out the essentials of local representative democracy. It fostered a degree of civic pride and the mayors, by their dignity and devotion to duty as first citizens, enhanced the status not only of the council but also of the city which they personified.

There were two principal reasons for the abolition of the council in 1974: firstly, the council had become too small a unit to administer efficiently a wide range of services at the high standard required in the last quarter of the twentieth century; secondly, the dichotomy between a town and its surrounding countryside, which was implicit in the legislation of 1835 and confirmed when local government was reorganized in 1888, proved an anachronism in the highly mobile society of the 1970s. The period since reorganization of local government in 1974 is too short a span of time for an evaluation of the work of the community council. Although it has little power, it has retained the dignified trappings of the former council and it has emerged as a champion of community needs and opinions. In its composition it would appear to be more representative of the community as a whole and more flexible and responsive to change.

There was one major ceremony to mark the centenary of the granting of the civic charter in 1883. Appropriately, it was one of thanksgiving for one hundred year of corporate life in Bangor and it was held in the cathedral around which the city has grown. A highlight of the service was the handing of the city's charter to a young person as a symbol that the civic trust must be passed on and that each generation must accept responsibility for the conduct of its own affairs. The generations between 1883 and 1983 established democratic government in Bangor on sound foundations; this book is a record of their achievements for future generations to emulate.

# APPENDICES

## Table 11
### Population and Housing Data

| Year | Population Bangor[1] | Tributary Area[6] | Inhabited Houses (Bangor)[1] |
|------|------|------|------|
| 1801 | 1,770 | 9,540 | 459 |
| 1811 | 2,383 | 10,678 | 678 |
| 1821 | 3,579 | 13,340 | 1,171 |
| 1831 | 4,751 | 16,939 | 1,542 |
| 1841 | 5,058 | 18,600 | 1,085 |
| 1851 | 6,338 | 20,934 | 1,228 |
| 1861 | 6,738 | 22,350 | 1,331 |
| 1871 | 7,722 | 25,742 | 1,672 |
| 1881 | 8,247 | 27,142 | 1,773 |
| 1891 | 9,892[2] | 25,771 | 2,122 |
| 1901 | 11,269[2] | 27,386 | 2,426 |
| 1911 | 11,236[3] | 26,929 | 2,536 |
| 1921 | 11,029 | 25,487 | 2,547 |
| 1931 | 10,960[4] | 24,688 | 2,668 |
| 1941 | | No Census taken in 1941 | |
| 1951 | 12,822[2] | 27,086 | 3,758 |
| 1961 | 13,993 | 26,155 | 4,292[7] |
| 1971 | 14,558 | 29,282 | 4,445[7] |
| 1981 | 14,346[5] | 33,503[5] | 4,872[7] |

*Source: Census Returns.*

1. (a) 1801-31    Data for parish of Bangor, i.e. present day parishes of Bangor and Pentir.
   (b) 1841-61    Data for Parliamentary Borough (Its western boundary ran along the Holyhead Road between the Station and the Look Out).
   (c) 1871-81    Data for Local Board District (for boundaries see Map 1).
   (d) 1891-1981 Data for Borough of Bangor (Boundary extended in 1883 to include Glanadda and again in 1934 to include the Penrhos Road area. See Map 2).
2. Students at city's colleges on vacation.
3. Only students at St Mary's College enumerated.
4. Only students at UCNW and St Mary's College enumerated.
5. See Chapter 1, footnote 34.

6. (a) 1801-81   Data for parishes comprising the Bangor and Beaumaris Poor Law Union, formed in 1834. Boundary extended in 1850s to include another four parishes in Anglesey.

   (b) 1891-1971 Data for Aethwy and Ogwen Rural Districts and Beaumaris, Menai Bridge, Bethesda and Llanfairfechan Urban Districts. Boundary of Aethwy R.D. extended in 1935 to include five parishes in S.W. Anglesey.

   (c) 1981      Data for same area as above.

7. Inhabited household spaces.

## TABLE 12

### List of Mayors

(a) THE MUNICIPAL BOROUGH COUNCIL, 1883-1974

| | |
|---|---|
| 1883 - 85 | Ald. Major Henry Platt, J.P. |
| 1885 - 87 | Ald. Thomas Lewis, J.P. |
| 1887 - 88 | John Pritchard, Esq. |
| 1888 - 90 | Ald. Charles Pierce, J.P. |
| 1890 - 91 | Ald. Dr John Richards, J.P. |
| 1891 - 92 | Cllr. Major Hugh Savage, V.D. |
| 1892 - 93 | William Arthur Dew, Esq. |
| 1893 - 94 | Ald. Donald Cameron |
| 1894 - 95 | Ald. Dr R. Langford Jones, J.P. |
| 1895 - 96 | Cllr. John Evan Roberts, J.P. |
| 1896 - 97 | Cllr. Dr Henry Grey Edwards, J.P. |
| 1897 - 98 | Cllr. Hugh Hughes |
| 1898 - 1900 | Ald. John Evan Roberts, J.P. |
| 1900 - 02 | Ald. Henry Lewis, J.P. |
| 1902 - 04 | Cllr. William Peter Mathews, J.P. |
| 1904 - 06 | Cllr. William Ewert Bayne |
| 1906 - 07 | Col. Henry Platt, C.B. |
| 1907 - 08 | Cllr. David Owen |
| 1908 - 11 | Cllr. Hugh Corbett Vincent, B.A. |
| 1911 - 12 | Cllr. John Pentir Williams, B.A. |
| 1912 - 13 | Cllr. Thomas John Williams |
| 1913 - 20 | Ald. Sir Richard John Williams, O.B.E., J.P. |
| 1920 - 21 | Cllr. Dr John Edward Thomas |
| 1921 - 22 | Ald. Owen Owen |
| 1922 - 24 | Cllr. William Thomas |
| 1924 - 26 | Cllr. Thomas Vallance |
| 1926 - 28 | Ald. Major John Roberts, T.D. |
| 1928 - 31 | Ald. W. R. Jones, J.P. |

| | |
|---|---|
| 1931 - 34 | Cllr. John Williams |
| 1934 - 35 | Ald. Richard Thomas |
| 1935 - 37 | Cllr. Rev. O. Madoc Roberts |
| 1937 - 39 | Cllr. William Owen, F.A.I. |
| 1939 - 41 | Cllr. Isidore Wartski |
| 1941 - 43 | Cllr. Mrs Elsie Chamberlain, J.P. |
| 1943 - 45 | Cllr. William Samuel Williams |
| 1945 - 47 | Ald. Ithel Williams |
| 1947 - 50 | Ald. Owen Glynne Owen |
| 1950 - 52 | Ald. Ioan Y. Glynne, M.C. |
| 1952 - 54 | Ald. Hugh John Jones, F.I.B., F.C.I.S. |
| 1954 - 56 | Ald. Frederick W. Pozzi |
| 1956 - 58 | Ald. Eirwyn Owen, M.P.S., M.R.S.H. |
| 1958 - 60 | Ald. Caradog R. Jones |
| 1960 - 62 | Ald. O. T. Pritchard |
| 1962 - 64 | Cllr. Emrys W. Edwards |
| 1964 - 66 | Cllr. Robert Owen |
| 1966 - 68 | Cllr. Eric Whitworth |
| 1968 - 70 | Cllr. Iorwerth Hughes |
| 1970 - 72 | Cllr. T. Vivian Lewis, LL.B. |
| 1972 - 74 | Cllr. Mrs Jean Dowling Christie |

(b) THE COMMUNITY COUNCIL, 1974-1983

| | |
|---|---|
| 1974 - 75 | Cllr. Mrs Jean Dowling Christie |
| 1975 - 76 | Cllr. Frank Woodcock |
| 1976 - 77 | Cllr. Miss Iris Parry |
| 1977 - 78 | Cllr. Charles A. Hainge |
| 1978 - 79 | Cllr. Mrs Jean Dowling Christie |
| 1979 - 80 | Cllr. Gareth Buckley Jones |
| 1980 - 81 | Cllr. Mrs Glenda Jones |
| 1981 - 82 | Cllr. Edward T. Dogan |
| 1982 - 83 | Cllr. John Haydn Jones |
| 1983 - 84 | Cllr. Frank Woodcock |

TABLE 13

*Principal Officers of the Council*

TOWN CLERK★

| | |
|---|---|
| 1883 - 1901 | Richard Hughes Pritchard, M.A. |
| 1902 - 12 | Huw Rowland |
| 1912 - 39 | John Pentir Williams, B.A. |
| 1939 - 68 | William Elwyn Jones, B.A., LL.B. |

1969 - 73      Edward J. Lloyd, F.C.I.S.
Jan.-Mar. 1974  Oscar D. Mathieson, B.A.
1974 -          Cecil George Gibbs
* Part-time 1883-1968 and 1974-77


CITY TREASURER
1884 - 1903    William Pughe, J.P. (E. Smith Owen, Accountant)
1903 - 35      E. Smith Owen
1935 - 38      Herbert Bell
1938 - 45      H. Livingstone
1945 - 47      N. S. Skeats
1947 - 50      V. M. Cragg
1950 - 66      Walter Stake
1966 - 74      F. W. Michael


CITY SURVEYOR & ENGINEER
1883 - 1924    John Gill
1925 - 29      T. P. Francis
1929 - 44      B. Price Davies
1945 - 66      Cyril Richard
1966 - 74      J. K. Birkett


ENGINEER & MANAGER, GAS DEPARTMENT**
1884 - 1908    John Smith
1908 - 41      Price F. White
1941 - 48      John R. Wood


ENGINEER & MANAGER, ELECTRICITY DEPARTMENT**
1899 - 1941    Price F. White
1941 - 48      F. O. Harber
** Gas and Electricity Departments merged 1908-1941


SANITARY/PUBLIC HEALTH INSPECTOR
1883 - 88      John Gill
1888 - 94      William Jones
1894 - 1921    William H. Worrall
1921 - 43      T. Rogers Jones
1943 - 74      G. W. Outram

LIBRARIAN (& Museum Curator to 1940)

| | |
|---|---|
| 1883 - 98 | Peter Williams |
| 1898 - 1907 | Miss Williams |
| 1907 - 1930 | Griffith Roberts |
| 1930 - 46 | W. R. Owen, B.A. |
| 1946 - 51 | Rev. Hugh D. Roberts, M.A. |
| 1951 - 53 | Leonard Owen Arridge, B.A. |
| 1953 - 74 | W. J. Jones, A.L.A. |

TABLE 14

*Honorary Freemen of the Borough*

| | |
|---|---|
| 1903 | General Baden-Powell |
| 1906 | Ald. Thomas Lewis, J.P. |
| 1911 | Sir John Pritchard-Jones |
| 1920 | Field-Marshal Lord Haig |
| | David Lloyd George, Esq., P.C., M.P. |
| 1921 | Sir Richard and Lady Williams |
| 1922 | Sir Henry Lewis, J.P. |
| 1926 | Edward Sholto Douglas-Pennant, Third Baron Penrhyn |
| 1931 | Dr Griffith Evans |
| 1933 | Ald. William Peter Mathews, J.P. |
| 1941 | Sir John Edward Lloyd |
| 1958 | 372nd Flint & Denbigh Yeomanry, Light Regiment, R.A. (T.A.) |
| | Sir Emrys Evans, M.A. |
| 1963 | Ald. Ithel Williams |
| | Ald. Glynne Owen |
| 1972 | William Elwyn Jones, Esq., B.A., LL.B. |
| 1974 | Ald. Ioan Y. Glynne, O.B.E., M.C. |
| | Ald. Hugh John Jones, F.I.B., F.C.I.S. |
| | Ald. Eirwyn Owen, M.P.S., M.R.S.H. |
| | Ald. Owen Thomas Pritchard |
| | Ald. Emrys Edwards |
| | Ald. Robert Owen (posthumously) |
| | Sir Michael Duff |
| | Angus MacDermid, Esq. |
| | University College of North Wales |
| | C. & A. Hospital      B.B.C. |
| | R.A.F. Valley      Deiniolen Silver Band |

TABLE 15

*Occupations of Council Members at Selected Dates*

#### 1883
Doctor
Solicitor
Postmaster
Chemist
Auctioneer (2)
Newspaper Editor
Landowner
Shipowner
Corn, etc. Merchant (3)
Wine and Spirits Merchant (2)
Brewers Agent
Hotelier
Draper
Ironmonger (2)
Jeweller
Coachmaker
Builder (2)
and one other

#### 1893
Doctor (3)
Solicitor
Dentist
Architect (2)
Newspaper Editor
Workhouse Governor
Works Proprietor
General Merchant (3)
Wine and Spirits Merchant
Brewers Agent
Flour Agent
Coal Merchant
Shipping Agent
Draper (3)
Butcher (2)
Coachmaker

#### 1903
Doctor (2)
Solicitor (3)
Headmaster
Chemist
General Merchant (2)
Wine and Spirits Merchant
Brewers Agent
Flour Agent
Slate Merchant
Proprietor, General Stores
Draper (4)
Butcher
Bookseller and Stationer
Builder
Coachmaker
Painter
and one other

#### 1913
Doctor (2)
Solicitor (2)
Architect
Accountant
Headmaster
Company Director
General Merchant
Slate Merchant
Flour Agent
Proprietor, General Stores
Draper (5)
Boot and Shoe Retailer
Tobacconist
Builder
Coachmaker
Painter
Railway Employee
and one other

## 1923

Doctor
Solicitor
University Professor
Headteacher (3)
Minister of Religion
Post Office Clerk
Auctioneer
Company Director
Coal Agent
Flour Agent
Draper (4)
Boot and Shoe Retailer
Painter
Printer
Tailor
Railway Employee (3)
and one other

## 1933

Solicitor
University Registrar
Headteacher (2)
Minister of Religion
Auctioneer
Company Director
Coal Agent
Flour Agent
Proprietor, General Stores
Draper (2)
Grocer
Jeweller
Painter (2)
Printer
Tailor
Railway Employee (3)
Railway Employee (wife of)
and two others

## 1943

Doctor
Solicitor (3)
College Lecturer (2)
Headteacher (3)
Schoolteacher
Minster of Religion
Bank Manager
Bank Employee
Chemist
Auctioneer
Coal Agent
Garage Proprietor
Garage Manager
Draper (2)
Greengrocer
Printer
Railway Employee
Railway Employee (wife of)

## 1953

Solicitor (3)
Headmaster (3)
Schooltecher (2)
University Professor (wife of)
Bank Manager
Branch Post Master
Insurance Agent
Local Government Officer
Chemist
Garage Proprietor
Flour Agent
Grocer
Fruit Merchant
Milk Retailer
Electrical Retailer
Baker and Confectioner (2)
Blacksmith
Plasterer
Upholsterer
Railway Employee (2)
and one other

| 1963 | 1972 |
|---|---|
| Doctor (wife of) | Doctor (wife of) |
| Solicitor (2) | Solicitor (2) |
| Headmaster (3) | Headmaster |
| Schoolteacher (3) | Schoolteacher |
| Bank Manager | University Lecturer (2) |
| Scientific Adviser | Bank Manager |
| Insurance Agent | Accountant |
| Hospital Secretary | Surveyor |
| Local Government Officer (2) | Local Government Officer |
| Chemist | Bus Inspector |
| Garage Proprietor | Chemist |
| Flour Agent | Garage Proprietor |
| Grocer | Flour Agent |
| Fruit Merchant | Baker and Confectioner (2) |
| Milk Retailer | Clerk of Works |
| Baker and Confectioner (2) | Printer |
| Blacksmith | Sales Representative (2) |
| Upholsterer | Railway Guard |
| Post Office Engineer | Post Office Employee (3) |
| Railway Employee (2) | Shopfitter |
| | Telephonist |
| | Porter |

TABLE 16

*Occupations of Mayors, 1883-1983*

| BUSINESSMEN | | SALARIED, FEE EARNING | | WAGE EARNING | |
|---|---|---|---|---|---|
| **1883 - 1913** | | | | | |
| Company Director | 3* | Solicitor | 3 | | |
| Grain, Flour Merchant | 2 | Doctor | 3 | | |
| Flour, Brewery Agent | 2 | Headmaster | 1 | | |
| Tailor, Draper | 4 | Auctioneer | 2 | | |
| **1914 - 1944** | | | | | |
| Company Director | 1* | Doctor | 1 | Railwayman | 1 |
| Draper, Boots & Shoes | 4 | Minister of Religion | 1 | Railwayman's wife | 1 |
| Coal Agent | 1 | Auctioneer | 1 | | |
| Painter, Printer | 2 | Headmaster | 1 | | |

## TABLE 16
*Occupations of Mayors, 1883-1983* [continued]

### 1945 - 1974

| | | | | | |
|---|---|---|---|---|---|
| Garage, Shop Proprietor | 3 | Solicitor | 3 | Rail Guard | 1 |
| Milk Retailer | 1 | Headmaster | 2 | | |
| Sales Representative | 1 | Doctor's Wife | 1 | | |
| Chemist | 1 | Bank Manager | 1 | | |

### 1974 - 1983

| | | | | | |
|---|---|---|---|---|---|
| Driving School Proprietor | 1 | Schoolteacher | 2 | Postman | 1 |
| Sales Representative | 1 | Doctor's Wife | 1 | Carpenter's Wife | 1 |
| | | Engineer | 1 | | |

*Note: Sir R. J. Williams enumerated in both 1883-1913 and 1914-44 column*

## TABLE 17
*Some Characteristics of the Mayors of Bangor*

| | Mayors Elected in | | |
|---|---|---|---|
| | *1883-1913* | *1914-44* | *1945-73* |
| Per cent male | 100 | 93 | 93 |
| Average age on taking office | 51 | 58 | 56 |
| Average length of service on Council at installation (years) | 8.8* | 13 | 16 |
| Per cent middle class | 100 | 86 | 93 |
| Per cent nonconformist | 65 | 64 | 71 |
| Per cent holding office in church or chapel | 93 | 93 | 71 |
| Per cent Welsh speaking | 85 | 86 | 79 |
| Per cent born within 5 miles of Bangor | 20 | 43 | 64 |

*Note: Sir R. J. Williams enumerated in both 1883-1913 and 1914-44 column*
* 1893-1913 only

TABLE 18

*Political Composition of City Council, 1883-1973*

| YEAR | COUNCILLORS | | | | ALDERMEN | | |
|------|------|------|------|------|------|------|------|
| | Con. | Lib. | Lab. | Ind. | Con. | Lib. | Ind. |
| 1883 | 11 | 7 | | | 3 | 3 | |
| 1884 | 10 | 8 | | | 3 | 3 | |
| 1885 | 9 | 9 | | | 3 | 3 | |
| 1886 | 8 | 10 | | | ★ | ★ | |
| 1887 | 10 | 8 | | | 2 | 4 | |
| 1888 | 8 | 10 | | | 2 | 4 | |
| 1889 | 7 | 10 | | 1 | 1 | 5 | |
| 1890 | 8 | 8 | | 2 | 1 | 5 | |
| 1891 | 9 | 8 | | 1 | 1 | 5 | |
| 1892 | 9 | 8 | | 1 | 1 | 5 | |
| 1893 | 9 | 8 | | 1 | 1 | 5 | |
| 1894 | 9 | 8 | | 1 | 1 | 5 | |
| 1895 | 9 | 8 | | 1 | 1 | 5 | |
| 1896 | 9 | 8 | | 1 | 1 | 5 | |
| 1897 | 9 | 8 | | 1 | 1 | 5 | |
| 1898 | 8 | 10 | | | 1 | 5 | |
| 1899 | 8 | 10 | | | 1 | 5 | |
| 1900 | 6 | 12 | | | 1 | 5 | |
| 1901 | 6 | 12 | | | 1 | 5 | |
| 1902 | 5 | 13 | | | 1 | 5 | |
| 1903 | 5 | 13 | | | 1 | 5 | |
| 1904 | 5 | 13 | | | | 6 | |
| 1905 | 4 | 13 | | 1 | | 6 | |
| 1906 | 4 | 12 | 1 | 1 | | 6 | |
| 1907 | 4 | 12 | 1 | 1 | | 6 | |
| 1908 | 5 | 12 | 1 | | | 6 | |
| 1909 | 5 | 12 | 1 | | | 6 | |
| 1910 | 5 | 11 | 1 | 1 | | 6 | |
| 1911 | 6 | 10 | 1 | 1 | | 6 | |
| 1912 | 4 | 12 | 1 | 1 | 2 | 4 | |
| 1913 | 4 | 12 | 1 | 1 | 2 | 4 | |
| 1914 | 4 | 12 | 1 | 1 | 2 | 4 | |
| 1915-18 | Elections suspended | | | | | | |
| 1919 | | | 6 | 12 | | | 6 |

★ See page 107-8

TABLE 18 [continued]
*Political Composition of City Council, 1883-1973*

| YEAR | COUNCILLORS | | | | ALDERMEN | | |
|---|---|---|---|---|---|---|---|
| | Con. | Lib. | Lab. | Ind. | Con. | Ind. | Lab. |
| 1920 | | | 5 | 13 | 6 | | |
| 1921 | | | 5 | 13 | 6 | | |
| 1922 | | | 4 | 14 | 6 | | |
| 1923 | | | 4 | 14 | 6 | | |
| 1924 | | | 5 | 13 | 6 | | |
| 1925 | | | 5 | 13 | 6 | | |
| 1926 | | | 5 | 13 | 6 | | |
| 1927 | | | 5 | 13 | 6 | | |
| 1928 | | | 4 | 14 | 6 | | |
| 1929 | | | 3 | 15 | 6 | | |
| 1930 | | | 5 | 13 | 6 | | |
| 1931 | | | 4 | 14 | 6 | | |
| 1932 | | | 4 | 14 | 6 | | |
| 1933 | | | 4 | 14 | 5 | 1 | |
| 1934 | | | 4 | 14 | 5 | 1 | |
| 1935 | | | 3 | 15 | 5 | 1 | |
| 1936 | | | 3 | 15 | 5 | 1 | |
| 1937 | | | 2 | 16 | 5 | 1 | |
| 1938 | | | 3 | 15 | 5 | 1 | |
| 1939 | | | 3 | 15 | 5 | 1 | |
| 1940-44 | Elections suspended | | | | | | |
| 1945 | | | 3 | 15 | 5 | 1 | |
| 1946 | | | 5 | 16 | 6 | 1 | |
| 1947 | | | 7 | 14 | 6 | 1 | |
| 1948 | No Elections | | | | | | |
| 1949 | | 2 | 4 | 15 | 6 | 1 | |
| 1950 | 4 | 3 | 14 | | 6 | 1 | |
| 1951 | 6 | 2 | 13 | | 6 | 1 | |
| 1952 | 6 | 2 | 13 | | 6 | 1 | |
| 1953 | 6 | 5 | 11 | | 6 | 1 | |
| 1954 | 5 | 3 | 13 | | 6 | 1 | |
| 1955 | 6 | 3 | 12 | | 6 | 1 | |
| 1956 | 6 | 3 | 12 | | 6 | 1 | |
| 1957 | 5 | 3 | 13 | | 6 | 1 | |
| 1958 | 4 | 4 | 13 | | 7 | | |
| 1959 | 4 | 4 | 13 | | 7 | | |

TABLE 18 [continued]

*Political Composition of City Council, 1883-1973*

| YEAR | COUNCILLORS | | | | ALDERMEN | |
| | Con. | Lib. | Lab. | Ind. | Ind. | Lab. |
|------|------|------|------|------|------|------|
| 1960 |   |   | 4  | 14 | 7 |   |
| 1961 |   |   | 5  | 13 | 7 |   |
| 1962 |   | 3 | 5  | 13 | 7 |   |
| 1963 |   | 3 | 4  | 14 | 7 |   |
| 1964 |   | 3 | 5  | 13 | 7 |   |
| 1965 |   | 3 | 6  | 12 | 7 |   |
| 1966 |   | 2 | 6  | 13 | 7 |   |
| 1967 |   | 2 | 8  | 11 | 7 |   |
| 1968 | 4 | 1 | 7  | 9  | 7 |   |
| 1969 | 4 | 1 | 7  | 9  | 7 |   |
| 1970 | 4 | 1 | 7  | 9  | 7 |   |
| 1971 | 2 |   | 10 | 9  | 6 | 1 |
| 1972 | 2 |   | 12 | 7  | 6 | 1 |

Con. = Conservative
Lib. = Liberal
Lab. = Labour
Ind. = Independent

TABLE 19

*Details of the Council's Housing Programme 1905-1974*

| Housing Scheme | Housing Act under which built | Date completed | No. of Houses | Maisonettes | Flats | Superficies (sq. ft.) | Average Construction Price per unit (£) | Average Gross Rateable Value (1963 valuation) | Per cent of houses sold to tenants at 31 December 1983 |
|---|---|---|---|---|---|---|---|---|---|
| 1. Sackville Rd.-Treflan-Minafon | 1890 | 1905 | 43 | | | | 176 | 59 | 7 |
| 2. Pennant Crescent | 1919 | 1921 | 18 | | | | 960 | 85 | 33 |
| 3. Penchwintan No. 1 | 1923 | 1924 | 16 | | | 1000 | 470 | 75 | 6 |
| 4. Caerdeon | 1923 | 1926 | 8 | | | 900 | 488 | 70 | 50 |
| 5. (a) Maes-y-Dref–(b) Penlon | 1923 | 1926 | 42 | | | 850 & 950 | 500 & 540 | 79 | 38 |
| 6. Penchwintan No. 2 | 1923 | 1928 | 66 | | | | 493 | 73 | 20 |
| 7. Tyn-y-Caeau | 1924 | 1932 | 63 | | | 830 | 353 | 70 | 11 |
| 8. Maes-y-Llan | 1924 | 1933 | 70 | | | 830 | 347 | 70 | 27 |
| 9. Maes Isalaw | 1924 | 1933 | 35 | | | 760 | 335 | 65 | 30 |
| 10. Maes Tryfan | 1930 | 1935 | 164 | | | | 319[1] & 370[2] | 68 | 15 |
| 11. Tan-y-Maes – Gernant | 1930 | 1938 | 18 | | | | 362 | 65 | 0 |
| 12. Brynllwyd | 1930 | 1938 | 54 | | | | 362[1] & 404[2] | 66 | 13 |
| 13. Maesgeirchen | 1930 | 1939 | 304 | | | 771 | 359[1] / 390[1]* | } 60 | 3 |
| 14. Dean St. (Redevelopment) | 1930 | 1939 | 42 | | | 860 / 1106 | 452[2] | 80 | 10 |
| 15. Maesgeirchen (50) and Brynllwyd (10) – temporary bungalows, removed 1966-7. | | | | | | | | | |
| 16. Hirael (Redevelopment) | Various | 1946-66 | 40 | 16 | 40 | | 1245[3] | 85[6] & 48[7] | 36 |
| 17. Coed Mawr | 1946 | 1947-62 | 258 | | 16 | 900 | 1245-1500 | 84 | 23 |
| 18. Caernarfon Road | 1946 | 1947 | 5 | | | 900 | 1230 | | 20 |
| 19. Britannia Square | 1946 | 1951 | | | 12 | | 1150 | 55 | 0 |
| 20. Maesgeirchen | 1952 | 1953-58 | 238 | | 36 | 750 & 850 | 1400[4]-1650[5] | 65[6] & 45[7] | 11 |
| 21. Pen-y-Ffridd | 1952 | 1957 | 26 | | 18 | | 1650 | 91 | 50 |
| 22. Caernarfon Road | 1956 | 1961 | | | 13 | | } 3545 | 55 | 0 |
| 23. Ffordd Cynfal – Maes Tryfan | 1956 | 1963-64 | | | | | | 55 & 65 | 0 |
| 24. Tan-y-Bryn | 1961 | 1968 | 102 | | | | | 76 / 77.5 / 80 | 16 / 0 / 0 |
| | | | | 48 | 84 | | | | |

Notes:
| 1 | 3-bedroom | 1* | 3-bedroom parlour |
|---|---|---|---|
| 2 | 4-bedroom | 3 | Ambrose St. and Seiriol Rd. |
| 4 | 1953 | 5 | 1958 |
| 6 | Houses | 7 | Flats |

# BIBLIOGRAPHY

A. MANUSCRIPTS, MICROFILMS AND UNPUBLISHED WORKS.
  (i) Library, U.C.N.W., Bangor.
    Belmont Collection.
    Carter Vincent Collection (Bangor documents).
  (ii) Gwynedd Record Office, Caernarfon.
    Microfilms of the enumerator's schedules for the parish of Bangor, censuses of 1851 to 1881 (inclusive).
    Bangor Borough Council Collection, LBX2/115 including Minutes of the Bangor Local Board of Health, 1855-83, Minutes of the Borough of Bangor, 1889-1959, Minutes of the Finance etc. Committee, 1887-1958, printed minute books, 1897-1969, Abstracts of Accounts, Rate Books, etc.
    Penrhyn Quarry Collection, PQ 65/1-18 and Port Penrhyn Shipping Books, PQ 66/1-11.
  (iii) Public Record Office.
    Correspondence between Bangor Local Board of Health and General Board of Health, 1848-71. Ref. M.H.13/13.
  (iv) Broncastell Community Centre, Bangor.
    Minutes of the Community Council, 1974-83.
  (v) Unpublished theses:
    Peter Ellis Jones, 'Bangor: A Study in Urban Morphology and Social Geography', Ph.D., University of Wales, 1973.
    D. Dylan Pritchard, 'The Slate Industry of North Wales: a study of change in economic organization from 1780 to the present day', M.A., University of Wales, 1935.

B. PUBLISHED SOURCES.
  (i) Newspapers.
    *North Wales Gazette*, 1808-28.
    *North Wales Chronicle*, 1829-1983.
    *Caernarvon and Denbigh Herald*, 1831-1983.
    *North Wales Observer and Express*, 1880-1900.

(ii) Reports.

F. W. Barry, Report on an outbreak of enteritic fever in Bangor and its neighbourhood, 1883.

G. T. Clark, Report to the General Board of Health on a preliminary enquiry into the sewerage, drainage and supply of water and the sanitary conditions of the inhabitants of the Borough of Bangor, 1849.

G. L. Travis, Report on the sanitary conditions of Bangor for the year ending 31 December 1911, 1912.

Report of a housing census and survey made March-August 1926 under the auspices of Bangor City Council and the Bangor COPEC group, Bangor, 1926.

Report and Proposals of the Local Government Commission for Wales, HMSO, 1963.

Report of Royal Commission on Local Government in England, 1966-69, 3 Vols., Cmnd. 4040, HMSO.

The Reform of Local Government in Wales: consultative document HMSO, Cardiff, 1971.

(iii) Books and articles.

H. Anthony, *Menai Bridge and its Council* (Menai Bridge 1974).

Bangor City Council, *The Development of Bangor* (Bangor 1935).

Frank Bealey, 'Municipal politics in Newcastle-under-Lyme, 1872-1914' in *North Staffordshire Journal of Field Studies*, Vol. V, 1965.

A. H. Birch, *Small Town Politics: A study of the political life of Glossop* (Oxford 1959).

A. H. Birch, *Representation and Responsible Government.* (London 1964).

A. H. Birch, *The British System of Government* (London 1967).

T. Brennan *et al.*, 'Party Politics in Local Government in Western South Wales' in *Political Quarterly*, 1954, pp. 76-83.

Asa Briggs, *Victorian Cities* (Harmondsworth 1963).

J. G. Bulpitt, *Party Politics in English Local Government* (London 1967).

John Burnett, *A Social History of Housing, 1815-1970* (London 1980).

R. J. Buxton, *Local Government*, 2nd. edn. (Harmondsworth 1973).

David Cannadine, *Lords and Landlords: the Aristocracy and the Towns, 1774-1967* (Leicester 1980).

R. V. Clements, *Local Notables and the City Council* (London 1969).

C. A. Cross, *The Local Government Act, 1972* (London 1973).

J. B. Cullingworth, *Housing and Local Government in England and Wales* (London 1966).

M. J. Daunton, *Cardiff, Coal Metropolis, 1870-1914* (Leicester 1977).

H. J. Dickman, *History of the Council: Haverfordwest Rural District Council, 1894-1974* (Haverfordwest 1976).

A. H. Dodd, *A History of Caernarvonshire, 1284-1900* (Denbigh 1968).

P. J. Dunleavy, *The Politics of Mass Housing in Britain, 1945-75* (Oxford 1981).

D. Fraser, *Power and Authority in the Victorian City* (Oxford 1979).

D. Fraser, *A History of Modern Leeds* (Manchester 1980).

J. F. Garner 'Aldermen in English Local Government' in *Journal of Local Administration Overseas*, Vol. 3, 1964.

R. Glass, 'Urban Sociology in Great Britain' in R. Pahl (ed.) *Readings in Urban Sociology* (Oxford 1968).

E. P. Hennock, 'Finance and Politics in Urban Local Government in England, 1835-1900' *History Journal*, Vol. 6, No. 2.

E. P. Hennock, 'The social composition of Borough Councils in two large cities, 1835-1914' in H. J. Dyos (ed.), *The Study of Urban History* (London 1968).

E. P. Hennock, *Fit and Proper Persons: ideal and reality in nineteenth century urban government* (London 1973).

D. M. Hill, *Democratic Theory and Local Government* (London 1974).

P. W. Jackson, *Local Government*, 3rd edn. (London 1976).

W. Ivor Jennings, *Principles of Local Government Law*, 4th edn. (London 1976).

G. W. Jones, *Borough Politics: a Study of Wolverhampton Town Council, 1888-1964* (London 1969).

P. E. Jones, 'The City of Bangor at the time of the Tithe Survey, 1840' in TCHS, Vol. 31, 1970.

P. E. Jones, 'Bathing facilities in Bangor, 1800 to the present day' in TCHS, Vol. 36, 1975.

P. E. Jones, 'The Bangor Local Board of Health, 1850-83' in TCHS, Vol. 37, 1976.

B. Keith-Lucas, *The English Local Governmental Franchise: a short history* (Oxford 1952).

J. M. Lee, *Social Leaders and Public Persons: a study of county government in Cheshire since 1888* (London 1963).

K. O. Morgan, *Rebirth of a Nation, Wales 1880-1980* (Oxford and Cardiff 1981).

D. Morris and K. Newton, 'Profile of a local political élite: businessmen and community decision makers in Birmingham, 1838-1966' in *New Atlantis*, Vol. 1, 1970.

Lawrence Orbach, *Homes for Heroes* (London 1977).

Open University, Course D202, Urban Development, Unit 26, Housing.

Gwen Owen, 'The Bangor Typhoid Epidemic of 1882' in TCHS, Vol. 26, 1965.

Cyril Parry, 'Fabianism and Gwynedd Politics, 1890-1918' in TCHS, Vol. 29, 1968.

Cyril Parry, 'Gwynedd Politics and the rise of a Labour Party' in *Welsh History Review*, Vol. 6, No. 3, 1973.

C. J. Pearce, *The machinery of change in Local Government, 1884-1974* (London 1980).

Lord Redcliffe-Maud and B. Wood, *English Local Government Reformed* (Oxford 1974).

A. M. Rees and T. A. Smith, *Town Councillors: a study of Barking* (Acton Society Trust 1964).

P. G. Richards, *The New Local Governmental System* (London 1968).

Glyn Roberts, *The Municipal Development of the Borough of Swansea to 1900* (Cardiff 1940).

W. A. Robson, *Local Government in Crisis*, 2nd edn. (London 1968).

Peter Saunders, *Urban Politics: a sociological interpretation* (London 1979).

L. J. Sharpe, 'Elected representatives in local government' in *British Journal of Sociology*, Vol. 13, 1962.

K. B. Smellie, *A History of Local Government* (London 1969).

B. D. White, *A History of the Corporation of Liverpool* (Liverpool 1951).

J. E. Williams, 'Paternalism in local government in the nineteenth century' in *Public Administration*, Winter 1955.

W. Ogwen Williams, 'The Platts of Oldham' in TCHS, Vol. 17, 1956.

E. A. Wrigley (ed.), *Nineteenth Century Society* (Cambridge 1972).

(iv) Other Published Works

Library, U.C.N.W., Bangor.

By-laws made . . . by the Bangor Local Board of Health, 1861.

The Charter of Incorporation of the City of Bangor.

Bangor Corporation: By-laws for new streets, etc., 1887.

Bangor Corporation: By-laws for good rule and government, 1889.

# INDEX